CREDIBLE FISCAL POLICY COMMITMENTS AND MARKET ACCESS—CASE STUDIES OF ARGENTINA, CHILE, AND MEXICO, 1980-1995

Credible Fiscal Policy Commitments and Market Access—Case Studies of Argentina, Chile, and Mexico, 1980-1995

Rosa Gomez Dierks

Studies in Political Science
Volume 7

The Edwin Mellen Press
Lewiston•Queenston•Lampeter

Library of Congress Cataloging-in-Publication Data

Gomez Dierks, Rosa.
Credible fiscal policy commitments and market access--case studies of Argentina, Chile, and Mexico, 1980-1995 / Rosa Gomez Dierks.
p. cm. -- (Studies in political science ; v. 7)
Includes bibliographical references and index.
ISBN-0-7734-6939-7
I. Title. II. Series. III. Studies in political science (Lewiston, N.Y.) ; v. 7.

This is volume 7 in the continuing series
Studies in Political Science
Volume 7 ISBN 0-7734-6939-7
SPS Series ISBN 0-7734-7434-X

A CIP catalog record for this book is available from the British Library.

The Edwin Mellen Press
Box 450
Lewiston, New York
USA 14092-0450

The Edwin Mellen Press
Box 67
Queenston, Ontario
CANADA L0S 1L0

The Edwin Mellen Press, Ltd.
Lampeter, Ceredigion, Wales
UNITED KINGDOM SA48 8LT

Printed in the United States of America

"Let us consider the way in which we spend our lives."
Henry David Thoreau

When I embarked on this journey, I had the unabated support of my husband, Clark. His love, patience, and encouragement never wavered. He gave me the courage to forge ahead and arrive at my destination. His wisdom, vision, and humor brighten all days of our lives.

Table of Contents

List of Figures

List of Tables

Preface

This book makes both theoretical and empirical contributions to the field of comparative public policy. Specifically, this study examines how and with what consequences budget institutions and fiscal policy choices shaped the ability of Argentina, Chile, and Mexico to access private market financing and issue bonds in the international sovereign debt market from 1980 to 1995. The study relies on qualitative and quantitative comparison to examine the effects of budget institutions and fiscal policy choices. It explains how a government's access to the international sovereign debt market can translate into a greater capacity to finance expenditures that contribute to a nation's economic growth. It concludes that governments able to access private capital markets to issue debt can strengthen their public finance capacity, stimulate economic growth, and secure higher and more equitable living standards for their citizens.

The author makes an important theoretical contribution by linking transparent budget institutions, credible fiscal policy choices, and sovereign market access to explain how a government can effectively gain access to private market financing. She develops a robust theoretical model by synthesizing the economic and historical-institutional approaches to public policy and incorporates elements of the advocacy coalition model to frame the political dimension of institutional choice. Furthermore, a qualitative comparison of the budget institutions and fiscal choices adopted by Argentina, Chile, and Mexico from 1980-1995 uncovers variance in market access in spite of similar histories, political cultures, and political institutions.

The period 1980-1995 is critical to an understanding of the significance of this study because Argentina, Chile, and Mexico had to prove that structural economic reforms and political liberalization could translate into greater fiscal credibility among both international financial market participants and domestic constituencies. The period was critical in reversing a decade long decline in fiscal accountability. Two decades later, many of the lessons drawn from this transition period remain an important benchmark for the institutional choices policy makers confront as they seek to finance growth.

In addition to qualitative analysis, this study applies quantitative data mining techniques designed to identify patterns in large, complex, disparate and often non-quantifiable data. The objective is to uncover patterns across each country in the choice of budgetary institutions, fiscal policy commitments, and subsequent access to the international sovereign debt market.

This quantitative analysis identifies the institutional and policy characteristics that facilitate market access. In addition, this set of qualities identifies the extent to which access to the sovereign debt market triggers an increase in public finance capacity, particularly in terms of education, health care, and infrastructure expenditures.

Previous applications of data mining have been limited to various scientific and business applications but have not included the comparative study of fiscal policy and financial flow patterns. In conjunction with data mining techniques, correlation analysis is used to test the hypotheses derived from the theoretical model. This application of data mining to the study of comparative public policy represents a path breaking approach and sets this study apart from other empirical studies in the field of public policy.

This book contributes to an understanding of contemporary political economy and public policy by examining the relationship between budget institutions, fiscal policy, and global finance. In identifying patterns that either facilitate or block government access to an increasingly important source of private market financing, policy makers could apply the comparative method of this study to evaluate budget institutions, fiscal policy choices, and conflicting domestic fiscal commitments. Specifically, policy makers could benefit from the findings of this study to address the current fiscal credibility crisis in Argentina by designing transparent budget institutions. In the coming decades, governments that find the appropriate balance of transparent budget institutions and credible fiscal policies will continue to benefit from access to private capital markets to strengthen public finance capacity, stimulate economic growth, and improve living standards for their citizens.

Dan A. Cothran, Professor
Northern Arizona University

Acknowledgments

This book originated as I pondered questions raised in various graduate seminars at Northern Arizona University. I wish to thank the faculty of the Political Science Department for providing an inspiring academic setting. In particular, I wish to thank the members of my dissertation committee for their contributions. Without the invaluable advice and support of my dissertation chair, Dr. Dan A. Cothran, this project would not have been brought to fruition. His guidance was invaluable in shaping this study. I am also deeply grateful to Dr. Carol Thompson for her thoughtful comments and suggestions. Her interest in my work helped me to improve this project in numerous ways. I also wish to thank Dr. Dean Smith for his outstanding statistical assistance and patience through seemingly endless revisions. In addition, I wish to thank Dr. Sheila Nair. I am very grateful to the members of my dissertation committee for their important contributions to this work. The responsibility, however, is solely mine for any flaws, errors, or omissions.

Upon completion of my dissertation, I received the Western Political Science Association 1999 Outstanding Dissertation Award. I wish to thank the members of the awards committee, Dr. Dan Smith, Dr. Diane Schmidt, and Dr. Carolyn Tolbert.

Other individuals provided insight and encouragement and it is difficult to name them all. Nevertheless, I would be remiss not to acknowledge and thank Dr. Bernard Carey and his colleagues at Northern Arizona University's Center for Data Insight (CDI). I also wish to acknowledge the wise counsel and encouragement of Dr. L. Earl Shaw, a special mentor who will be greatly missed. His seminars were a true source of inspiration and his memory will continue to motivate aspiring scholars.

Introduction

In today's global economy, governments increasingly rely on private capital markets to finance public expenditures. The surge of global capital flows since the mid 1970s can be partially explained as a result of the increasing financing demands of governments.[1] Although financial market participants play a pivotal role in determining a government's access to international capital markets, public policy makers hold the key to this access. The institutional and policy choices that governments make determine how, when and under what terms and conditions private capital market participants are willing to provide credit.

Government access to international capital markets is generally examined in the context of both fiscal and monetary policy choices. On the surface, these choices may appear to be grounded solely in economics, but they are not. These are political choices, often conflicting ones, rooted in domestic institutions. For example, budget institutions shape and are shaped by domestic policy commitments. In turn, policy commitments result in fiscal policies that can either facilitate or limit access to international capital markets. The nature of these commitments brings governments and global capital markets together – or keeps them apart.

Fiscal policy commitments that are credible to financial market participants signal both the ability and the willingness of a government to service its debt on a continuing and sustainable basis. Yet fiscal policy commitments that are credible to international creditors may not be desirable to domestic constituencies. Governments that implement and maintain fiscal restraint often cut deficits and balance budgets. These steps require spending cuts, a reordering of fiscal policy priorities and in some cases, tax and expenditure reforms that change the balance of political power. Governments following a path of fiscal restraint often gain access to the international sovereign debt market. Fiscal restraint increases the flexibility of governments to finance public expenditures through private capital markets. This flexibility, however, comes at a political price.

If access to the sovereign debt market translates into economic benefits, one needs to ask, whether there are any political costs associated with gaining greater public finance capacity. Asking about the political costs of gaining access to private market financing directs attention to the central questions of this study: (1) What is the effect of fiscal policy choices on a government's access to the international sovereign debt market? (2) How, why and with what consequences do credible fiscal policy commitments translate into public finance capacity?
(3) How does access to the sovereign debt market increase a government's capacity to finance expenditures leading to economic growth?

The politics of budgeting differ across national contexts. Public policy makers engaged in the budget process, however, share one common challenge in making fiscal policy choices, namely, balancing conflicting budget demands. Fiscal policy choices are grounded in budget institutions, the rules of the budget game.[2] Consequently, the design of budget institutions sets in motion the steps by which budget conflicts are resolved. Where budget conflicts are resolved matters.

When it comes to budgetary decisions, conflict resolution at the cabinet level differs from conflict resolution in the legislative arena. Fiscal policy choices made in different institutional settings may signal different levels of fiscal policy commitment and responsiveness to social demands. Insofar as fiscal policy choices are derived from either a hierarchical or collegial institutional framework, these choices differ in terms of their political costs, effectiveness in balancing conflicting budget demands and relevance to social needs.[3]

The ability to borrow through the international sovereign debt market empowers governments to finance human and capital investments leading to growth. The argument is that domestic fiscal policy commitments evolve from budget institutions. When fiscal policy commitments result in fiscal policies choices that are credible to international sovereign debt market participants governments are able to issue sovereign debt, an important source of public finance capacity. Specifically, this is the capacity to finance growth through bonds issued for education, health care and infrastructure expenditures. These kinds of expenditures require long term financing. Bonds are long term debt instruments ideally suited to finance long term projects. Bond financing reduces uncertainty for borrowers and creditors. Governments able to issue long term bonds can match revenue and expenditure flows, thus pursuing predictable and controllable financial management strategies.

When bonds are a source of debt financing, governments are in a better position to meet the information standards of the global capital markets.[4] Unlike loans, which are not securitized and do not trade in highly liquid secondary markets, bonds transmit instant information about economic fundamentals. Bond prices serve as signals of future economic activity and as such, represent leading indicators of economic cycles. In an age of instant global communications, bond prices serve as important signals of government performance.

Whereas loans keep bad economic news hidden from public view until borrowers and lenders publicly agree on loan restructuring terms, government bonds instantly reflect the underlying economic conditions of the issuer.[5] This instant price transmission of economic information offers governments able to sustain credible fiscal policy commitments greater flexibility to finance long term public expenditures, such as education, health care, and infrastructure.

Within the context of global finance, credible policy commitments matter. Financial market participants are forward-looking and discount the value of future events. Consequently, a government's past performance does not represent the only measure of fiscal policy credibility. Credible fiscal policy commitments represent the discounted present value of future government performance. Therefore, credible fiscal commitments anticipate a government's creditworthiness and pave the way for the issuance of government bonds in international capital markets. When governments are able to rely on the sovereign debt market to finance public expenditures, policy makers gain greater flexibility to finance growth through long term debt – a viable alternative to the regressive tax financing strategies favored by many governments.

Chapter One
The Political Economy of Institutional Choice

Why generalize about governments and not focus exclusively on liberal democracies? Generalizations about the relationship between fiscal and institutional choices and access to private market financing apply to all governments. Liberal democratic governments, however, face a higher degree of public pressure to deliver economic prosperity. Emerging liberal democracies are particularly vulnerable to popular expectations of accountability. This study does not focus on how public pressures affect fiscal policy choices, but recognizes that policy makers in emerging liberal democracies may face the conflicting demands of voters and private creditors. Although an analysis of voters' expectations and public pressures is beyond the scope of this study, it is recognized that fiscal choices involve economic, political and social considerations.

Why does this study target public finance capacity ? Why not generalize about government capacity? Government capacity is a broad concept that captures the ability to formulate, implement and evaluate policy and to allocate resources for those policies. Government capacity also refers to a government's power to make, apply, adjudicate and enforce rules. The point of departure for all these dimensions of government capacity is the capacity to finance public expenditures, government operations and programs.

Public finance capacity is an important component of overall government capacity.[6] The capacity to make rules without the capacity to apply, adjudicate and enforce them makes rules obsolete. The effort to implement policy without the capacity to pay for it makes policy obsolete. Without the capacity to finance public expenditures the capacity to implement policy initiatives quickly dissipates into thin air. Governments build public finance capacity when they finance public expenditures either through taxes or debt. For newly industrialized countries like Argentina, Chile and Mexico, tax financing alternatives are limited due to low income, savings and investment levels. To overcome these revenue hurdles, policy makers rely on consumption taxes to finance public expenditures. Regressive taxation perpetuates the great disparity in incomes, education, and health care access in Latin America.

In the last twenty years, debt financing alternatives from official sources have been reduced, as industrialized countries have become increasingly concerned about their own rising deficits. Money financing alternatives (i.e. monetizing the debt by either printing money or borrowing from the central bank) have been gradually abandoned due to their severe inflationary consequences. These public financing trends leave countries such as Argentina, Chile, and Mexico with few debt financing alternatives. The capacity to finance public expenditures by borrowing through private capital markets gives these governments a viable financing alternative. One source of private financing is the loan market and another is the sovereign debt market.[7]

Why focus on the international sovereign debt market? Governments increasingly seek financing in international bond markets. In Latin America, bonds represented merely 4.5 percent of total private capital flows to the region from 1977 to 1981. International bond financing represented 18 percent of total private flows in 1991 and by 1996 bonds represented 38 percent of total private capital flows.[8]

The surge of bond financing in Latin America during the last decade reflects the openness of the regional economies – a direct result of trade liberalization and financial deregulation. Open trade and free capital mobility, however, are not sufficient conditions for securing access to the sovereign debt market. Global finance opens new avenues for governments to seek private market financing, but these avenues require fiscal disclosure, transparent budgetary rules and procedures, and credible fiscal policy commitments.

As an economic institution, the sovereign debt market designs and applies its entry rules on the basis of various measures of government performance. In this context, fiscal policy becomes the focal point of credit assessments. Fiscal policy, however, does not evolve in an institutional vacuum. The rules of the budgetary game are inherently domestic and political. The politics of budgeting to a large extent determine government performance and the ability of policy makers to service debt obligations. Uncertainty about budget rules and government performance affects the expectations of financial market participants. Uncertainty about the ability of policy makers to make and sustain credible fiscal policy commitments shapes the responses of financial market participants to policy actions. In turn, these responses influence a government's access to the sovereign debt market. The political economy of institutional choice links fiscal policy choices, domestic fiscal commitments, and global finance.

Access to the sovereign debt market provides flexibility to fund public expenditures and strengthens a government's public finance capacity. The sovereign debt market differs from the corporate bond market, where credit is based solely on the borrower's ability to pay. In contrast, sovereign credit assessments are based on the expected ability and willingness of a government to service its debt. Ability to pay is based on objective measures, such as solvency, liquidity, and growth rates. Willingness to pay is based on subjective measures, such as the risk of policy makers reneging on their commitment to honor debt obligations. The ability and willingness of governments to service their debts are reflected in the credit ratings assigned to government bonds.

Cantor and Packer argue that the main factors affecting a government's sovereign ratings are "per capita income, GDP growth, inflation, external debt, level of economic development and default history."[9] Per capita income, GDP growth, external debt, default history and the level of economic development are functions of fiscal choices – financing and spending choices about consumption or long term investments. Governments that choose to rely on debt to finance consumption give up growth. Governments that choose to finance infrastructure development or education can contribute to higher per capita income and growth. In addition, inflation levels reflect monetary and fiscal policy choices while restrictive monetary policy and deficit financing are examples of inflationary policy alternatives. All of the factors affecting a government's credit ratings reflect policy makers' choices. These choices are about debt and tax financing, debt management and monetary and fiscal stability. In short, these are domestic economic policy choices that impact the terms and conditions under which governments can access private market financing.

Trust is the key ingredient in every financial market transaction. Financial market participants make the implicit assumption that transactions are binding commitments, not just enforced by the rule of law but sustained by mutual trust. In an age of instant communications, electronic market transactions among virtual strangers take place across national borders under the unwritten rule that one's word is one's bond. Markets hold governments to the same principles that market participants adhere to in executing transactions. These principles are loosely labeled "market discipline" and represent the convergence of three conditions, credibility, transparency, and accountability. These conditions are rooted in trust and constitute a key benchmark for assessing how the behavior of public policy makers signals a government's willingness to service its external debt. Ability and willingness to pay result in higher credit ratings and lower borrowing costs. Ability to pay without the willingness to pay results in lower, more speculative ratings and higher borrowing costs, but willingness to pay without the ability to do so is likely to block access to global capital markets.

A conventional definition of a government's willingness to pay involves the subjective evaluation of political and economic risks. Willingness to pay is closely connected to a government's credibility. Credibility can be defined as the ability to signal, make, and sustain policy commitments binding a government to fiscal restraint.[10] This narrow definition of credibility only refers to fiscal policy. In this context, a policy of fiscal restraint is considered credible when financial market participants trust the willingness of policy makes to service their debt obligations.[11] In addition, a history of respecting property rights leads to credibility. This is particularly true in the case of foreign direct investments, long-term investments, often in plant and equipment. The risk of expropriation reduces a government's credibility in terms of foreign direct investments, but this risk is nonexistent for bond investors. A single keystroke can electronically transfer ownership, location, and the amount of bond portfolios in a matter of seconds across the globe. This global capital mobility puts the burden of instant trust on governments. If ability to pay creates creditworthiness, willingness to pay creates trustworthiness. This study develops a more objective definition of willingness to pay. This definition is based on institutional credibility and represents the willingness to make, apply, and enforce transparent budgetary rules. Institutional credibility requires a careful consideration of what makes fiscal rules credible, how the transparency of financial markets relates to budget rules and why information is the vital link between credibility, transparency, and accountability.

Credibility, transparency, and accountability go hand in hand when policy makers confront the information standards of global financial market participants. For global capital market participants, institutional transparency and fiscal policy disclosure means less uncertainty – for public policy makers, information standards mean greater pressures for delivering fiscal restraint. Making fiscal policy commitments that are credible to financial market participants makes policy makers mainly accountable to international creditors. These same commitments, however, may or may not be desirable to domestic constituents. Examining how policy makers translate budget institutions and fiscal policy choices into access to the global debt markets contributes to a better conceptual understanding of institutional choice and credible fiscal commitment. More importantly, however, this inquiry leads to a better understanding of the political and economic consequences of these choices.

Scope of Study

This study compares the impact of institutional and fiscal policy choices on the ability of governments to access private market financing. From a comparative public policy perspective, this study focuses on Argentina, Chile, and Mexico (1980-1995) and selects three narrow dimensions of institutions, public policy and global finance. In terms of institutions, this study only examines budgetary institutions, defined as the formal rules and procedures by which national budgets are formulated, approved, and implemented. These institutions are linked to fiscal policy, defined as the outcome of fiscal decision-making and embedded in the approved budget itself. Alesina et al. suggest that "fiscal outcomes are not independent of institutions, that is, government [the executive branch] and legislatures must not be able to produce whatever fiscal outcome they (collectively) choose, regardless of the budget procedures which are in place."[12]

The emphasis on institutions means that this is not a comparative study of liberal democratic regimes in Latin America, but rather a comparative analysis of budget institutions and fiscal policies across three emerging liberal democratic states. From this perspective, fiscal policy is defined as fiscal outcome and is derived from the respective institutional settings. Consequently, the nuances of the emergence of liberal democracy across all three countries are acknowledged, but do not constitute a central point of analysis.

In terms of global finance, this study analyzes primarily financial flows related to the sovereign debt market. The sovereign debt market is the segment of the global private capital market where governments seek debt financing through the issuance of government bonds. This is where public finance and private capital markets intersect. This study considers private equity financing in terms of stock portfolio flows and foreign direct investments but ignores other forms of public debt financing, such as official and private loans. Also excluded are all short-term, private flows through the foreign exchange, derivative, and commodity markets. Some of the included capital flows such as equity portfolio flows may reflect the one time sale of state owned firms, but do not represent a recurring method of public financing. Other capital flows such as foreign direct investments represent long term, private sector equity financing. Nonetheless, both of these equity flows are considered in this study because credible fiscal policy commitments may affect the investment decisions of financial market participants in both bond and equity markets. Investment decisions do not have a distinct character for each one of these financial markets. Consequently, both bond and equity flows are taken into account. From the perspective of this study, the repeated and interactive choices of policy makers and financial market participants establish credibility patterns that evolve over time.

The multiple causes and effects inherent in the policy making process complicate any study of macroeconomic policy. In addition, the study of global finance involves a complex array of actors, processes, and outcomes that combine order and uncertainty.[13] To overcome these theoretical challenges, this study focuses on a single macroeconomic policy, namely, fiscal policy and concentrates on a single effect of fiscal policy, namely, access to the sovereign debt market. This inquiry singles out fiscal policy for two main reasons.

First, since the collapse of Bretton Woods in 1973, the global economy has increasingly consisted of open and interdependent national economies.[14] The openness of an economy is both a function of trade liberalization, the removal of trade barriers, and financial deregulation, the removal of capital controls. While industrial countries have largely adopted floating exchange rate regimes, developing countries have adopted fixed exchange rate regimes.[15] The main reason for developing countries to adopt fixed exchange rate regimes is to attract both trade and capital flows. When fixed exchange rates are set by the government, both exchange rate volatility and the need for a monetary mechanism are eliminated.

The contemporary post- Bretton Woods system represents a dual international monetary regime subject to the "unholy trinity" of international economics. This trinity holds that in the context of free capital mobility, a government cannot exercise monetary policy autonomy and at the same time adopt a fixed exchange rate regime.[16] Argentina, Chile, and Mexico abandoned capital controls and adopted fixed exchange rate regimes during the 1980-1995 period. Therefore, in each case, free capital mobility and the fixed exchange rates set by each government negated monetary policy autonomy. Without monetary policy autonomy, defined as the ability to manipulate prices, interest rates, exchange rates, the money supply and other key indicators of economic performance, fiscal policy becomes the most significant tool to achieve internal and external macroeconomic balance.

A recent study by Kontopoulos finds that compared to monetary policy, fiscal policy plays an equal or more significant role for economic stabilization. He argues that credible fiscal policy affects economic actors' expectations of economic activity faster than monetary policy. Moreover, his findings suggest that "while fiscal policy appears as a necessary condition for successful price stability, the same is not true for monetary policy."[17] These findings convey the centrality of fiscal policy suggesting that it represents an important policy determinant of economic stabilization, and as such may influence governmental access to private market financing.

Second, the significant relationship between fiscal policy and credible commitments has been largely ignored in both economic and political analyses. The bulk of existing research on credible policy commitments addresses monetary policy. The most recent studies are institutional and examine the significance of central bank independence in establishing credible monetary policy commitments.[18] This gap in the literature offers a unique opportunity for inquiring how and why fiscal policy commitments become credible. Credible commitments in monetary policy are attributed in large part to central bank independence. In this case, the credible part of the commitment depends on the depoliticization of monetary policy making. Such a simple, institutional solution is not a realistic alternative for building credible fiscal policy commitments.[19] The reason fiscal policy is central to how, why and under what terms governments gain access to private market financing is that financial market participants view fiscal policy as a key indicator of both government and economic performance. As such, fiscal policy is not only at the "heart of politics,"[20] as Mitchell contends, but at the very heart of economics.

Domestic budget institutions and processes are inherently political.[21] To extract the fiscal function of government from the realm of politics entails deep institutional changes that would carve out the very core of this function. Reforms designed to depoliticize budgeting are not likely to be probable institutional choices for contemporary liberal democratic governments. In democracies, the making of fiscal policy represents the very essence of Lasswell's concise definition of politics: "who gets what, when and how."[22] Fiscal policy – taxing and spending – is what governments do or fail to do regarding the allocation of scarce economic resources. Unlike monetary policy, fiscal policy is not removable from the political arena. As monetary policy opts out of politics, fiscal policy steps in and adopts a central role on the stage of global finance.

Methodology

This study relies on the comparative method to examine the effect of budget institutions and fiscal policy choices on a government's access to the sovereign debt market. The focus is on the systematic comparison of a limited number of most similar cases, Argentina, Chile and Mexico. These cases, however, are not perfectly matched. For example, during the late 1980s all three countries reduced fiscal deficits and demonstrated fiscal restraint in managing their debts, but following these policy choices, only Argentina and Mexico experienced a sharp rise in sovereign debt issues. The comparison of similar cases is commonly used for regional studies but confronts what Collier calls "the problem of over-determination - the design fails to eliminate many rival explanations, leaving the researcher with no criteria for choosing among them."[23]

In an attempt to address the problem of over-determination, this study combines qualitative and quantitative analysis. The research questions are answered both in terms of historical interpretation and a variable-oriented approach. The historical interpretation approach is qualitative and allows for modest generalizations usually about causes and effects of narrow phenomena. This approach combines concept formation, causal, and interpretive analysis and is designed to uncover patterns of variance.[24] Historical interpretation is used to compare the economic and political context of institutional and policy choices in Argentina, Chile, and Mexico from 1980 to 1995.

In contrast, the variable-oriented method is quantitative. The first step is to specify three hypotheses derived from a deductive model founded on institutional, public policy and political economy theoretical approaches. The hypotheses derived from this model are: a) *credible fiscal policy commitments - commitments signaling fiscal restraint to financial market participants - increase access to the sovereign debt market;* b) *budget institutions and fiscal policy commitments lead to fiscal policy choices that can either strengthen or weaken a government's public finance capacity,* and c) *access to the sovereign debt market increases a government's capacity to finance public expenditures that can contribute to economic growth.*

The second step is to test these hypotheses through data mining techniques and correlation analysis. Data mining allows for starting the analysis with a very large number of variables. Through an iterative process driven by data mining algorithms, the large pool of variables is filtered down to the most important explanatory variables. This filtering process helps to eliminate rival explanations and enhances one's ability to identify relevant patterns of association.

One needs to be cautious about making empirical generalizations. Nevertheless, qualitative and quantitative comparisons allow for concept formation, contextual analysis, quantitative measurement and hypotheses testing. These analytical steps may be modest and preliminary but constitute the necessary building blocks of theory developed in this study. Collier states that

> Comparison is a fundamental tool of analysis. It sharpens the power of description, and plays a central role in concept formation by bringing into focus suggestive similarities and contrasts among cases. Comparison is routinely used in testing hypotheses, and it can contribute to the inductive discovery of new hypotheses and to theory building."[25]

This statement implies that comparison does not necessarily provide final answers to research questions. Ultimately, the power of this method lies in its strength to lead to the formulation of new questions – the very frontiers of new knowledge.

Rationale, Significance, and Implications of Study

Governments increasingly rely on global debt markets to finance public expenditures. The capacity to borrow through these markets empowers governments to finance infrastructure development, education, and other public expenditures that contribute to economic growth. Therefore, it is important to understand how and why institutional and policy choices enable governments to tap private market financing sources. When these choices signal credible commitments, financial market participants tend to trust both the ability and the willingness of policy makers to service debt obligations. Market access is predicated on trust. Therefore, it is necessary to better understand the interactive choices between financial market participants and public policy makers to build and sustain this trust.

In chapter two, the justification for this study flows out of the main gaps in definitions and analysis of credible fiscal policy commitment and the weakness of one-dimensional institutional approaches to public policy. In regards to the credible commitment problem, this study introduces a policy commitment typology. The typology represents a first step in developing a more robust concept than those currently available. In addition, credible commitment is analyzed in the context of fiscal rather than monetary policy. Given that credible monetary policy largely results from central bank independence, the study of credible fiscal policy allows for a more detailed political analysis. The conflicting nature of fiscal commitments requires one to pay particular attention to budget institutions. Institutional models based on either economic or historical explanations only capture particular fragments of institutional effects on policy. Separately, each approach has much to contribute to our understanding of institutional choice. Combined, however, these approaches provide a theoretical lens larger than the sum of their individual parts.[26]

Chapter three introduces a theoretical model of institutional choice and presents the comparative method as a means to study how, why and with what consequences Argentina, Chile, and Mexico gained access to the sovereign debt market from 1980-1995. The first step is to develop the model by synthesizing the economic and historical institutional approaches to public policy. The second step is to introduce elements of the advocacy coalition model to frame the political dimension of institutional choice. Furthermore, some elements of game theory are used to frame the economic and interactive dimension of institutional choice. The goal is to establish a framework capable of explaining how, why and with what consequences governments gain access to private market financing. The third step is to present an overview of the comparative method and to define how the comparative method applies to the analysis of budget institutions and fiscal policy choices in Argentina, Chile and Mexico. Qualitative and quantitative comparison are complementary methodological approaches and this study relies on both.

In chapter four, the comparative method is used from a qualitative perspective to assess the political economy of institutional choice in Argentina, Mexico, and Chile. In comparing the paths of fiscal policy and budget institutions from 1980-1995, the goal is to find variance in market access across similar histories, political cultures and institutions. This chapter describes the political, economic, and social contexts surrounding the institutional and fiscal policy choices made by policy makers in each country.

The period 1980-1995 is critical to an understanding of the significance of this study for three reasons. First, during this period Latin America experienced profound structural reforms in the areas of trade, tax, financial, and privatization policy. Recent research suggests that these combined reforms caused capital flows to the region.[27] The timing of reforms varied in each country but in each case, economic reforms contributed to the ability of each government to project greater credibility in the international sovereign debt markets.

Second, financial reforms appear to rank high in the list of priorities for newly elected presidents of emerging democracies. From the mid-1980s to the mid-1990s, Argentina, Chile, and Mexico experienced political liberalization that paralleled the economic revolutions in each country. The shift from authoritarian to democratic regimes in Argentina and Chile as well as the greater political liberalization of Mexico's one party rule marked a significant turning point for the credibility of these governments both in terms of domestic constituencies and international financial market participants.

Third, during the mid-1990s Latin American countries including Argentina, Chile, and Mexico began to negotiate bilateral agreements to develop regional regulatory cooperation in financial policy. Given the weak link between these individual economies and international financial markets, the cooperative regulatory arrangements in the region contributed to the increased access to sovereign debt markets experienced by each country during this critical transition period.

From 1980 to 1995, Argentina, Chile, and Mexico had to prove that structural economic reforms and political liberalization could translate into greater fiscal credibility among both international financial market participants and domestic constituencies. The period was critical in reversing a decade long decline in fiscal accountability. Two decades later, many of the lessons drawn from this transition period remain an important benchmark for the institutional choices policy makers confront as they seek to finance growth.

Chapter five presents quantitative data mining techniques designed to identify patterns in large, complex, disparate and often non-quantifiable data.[28] This chapter applies data mining techniques and correlation analysis to uncover patterns across the choice of budgetary institutions, fiscal policy choices, and access to the sovereign debt market in Argentina, Chile, and Mexico.

The primary goal is to determine what combination(s) of budget institutions and fiscal policy choices led to sovereign debt market access in Argentina, Chile, and Mexico.[29] This analysis identifies the institutional and policy mix facilitating market access. A secondary goal is to identify the extent to which access to the sovereign debt market triggers an increase in public finance capacity, particularly in terms of education, health care, and infrastructure expenditures. In addition to data mining tools, correlation analysis is used for the specific task of identifying how access to the sovereign debt market affects public finance capacity. Expenditure patterns are then matched to social development indicators in order to examine the social effects and political costs of market access.[30] Previous applications of data mining have been limited to various scientific and business applications but have not included the comparative study of fiscal policy and financial flow patterns. In conjunction with data mining techniques, correlation analysis is used to test one of the hypotheses derived from the theoretical model.

Chapter six summarizes the main points and findings of each chapter and presents the implications of the study for future research. The recent surge in global bond financing for developing countries marks not so much a discovery, but a rediscovery of sovereign debt markets in the twentieth century. During the rapid expansion of global capital markets from 1870-1914, Argentina, Canada, the United States, and Russia were the top four recipients of global capital flows.[31] During the next century, governments that find the appropriate institutional and policy mix to access private capital markets will strengthen their public finance capacity, stimulate economic growth and secure higher and more equitable living standards for their citizens.

Perhaps one of the most significant contributions of this study is the potential fusion of theory and practice. Theory provides the foundation for formulating the hypotheses to be tested in the comparative analysis of institutional and policy choices. This study contributes to our conceptual understanding of contemporary public policy by examining the relationship between budget institutions, fiscal policy, and global finance. In identifying patterns that either facilitate or block government access to an increasingly important source of private market financing, we gain a better understanding of public finance capacity. At a practical level, policy makers could apply the empirical theory and comparative method of this study to evaluate their budget institutions, fiscal policy choices, and conflicting commitments.

Chapter Two

Choice and Institutions

In this study, fiscal policy makers and financial market participants are defined as rational actors, situated within institutions that inform both intention to act and strategic action, thus leading to anticipated and unanticipated consequences. It is assumed from a rational choice perspective, that domestic budgetary rules and the rules of global finance define the rational interactive choices of policy makers and financial market participants. It is further assumed that these rules delineate the extent to which domestic budget and global finance games run parallel to each other.[32] These parallel games converge, however, when governments gain access to the financial markets. How policy makers and financial market participants influence each other's choices depends on the formal rules of the game each plays, rules firmly grounded in history, culture, and society.

In studying the policy choices made by policy makers in the context of budget institutions, it is useful to adopt the concept of bounded rationality because it highlights important constraints on individual choice. These constraints are particularly relevant to fiscal decision making. Time constraints such as budget cycles, limited information, the cognitive limitations of policy makers to evaluate information, and formal budget rules restrict fiscal policy action. This means that rational fiscal policy makers are not necessarily free agents able to ignore time, information, cognitive constraints and formal budget rules to pursue their individual fiscal policy agendas. Furthermore, when policy makers choose to access the international sovereign debt market to finance public expenditures, formal market entry rules add another institutional constraint layer. Market entry rules such as credibility, transparency, and accountability define access terms.

Within the confines of formal institutions, however, policy makers have discretion to make policy choices reflecting both their individual preferences and those of their constituents. For example, policy makers can choose not to access the international sovereign debt market but once they make this choice, they need to play by the rules of the capital markets. Formal institutions and bounded rationality set the parameters of institutional and policy choice.[33] The concept of limited rationality has been influential in the development of institutional theories.

Rothstein suggests that by the mid-1980s several trends contributed to the rediscovery of institutions.[34] The "new" institutionalism has proved to be diverse and distinct from the "old" institutionalism – diverse in the sense that it represents three separate schools of thought, namely the historical, economic and sociological approaches and distinct in that it is theory driven. The central themes that emerge in the vast literature on institutions are stability and change. These are themes that political theorists have grappled with since Aristotle attempted to develop a typology of political regimes.

This study attempts to draw from the cumulative knowledge of all three new institutional perspectives to examine the political economy of institutional choice. The "new" institutionalism borrows analytical tools from economics, sociology and history, thus it is less of an indigenous political science approach. Additionally, unlike their predecessors, the new institutionalists tend to define institutions as "rules of the game" rather than defining institutions as organizations. This consensus across all three branches of the new institutionalism, however, does not extend to an agreement about the rules to be included and excluded.

For Lijphart, Wildavsky and Olsen, institutions are defined as both informal (cultural) and formal rules, routines, norms of behavior and standard operating procedures. For North, who has pioneered institutional analysis from an economic perspective, formal rules are the key. In his work, however, North recognizes that informal incentives play a part in shaping behavior and outcomes and begins to consider cultural norms.[35] In contrast, Tsebelis and Hall focus only on formal rules. I adopt Tsebelis and Hall's definition to characterize institutions as formal rules and procedures.[36]

In addition to defining institutions, it is also important to consider the role of institutions. Scholars differ in their explanations of institutions, but there is a general consensus that institutions influence strategy, preferences, and social capital.[37] None of the contemporary institutional literature, however, links strategy, preferences, and commitment.

Strategy is closely linked to commitment. Institutions determine who gets to be an actor, in what order actors move (according to Ostrom, sequence of action influences outcomes) and what actors have veto power.[38] I define veto power as the unilateral power institutional actors have to make or not to make binding policy commitments and their subsequent policy choices. In this context, veto power relates to the ability to either make or stop a budget decision. For example, the executive branch yields its veto power when it makes a fiscal policy commitment to reduce deficit spending without congressional approval. In contrast, the legislative branch exercises veto power over a budget decision when it rejects a budget proposed by the executive branch.

In terms of preferences, two views dominate. One view holds that preferences can only be attributed to individuals. This is the position of economic institutionalists and rational choice theorists such as Olson, Riker, and Ostrom. Another view holds that preferences emanate from culture and society. The society-centered view is represented by the work of sociological institutionalists such as Powell and Di Maggio, and March and Olsen.[39] The sociological argument is weak for two reasons. First, it equates institutions with organizations providing no clear explanation of where preferences originate. A definition of institutions as formal "rules of the game" provides a firmer grounding for arguing that institutions constrain actions. Organizations are merely the infrastructures within which formal rules are made, applied and adjudicated. Second, when informal, social norms are considered sources of institutional constraint it is difficult to explain exactly how society constrains action.

In contrast, formal rules are well delineated and can more accurately explain how institutions constrain action. For example, budget institutions may define specific limits on spending and borrowing. These formal budget rules constrain the actions of policy makers who may have a preference for open ended expenditures. While formal rules can impose specific costs and penalties for non-compliance, social norms can be more amorphous regarding sanctions for non-compliance. In sum, this argument leads to an acknowledgment that a focus on formal rules and an economic institutionalist explanation is more likely to uncover the linkages between preferences, commitment and action.

Economic institutionalism ignores the influence of society, culture and history on formal rules. The strength of this approach lies in its simplifying assumption, a focus on individual preferences – rules and organizations do not have preferences, individuals do. On the other extreme, the sociological explanation adopts the view that informal social norms constrain action. The strength of this perspective is its acknowledgment of culture, but the exclusion of history is a weakness.[40]

In contrast, historical institutionalism offers potential explanations of the origin of preferences by introducing path dependence to the analysis of institutions. This approach combines historical analysis with assessments of strategic behavior- what six decades ago Friedrich labeled "the rule of anticipated reactions."[41] The works of Steinmo, Immergut, Skocpol, Weir and Orloff represent the historical institutionalist approach, but this body of literature largely ignores the question of preferences and the problem of commitment.[42]

This study develops a hybrid, economic-historical approach focusing on formal rules implicitly rooted in culture and explicitly grounded in history (path dependence). For the sake of parsimony, this eclectic institutional approach leaves out sociological explanations of institutions. The weakness of economic institutionalist explanations is that they say nothing about where preferences originate. From the economic perspective, preferences are deduced from individual behavior, indicating where preferences lead, but not where they originate. This is the crux of the problem of commitment. Commitment constitutes a higher order of preferences. This perspective departs from the conventional wisdom that places preferences ahead of policy commitment. Here, the assumption is that a policy commitment carries economic and political values that shape preferences. In turn, preferences influence policy choice. Therefore, policy commitments precede both preferences and policy choice. These concepts are further developed in the theoretical framework of this study.

The Problem of Commitment

The concept of "credible commitment", originated with Oliver Williamson.[43] He focuses on transaction costs and views "credible ways" as costs to which partners could commit themselves to "nonopportunistic behavior." From this perspective, a commitment represents a promise of future performance. If broken, this promise carries an economic cost that discourages those exchanging promises from breaking their commitment. Williamson's definition of credible commitment focuses on economic constraints and is narrower than the definition of commitment adopted in this study. Here credible commitment is defined in terms of both constraints and incentives. The definition moves beyond binding economic constraints that impose costs on those who break commitments. Fiscal policy commitments that are credible to financial market participants not only bind policy makers to a specific course of action (e.g., reducing debt) but generate incentives (e.g., lower borrowing costs) that reward those choices. In this context, policy commitments represent a point of departure for both preferences and policy choice. Commitments that are credible to financial market participants carry specific political values such as respect for the rule of law and private property and political and economic goals such as stability and growth.

In the late 1970s and early 1980s, economic studies of political institutions focused on the effects of institutions on choice. In the early 1980s, North linked the concept of credible commitment to the study of political rulers and economic development. North addressed the problem of constitutional economic constraints on rulers. According to Miller, North's interpretation of commitment abandons the assumption of self-interested choices of political actors in favor of an explanation that constitutional commitments restrict the self-interested choices of rulers.[44] Once again, however, the definition of credible commitment is limited to an economic interpretation. The focus shifts from economic constraints to economic goals. North incorporates economic goals into his definition but leaves out political goals and values.

In the 1990s, North and Weingast continue to focus on a narrow economic definition of credible commitment and examine the beneficial effects of constitutional commitment on the emergence of financial markets during England's Glorious Revolution of 1688. The authors argue that one of the determinants of England's financial markets was the creation of credible constraints on the king, who had incentives to infringe on property rights and violate contracts.[45] The shift in focus from economic to constitutional constraints does not clarify the problem of commitment, it merely shifts attention from economic rules to a higher order of formal political rules.

By the mid 1990s, institutional analysis links institutional choice, change and policy commitment. Examples of such work include studies by Weingast and Milgrom connecting credible commitments to international trade and the works of Levy, Spiller, Sampson, Vogelsand, Galal, Hill, Esfahani and Abdala connecting regulatory policy, institutions and commitment.[46] These combined studies, however, do not link the problem of commitment to fiscal policy choices and access of governments to the sovereign debt market. Furthermore, none of these studies provides a careful definition of what constitutes a fiscal policy commitment or explains what makes such a commitment credible.

One of the most comprehensive attempts to define credible fiscal policy commitment is the work of Patashnik. He constructs a typology of credible budget contracts ranging from "strong to weak" based on the level of institutional protection and officeholders' incentives to maintain promises.[47] His solution to the credible commitment problem, however, does not specify the thresholds that trigger a weak commitment to become strong or a strong one to become weak. Patashnik emphasizes transaction cost theory to address the problem of government commitment but underestimates the role of conflict and conflict resolution inherent in the politics of budgeting.

By leaving out the conflicting nature of political commitments, the literature on credible commitments avoids confronting the questions of how we know when policy commitments are credible and to whom policy commitments are credible. For example, fiscal policy commitments that are credible to global financial market participants may not be credible or desirable to labor unions or voters. My study closes this gap by focusing on the political values and goals that fiscal policy commitments carry when they are credible to financial market participants.[48] In this context, I acknowledge the conflicting nature of fiscal policy commitments and suggest that commitment is the point of departure for preferences.

Commitment is defined as a decision by policy makers to settle on a strategic course of action. Action is the choice of tactical policy alternatives resulting from that decision. The process of settling on a course of action is influenced by formal rules. For example, budget institutions influence fiscal policy commitments and fiscal policy choices. Budget institutions, however, are not static and the process by which rules change is incremental and adaptive. In the context of a global political economy, governments that seek private market financing undergo institutional change through rule learning. Budgetary rule learning and fiscal policy commitment in the context of global finance can best be understood from a subsystems perspective, one of several approaches to studying the policy process.

Policy Process

The study of the policy process is closely linked to the study of political institutions. The literature on policy implementation in general, and the subsystems literature in particular, are relevant to the study of institutions. Sociological institutionalists, for example, ground their work in organizational theory, a major theoretical approach in the field of policy implementation. The connection between institutions and policy process is explicit in this study – how fiscal policy is implemented flows from formal budgetary rules and procedures. These rules and procedures are inherently political, domestic, rooted in history and political culture. The policy process, however, evolves within the contexts of domestic politics and a global political economy that transcends national borders. When policy makers choose to finance public expenditures through private capital markets, such as the sovereign debt market, market rules cannot be ignored. The dual context of the policy process is characteristic of open and interdependent national economies that coexist with closed, domestic political systems.[49]

This study views domestic budget institutions as endogenous factors linked to the domestic fiscal policy process and to the global political economy. This is an attempt to solve a decision-making problem involving interactive choice, uncertainty, and imperfect information.[50] Interactive choice applies to problems of bargaining, organizations, institutions, and cultural exchange. Unlike individual choice, which concentrates on a single rational agent and collective choice, which examines decision- making by groups constrained by social norms that ensure that agreements are carried out, interactive choice explores "non-cooperative games."[51] Such games involve actors who choose independent strategies and are not necessarily bound by prior commitments, bargains, or arrangements.

Policy makers have autonomy to chose budget institutions and fiscal policy within the borders of their sovereign states. When, however, policy makers choose to finance domestic public expenditures through international private capital markets, domestic choices are subject to the close scrutiny of global financial market participants. This does not mean that financial market participants dictate institutional or policy choices, it means that policy makers that choose private market financing have to comply with market rules to access and maintain this type of financing. Policy makers who renege on their fiscal commitments and fail to be accountable for their fiscal actions forfeit their access to private market financing.

Within the literature that views global financial markets as sources of constraint on domestic political autonomy and choice, one argument prevails: credit rating agencies are gate keepers that block government access to global financial markets.[52] This argument is flawed. Credit rating agencies and other financial market participants such as underwriters have much to lose (e.g., underwriting fees) and little to gain when governments are kept out of global capital markets. Furthermore, fiscal and monetary policies are not formulated, approved and implemented by financial market participants."[53]

Fiscal choices are made by budget veto players. Elected and appointed government officials make budget choices that determine fiscal outcomes. These outcomes, in turn, influence the actions of financial market participants, but policy makers rather than economic actors determine the composition of the budget. From this perspective, public finance capacity is derived from institutional and policy choices. Choices that are credible to financial market participants can lead to sovereign debt market access. *Ceteris paribus*, rather than eroding financing capacity, the sovereign debt market, empowers governments to make investments that may lead to economic growth.[54]

A comparative study of budget institutions and fiscal policy choices made by Argentina, Chile, and Mexico from 1980-1995 cannot ignore the contours of the global political economy. When the focus of analysis is the effect of institutional and policy choices on the ability of governments to access the international sovereign debt market, the political economy is a pivotal contextual variable. Albeit narrow, the political economy approaches used in this study contribute to the overall objective of this inquiry.

Theoretical Approaches

Theories of political economy provide a contextual backdrop for the public policy and institutional approaches used in this study. Consistent with the selection of public policy theories, the selection of political economy theories focuses on two complementary approaches. These two approaches are combined within the framework of neoclassical economic theory: an economic approach to politics, and a state-centered approach to political economy.

These two approaches capture important political and economic variables affecting institutional and policy choices. The economic approach to politics adopts a key concept, the notion of constrained choice. This perspective retains the neoclassical assumptions about individual rational choice, but qualifies those choices with a given set of available resources, technology, and existing rules.[55] This perspective expands the concept of bounded rationality, adding technology and existing rules as sources of constraint. Given the importance of technology in the functioning of global finance, the economic approach to politics is a useful theoretical tool. Furthermore, the recognition of existing rules as sources of constraint does not exclude the probability of rule learning and institutional change. The weakness of this approach lies in its lack of political focus.

Economic theories of politics are primarily centered on the economy and view the state in instrumental terms. In contrast, the state-centered approach to political economy adopted by Nordlinger acknowledges that the autonomy of the state involves the capacity of policy makers to execute their preferences. These preferences translate into public policy, regardless of the support or opposition of non-office holders.[56] This argument needs to be qualified to acknowledge that public pressures may influence preferences. When we view fiscal policy in the context of global finance, however, financing pressures may take precedence over public pressures.

The strength of this approach lies in its simplifying assumption – policy makers order their preferences and make autonomous choices that translate into public policy. One weakness is that the state-centered approach ignores constraints on the choices of policy makers. The main weakness of this approach, however, is methodological. When translating preferences into policy, it is problematic to measure preferences and then infer that specific policy choices resulted from these preferences. It is particularly difficult to isolate what part of the policy choice results from policy makers' unconstrained choice and what part results from institutional constraints.[57]

The state-centered approach to political economy is compatible with the theoretical framework of this study. In particular, this view of policy makers is consistent with the selected concepts of historical institutionalism. The notion that government has the capacity to structure the character and the resolution of conflicts implies that policy makers are not neutral and have the power to influence political outcomes. I define this power in institutional terms – the power to learn, make, and apply the rules of the game.[58]

The economic approach to politics can be applied to problems of public choice, policy efficiency, and institutions. The latter application is the most relevant for the purposes of this study. The state-centered approach recognizes that the state is not an abstract entity; it consists of individuals with specific preferences.[59] On their own, the economic and state -centered approaches to political economy are one-dimensional – either explaining economic or political phenomena. Combined, however, these approaches provide a wider, two-dimensional theoretical lens. The study of institutional choice requires such a lens capable of capturing the political and economic context in which choices are made by policy makers and financial market participants.

Theoretical Framework

The central question of this study is: What is the effect of fiscal policy on a government's access to the sovereign debt market? The subquestions are: 1) How, why and with what consequences do credible fiscal policy commitments translate into public finance capacity? 2) What are the political costs involved in gaining greater public finance capacity? Following Rosenau and Durfee's prescription for thinking theoretically, it is important to ask: "Of what is this [study] an instance".[60] The answer to this question forces us to envision a larger universe of political and economic phenomena of which this particular study is a case. This is a study of interactive choices: choices about budget institutions, fiscal policy and government access to private market financing. The interactive choices of policy makers and sovereign debt market participants are instances of decision-making . On the part of policy makers, these choices involve decisions about budgetary rules, procedures, fiscal commitments, and fiscal policy choices. On the part of sovereign debt market participants, these choices involve decisions about credit ratings, assessment of credible policy commitments and willingness to lend. These interactive choices take place within the context of a domestic policy process and a global political economy.

Three public policy theoretical approaches are relevant to the study of decision making. These approaches are suited to the central question of this study, because they offer complementary explanations of institutional choice and public policy making. These approaches include an advocacy coalition framework developed by Sabatier, a theory of interactive choice, and a theory of institutions that combines historical and economic concepts.[61] Sabatier's model explains the process of policy change over a period of one or several decades.[62] Some elements of this framework apply to the comparative study of institutional and fiscal policy choices implemented in Argentina, Chile, and Mexico from 1980-1995. Sabatier's important contribution links policy choices to policy-oriented learning and shifts the focus of policy subsystems from description to analysis. The concept 'advocacy coalition' as the unit of analysis allows for the aggregation of actors, who share a set of beliefs and coordinate their activities over time.[63]

Viewed through this particular theoretical lens, economic policy makers choose fiscal policy alternatives and financial market participants evaluate policy choices to determine the terms and conditions under which governments can access the sovereign debt market to finance public expenditures. Assuming that these actors share a set of basic economic values, such as economic growth, one can argue that policy makers and financial market participants conform to different sets of rules in their respective institutional settings. Shared economic belief systems do not necessarily translate into a mutually accepted and credible fiscal policy.

The simplifying assumption of shared economic growth values is parsimonious but ignores political values such as economic and political equality. A review of the vigorous debate over the trade-offs between economic growth and equitable distribution of resources is beyond the scope of this study. Nevertheless, it is necessary to acknowledge that policy makers and financial market participants who focus on economic growth largely do so at the expense of economic equity while completely ignoring political equity.[64]

Equitable growth remains elusive for much of the world but recent normative research on the growth-efficiency debate moves towards a synthesis of growth and equity. From this perspective, equity and efficiency can be compatible within the context of educational, financial and judicial reforms. For example, writing about growth and equity in Latin America, Shehan and Iglesias contend "low quality of mass education, high concentrations of asset ownership and great resistance to progressive taxation" block progress toward greater equality.[65]

Sheahan and Iglesias' prescribe an increase in labor skills and wages and a reduction of regressive taxes. They focus on economic and social policies that deliver equity and growth in the long run. Their argument aims to reverse the conventional argument that growth causes inequality and emphasizes the long run beneficial effects of growth- oriented policies on social equity. This line of argument is also evident in a recent article by King who claims: "although higher growth rates do seem to exert a negative impact upon basic needs outcomes in the short term of roughly half a decade, the longer term impact of growth upon basic needs appears to be negligible..."[66] These explanations remain narrowly focused on the short and long term effects of growth policies on social equity and leave out the intricacies of institutional and political choices.

Policy makers do not make choices about budget institutions and fiscal policy in a political vacuum. Fiscal policy choices are made in the context of conflicting domestic, political commitments. Because interactions between economic policy makers and financial market participants do not always result in cooperation, the advocacy coalition framework has limited explanatory power. Although Sabatier accounts for policy conflicts, he does not elaborate on how these conflicts affect policy choices. He accounts, however, for policy oriented learning, an important factor linking government and nongovernment actors.

Policy learning can contribute to an explanation of how fiscal policy choices affect a government's access to the sovereign debt market. If policy choices can be learned, it is possible that over time the policy learning process smoothes out conflict by reinforcing shared core values. Policy learning is particularly relevant to a comparison of the fiscal policy choices of Argentina, Chile, and Mexico from 1980-1995. Gradually, over this period of time, each government reached a fiscal policy consensus that opened access to the international sovereign debt markets. According to Sabatier, policy learning is an important factor in understanding policy changes over time. The concept of policy learning is relevant in the analysis of budget institutions. Rules are not static. Specifically, budget rules can and do change over time. Thus, it is necessary to extend Sabatier's policy learning concept to the process of budgetary rule learning.

Sabatier identifies three dimensions of policy oriented learning. First, he argues that this process entails "improving one's understanding of the state of variables defined as important by one's belief system (or secondarily by competing belief systems)."[67] Second, he contends that the process involves the search for improved mechanisms to attain core values in their order of priority. He defines these core values as basic and normative, such as freedom, security, welfare or health. These core values can be interpreted as policy goals and in this context, one can add economic growth as a core value. Third, Sabatier introduces the possibility that external events motivate revisions in one's belief system. In his view, the structure of policy belief systems consists of three levels, a core, a near core representing the fundamental policy positions for a given policy area (e.g. fiscal policy) and secondary aspects defined as the instrumental decisions and information searches necessary to implement the policy core. Examples of the secondary aspects include decisions about administrative rules, budgetary allocations and even statutory revisions. Sabatier summarizes the interactive process of policy learning:

> "Policy-oriented learning, then, is an ongoing process of search and adaptation motivated by the desire to realize core policy beliefs. When confronted with constraints or opportunities, actors attempt to respond in a manner which is consistent with their core. Although exogenous events or opponents' activities may eventually force the reexamination of core beliefs, the pain of doing so means that most learning occurs in the secondary aspects of a belief system and/ or a governmental program."[68]

Sabatier places core policy values ahead of the secondary aspects of a policy belief system. His suggestion that learning takes place mainly in terms of administrative rules, budget allocations and statutory revisions imply that a major portion of what he labels policy learning is actually rule learning. Rule learning like policy learning is an adaptive process. For Sabatier, this process takes place at the periphery of core policy values.

If we extend Sabatier's definition of policy core values, to include policy commitment – defined as a decision to settle on a course of action– Sabatier's core policy values can be interpreted in a narrow sense, as both policy commitments and policy goals. From this perspective, fiscal policy commitments, core fiscal policy values, and fiscal policy goals are one and the same. This simplifying assumption recognizes that fiscal policy commitments can be conflicting and internally self-contradicting. For example, concurrent fiscal policy commitments to advance social welfare and implement fiscal discipline may be difficult to implement simultaneously.[69]

Sabatier simplifies the structure of policy belief systems and in doing so, he provides a limited explanation of institutional and policy change. Nevertheless, his framework provides a useful point of departure for a more comprehensive institutional analysis. Policy oriented learning, a major component of Sabatier's advocacy coalition framework, can be adapted to explain both institutional and policy choices. Policy learning in the context of global finance involves interaction over time between policy makers and financial market participants.

Institutions and policy are not static. Change is an integral part of institutional and policy choices. In this context, learning is a vital component of rule and policy making. In particular, for governments of newly industrialized economies such as Argentina, Chile, and Mexico, both rule and policy learning play an important role in the choice of budgetary institutions and fiscal policy alternatives. Rule and policy learning also play an important role in the interactions of policy makers and financial market participants.

The interaction between economic policy makers and financial market participants is not linear and involves a complex array of independent strategies that can either converge, diverge, or cycle. Game theory is a useful theoretical lens for this situation because it explains decision making when the actions of one actor depend on other actors' decisions.[70] This actor choice theory has been applied to the study of public policy actors in diverse settings such as voting, foreign policy decision-making, and bargaining situations.

Game theory is a powerful analytical tool grounded in rational choice. This tool can turn the informal understanding of a decision-making problem into a formal theoretical statement. This is not to say that by formalizing a problem one can arrive at a comprehensive explanation of a choice-centered process. Game theoretic models seek "to capture the general characteristics of a situation rather than the specific decisions of a particular event."[71] In this sense, game theory, as most theory in the social sciences, provides simplified and partial explanations.

There are five elements inherent in each game theoretic problem. These elements specify a game. First, one needs to determine who makes decisions. Who are the players? In the case of this study there are two types of players, policy makers and financial market participants. Second, one defines the strategies available to decision-makers. For example, policy makers can choose between debt financing and tax financing strategies. Another choice might be strictly debt financing and the strategies would be bond financing or loan financing.

Third, one determines whether binding agreements are feasible between players. Assuming that a bond financing strategy is selected, are financial market participants willing and able to lend and are policy makers willing and able to service the debt? Here, one first confronts the problem of commitment. How credible are the commitments? The process of reaching binding agreements entails both conflict and bargaining. At the end of this process is the point where coalitions are formed. When agreements are binding and commitments credible, policy makers and financial market participants form a coalition to implement the agreed strategy.

The fourth element addresses the consequences, pay-offs, of all possible combinations of strategies for each player. At this point, one specifies the players' order of preferences. This ordering represents objectives and the pay-off represents the extent to which objectives are met given a particular outcome. The fifth element deals with the kind of information each player has about each other's strategy and pay-offs. The level of information known to players determines levels of uncertainty. Information known to all players is considered common knowledge. Common knowledge allows players to anticipate the reactions of other players. In contrast, when players do not share knowledge about strategies and pay-offs, the game is played under conditions of incomplete information .[72]

Game theory has been used to solve collective action and public choice problems. The work of Morrow focuses on the application of game theory to problems in political science. Two of these problems are relevant to the study of institutional choice. One is the problem of why rules are adopted and what the consequences of rules are and another is the problem of bargaining, which game theory treats as a sequence of strategic moves.[73] Game theory serves as a descriptive building block for the theoretical framework of this study.

Game theory tools and applications can help in understanding a sequence of plausible preferences and choices over outcomes that economic policy makers and financial market participants may hold. This study builds a deductive decision making model that captures the essence of how, why and with what consequences democratic governments gain access to private market financing. This model assumes that political behavior results from rational, strategic choices that best satisfy policy makers' objectives given the relevant constraints. From this perspective, choice is driven by procedural rationality - a short-cut device that employs rules of thumb to guide action.

This interpretation of rationality adopts Simon's concept of bounded rationality. Bounded rationality recognizes that decision makers are not always fully informed, may face time constraints and may lack the cognitive capacity to process all relevant information. For example, this approach to decision making uses adaptive expectations, which base future expectations on actual outcomes observed during recent periods.[74] Bounded rationality simplifies the problems of ranking present choices solely on the basis of rational expectations that involve the discounted present value of future actions. Fiscal policy makers who adopt rules of thumb and standard operating procedures do not necessarily ignore transaction, search and uncertainty costs. In fact, transaction cost theory complements the implicit assumption of incrementalism embedded in bounded rationality.[75]

Bounded rationality allows rational actors to move beyond the inadequacies of instrumental rationality which separates the individual from the social, historical and cultural context. The use of rules helps to locate the individual within this context, but does not negate individual agency.[76] Furthermore, the connection between rules and choice means that institutions shape the strategies, actions and outcomes of the decision making process. Given the centrality of institutions in the study of choice, this study adopts two complementary views of institutions.

Since the mid 1980s, the historical and economic schools of thought on institutions have evolved in relative isolation from one another. In a recent article, Hall and Taylor call for a synthesis of these approaches, while recognizing that since the early 1990s, Garrett, Weingast, Scharf and Bates have been moving towards an integration of new institutional approaches.[77] This study builds on the recent trend of selectively combining historical and economic approaches to provide a more complete explanation of institutional effects. The strengths of each approach are points of departure for selecting the factors to be integrated into a conceptual model of institutional choice.

Historical institutionalism, group theory, and structural functionalism share the assumption that conflict is at the center of politics. Historical institutionalists adopt the view that governments have the capacity to structure the "character and outcome" of conflict and view institutions as instrumental in the distribution of power.[78] This perspective is advantageous in the analysis of budget institutions and fiscal policy choices because conflicting commitments are at the center of budgetary politics. In addition, path dependence emphasizes the historical continuity of institutions complementing the argument that institutions reduce uncertainty for forward looking individual actors engaging in strategic behavior. In providing guidelines for action, institutions reduce uncertainty about behavior. These views are shared by some economic institutionalists.[79]

The main strength of the historical approach to institutions is that it connects actors' behavior to institutions through history and future-oriented strategic calculus. In contrast, the economic approach to institutions emphasizes forward looking behavior at the expense of historical path dependence. The strengths of economic institutionalism are a recognition that politics involves the management of uncertainty and that information affects political relations and outcomes.[80]

The main weakness of the economic and historical institutional approaches is that neither acknowledges the role of culture in shaping formal and informal rules. For example, formal budget institutions do not exist in isolation from the culture in which they evolve. One possible explanation for Latin America's predominance of hierarchical budget institutions may well be that these formal institutions are rooted in the cultural traditions of the region.[81]

An additional weakness of the economic and historical approaches is derived from the exclusion of cultural variables. When cultural context is ignored, institutional analysis may lead to weak cross- regional generalizations. By limiting this study to Latin America, it is possible to exclude culture because it represents a common denominator across all three countries to be compared. In excluding cultural context, however, economic and historical institutional analysis limits the scope of generalizations to the region. In spite of inherent weaknesses, the historical and economic approaches provide fertile theoretical ground to develop a model of institutional choice.

The combined strengths of the historical and economic institutional approaches complement public policy approaches. Combining institutional approaches with the selected components of Sabatier's advocacy coalition framework and game theory, results in the initial contour of a theoretical model of institutional choice. The selected theoretical approaches and their components are the point of departure for building the foundation of this model.

A Comprehensive Approach

To study either public policy or political economy in isolation from each other is to negate their interdependence. In order to combine these subfields, however, it is necessary to draw instruments from different theoretical traditions. This requires a careful selection of approaches and concepts.

The goal in selecting concepts is to find shared or compatible, simplifying assumptions. These assumptions link diverse theoretical perspectives into a simplified framework. Shared assumptions do not differ across theoretical approaches. Compatible assumptions differ but their differences can be reconciled. Both shared and compatible assumptions lead to compatible concepts.[82] Selected concepts are then qualified (e.g. bounded rationality) or extended (e.g. rule learning). In qualifying and extending concepts one can tailor concepts to the specific problem of institutional choice.

The selected components of each theoretical approach form the basis for qualifying or extending the main concepts used to build a theoretical model of institutional choice. The extended and qualified concepts are core theoretical building blocks linked together across approaches. Public policy approaches such as the advocacy coalition framework, rational choice theories of decision making such as game theory and institutional theories help answer the central question and the subquestions of this study.

Theoretical Approach	Selected Component	Concept Extension or Qualification
Advocacy Coalition	Policy-oriented Learning	Rule Learning
	Core Policy Value	Policy Goal and Commitment
Game Theory	Interactive Choice	Bounded Rationality
Historical Institutionalism	Path Dependence	Rule and Policy Learning
	Uncertainty	Link to Interactive Choice
	Strategic Calculation	Interactive Choice
Economic Institutionalism	Management of Uncertainty	Link to Rule Learning and Interactive Choice
	Information	Rule and Policy Learning

Figure 2.1 Theoretical Approaches.[83]

Institutional and policy choices, particularly choices about budget institutions and fiscal policy evolve within the boundaries of domestic politics. Outside of these boundaries, the global political economy serves as the backdrop for domestic choices. As acknowledged by Sabatier, policy choices are influenced by external socio-economic and political factors. When one asks about the effects of fiscal policy on a government's access to the sovereign debt market, domestic institutional and policy choices need to be understood in the context of the global political economy.

Three gaps identified in the literature review provide the keys for selecting the theoretical tools of this study. First is the problem of commitment. Definitions of policy commitment ignore the relationship between budgetary institutions, fiscal policy choices, and access to the sovereign debt market. Additionally, attempts to classify credible fiscal commitments fail to consider how commitments that are credible to economic actors may not be credible to political and social actors. Second, in contrast to approaches that attempt to describe or explain public policy from either a process, institutional or rational choice perspective, this study combines these perspectives. Third, in addition to applying economic reasoning to explain the policy process, this study seeks to integrate explanations of what happens when political and economic choices intersect. The focus of this analysis is interactive choice and it connects theories of public policy and theories of political economy.

In combining theoretical approaches, an important step is to select the components providing the most effective lens for examining institutional and policy choices. The next step is to either extend or qualify available concepts in order to tailor them to the object of our inquiry. These steps are presented in Figure 2.1 and are subsequently integrated into a broader framework. Theories of public policy and theories of political economy can be combined to arrive at a hybrid theory of institutional choice. The main components of this theoretical framework include institutions, policy process, and political economy. Each component constitutes a concentric sphere, where policy makers and financial market participants interact.[84] The main concepts for each selected theoretical approach are clustered and linked to three interaction spheres. These spheres are budget institutions (rules), policy process, and political economy (Figure 2.2).

As indicated by the dotted line, all three spheres are interconnected. The core budget institutions circle represents the formal rules of the budget game. Within the budget institutions circle, policy makers line up in a given order to formulate, approve, and implement budgets. Concept clusters representing both the advocacy coalition framework and the historical and economic institutionalisms are most directly related to the budget institutions circle. These concepts, however, also relate to the policy process sphere. The middle sphere is where fiscal policy makers confront conflicting commitments and choose fiscal policy strategies.

This is where concepts related to game theory and political economy converge. The policy process arena brings together all of the concept clusters representing the selected theoretical approaches.

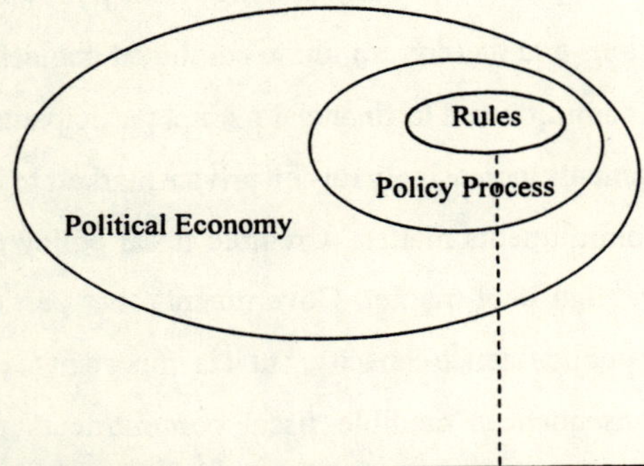

Theoretical Approach	
Advocacy Coaltion:	Rule Learning, Policy Goal and Commitment
Game Theory:	Interactive Choice, Bounded Rationality
Institutionalism:	
Historical	Path Dependence
Economic	Uncertainty, Information

Figure 2.2 A Comprehensive Approach showing selected theoretical approaches, related concepts and their connection to three spheres representing budget institutions, policy process and political economy.

The outer circle, political economy, is where financial market participants are located. This is the arena of global finance, where decisions are made about the credibility of governments and their access to the sovereign debt market.

This framework does not intend to mark the lines separating or uniting public and private spheres of political and economic action. The debate on where this line belongs is far from settled. I make no claim to contribute to this debate. I claim, however, that a point of departure for understanding fiscal policy choices is the choice of budget institutions and that in turn, these combined choices signal either credible or non-credible commitments to financial market participants.

Given that governments increasingly rely on private markets to finance public expenditures, credible commitments matter. Credible fiscal policy commitments create access to the sovereign debt market. Governments that participate in this market can increase their public finance capacity, but it is important to examine how, why and with what consequences credible fiscal commitments translate into increased public finance capacity. It is to these specific questions that we now turn.

Chapter Three

A Conceptual Model of Institutional Choice

This chapter proceeds with a description of a conceptual model of institutional choice followed by a description and justification of the qualitative and quantitative comparison used in this study. The institutional, policy process and political economy perspectives constitute a theoretical platform from which a simple conceptual model evolves. This model is grounded in the interrelated concepts presented in Figure 2.2. While these concepts provide a foundation, it is necessary to identify significant variables and their relationships.

Concepts are elusive, particularly as one "moves up the ladder" of theoretical abstraction.[85] This movement, however, is imperative when one builds a conceptual model. The first step is to highlight the conceptual path from interactive choice to sovereign debt market access. The second step is to define four key concepts: fiscal rules, policy choice, policy commitment and sovereign debt market access. The third step is to turn these concepts into variables and draw hypotheses about their relationships. These steps lead to a conceptual model of institutional choice.

Method follows and complements theory. Different methods suggest how to solve a problem and point out the research direction to be taken – either the empirical-causal approach or the value-interpretive approach.[86] Comparative analysis is useful to test the general applicability of theoretical models. Theory provides guidelines to organize and interpret data. Comparative analysis allows one to test hypotheses derived from theory across different cases. This study adopts what

Hauge *et al.* label "focused comparisons"– an approach using a systematic comparison of a limited number of cases and relying on less detail than a case study.[87] With this approach, each hypothesis derived from the conceptual model is subjected to qualitative and quantitative comparison.

The path from institutional choice to the sovereign debt market consists of four related concepts. Each concept, in turn, is linked to specific subconcepts derived from the selected theoretical approaches (Figure 2.2). A reordering of these elements into four concept clusters yields a sketch of the main components of the model. A brief definition of each component follows this sketch:

Budget Rules	Policy Choice	Policy Commitment	Market Access
• Interactive Choice	Interactive Choice	Interactive Choice	Interactive Choice
• Path Dependence	Uncertainty	Agency of	Uncertainty
• Culture Specific	Information	Policy Makers	Information
• Rule Learning	Conflict	Conflict	

Figure 3.1 Key concepts defining the path from institutional choice to the sovereign debt market.

Budget rules are defined as the domestic, formal rules used to formulate, approve, and implement budgets. Budget rules determine who participates at each level of the budget process, in what order budget participants make fiscal policy choices and who has veto power over budget choices. These rules are embedded in the political culture and historical path of each and every government.[88] Budget rules define the scope of conflict and determine where these conflicts get to be resolved. Hierarchical budget institutions, resolve these conflicts within the confines of the executive branch, often with a limited number of actors (e.g. cabinet ministers). Collegial budget institutions resolve these conflicts in a broader arena, legislatures influenced by domestic public opinion. Path dependence influences how and to what extent rules change over time.[89]

Rule learning is an adaptive process because of path dependence. In the context of budget rules, new rules are incorporated or may replace existing institutional frameworks. Therefore, rule learning can be defined as an incremental process. This view of rule learning forces us to look beyond the process and examine the actions of policy makers. The process of rule learning involves the interactive choice of policy makers at three levels, namely within budget institutions, the policy process, and the global political economy.

Communications technology accelerates the diffusion of information and technical knowledge and in doing so expands the scope and depth of rule learning. Newly industrialized countries, better defined as new globally linked countries, are increasingly adopting transparent budget rules.[90] Transparent budget rules are rules that disclose information about how budget choices are made. Transparent rules are credible to financial market participants because they eliminate the uncertainty of figuring out how budgets will be formulated, approved and implemented. More importantly, transparency suggests how conflicts will be resolved.

The process of rule learning, however, largely depends on who learns and how domestic politics affect the learning process. Policy makers who are willing and able to learn transparent budget rules position their governments to become more competitive in accessing international debt markets. Policy makers unwilling or unable to learn transparent budget rules face higher borrowing costs, limited or no market access. Budget rules shape policy choices and commitments.

Budget commitments are inherently domestic. Budget rules frame conflicting budget commitments within the domestic policy process. Conflicts over budget commitments are played out within the context of the fiscal policy process. Policy choice can be defined as a preferred course of government action resulting from policy commitments. A fiscal policy commitment is the decision to settle on a given course of fiscal action, be it debt financing or tax financing. Commitment entails the willingness to accept the political, economic and social consequences of a policy choice. Commitment is the willingness to see policy action through to its conclusion. From the standpoint of financial market participants, credible fiscal policy commitments are those that signal fiscal restraint. For example, a commitment to reduce deficit financing entails the implementation of debt reducing steps until targeted deficit reductions are reached.

Policy makers are defined as rational individuals bounded by imperfect knowledge, incomplete information, limited cognition and transaction costs.[91] Policy makers adopt new budget rules within existing, domestic institutional settings. Rules to formulate, approve and implement budgets are applied within a policy process characterized by multiple advocacy coalitions - policy subsystems consisting of various actors from government and the private sector who influence policy actions. Sabatier's definition of policy subsystem is useful to portray the multiple areas of policy concern inherent in the budget process. From Sabatier's perspective, public and private actors can be aggregated into coalitions representing a set of core policy beliefs.[92]

Policy makers operating within hierarchical or collegial budget institutions, however, increasingly make fiscal policy choices within the context of the global political economy. When policy makers seek private market financing in global bond markets, their fiscal policy choices become important factors determining access to these markets. Fiscal choices influence the decisions of financial market participants who provide access to the sovereign debt markets. Access, in turn, provides governments with increased public finance capacity. Policy choice and market access are linked through parallel interactive choices. These choices are influenced by uncertainty and information.[93]

Most policy decisions are made under conditions of uncertainty. Information is mostly incomplete due to limits in the cognitive capacity of decision makers and the time or cost constraints of collecting all possible information. Uncertainty is defined as what is unknown about future outcomes. Incomplete information is defined as what is known about the probability of a given outcome. Uncertainty and incomplete information are conditions of interactive choice.

Interactive choice takes place in three arenas, namely, budget institutions, the policy process and the global political economy. Rule learning, path dependence, culture, conflict, uncertainty and information represent conditions of interaction. Last but not least, it is important to consider the possible effects of interactive choice. This task requires the most simplification. The model specifies only two possible effects, namely public finance capacity and economic growth. The model unfolds along a matrix consisting of spheres of interaction, actors, interactive choice, conditions of interaction and effects of interactive choice.

In building a conceptual model, the first steps are to articulate some simplifying assumptions and to operationalize each variable. The first assumption is that budget institutions shape fiscal policy commitments. In turn, commitments originate before or at the formulation stage of fiscal policy. This means that budget cycles can provide a time horizon for identifying the inception of a policy commitment. For purposes of simplification, recurring and overlapping events in the budgeting and spending process are ignored. Given that budgeting is incremental, this assumption allows for the establishment of an analytical marker to facilitate the evaluation of policy commitments over time. When policy shifts take place, new policy commitments are assumed to replace existing ones. For example, tax reforms may be signals of new fiscal policy commitments.

The second assumption is that policy makers expectations of how private market actors will react to policy outcomes shape policy commitments. Rational expectations motivate policy makers to reduce policy uncertainty.[94] The assumption that only private actors are forward-looking is incomplete. The conventional wisdom holds that it is not possible to analyze the effects of policy makers' behavior without taking into account the reactions of economic actors. The behavior of economic actors such as financial market participants is grounded in expectations about anticipated public policies, knowledge of the structure of the economy and knowledge of data and information relevant to the functioning of the economy.[95]

Consistent with this interpretation of expectations, Simmons argues that rational forward looking markets search for evidence of a government's commitment to economic stability.[96] Simmons, however, ignores the possibility that economic policy flows from the expectations of forward looking policy makers. Policy makers act on the basis of both adaptive and rational expectations. Adaptive expectations lead policy makers to base their actions on actual outcomes observed during recent periods.[97] Rational expectations lead policy makers to anticipate desired responses to policy by financial market participants. These desired responses may be the inflow of capital, the avoidance of capital flight, increased market capitalization and lower borrowing costs.

The third assumption is that credible fiscal policy commitments lead to higher credit ratings, lower financing costs and greater flexibility to finance public expenditures. These factors represent incentives for policy makers to chose institutions and policies that facilitate market access.

The conceptual model provides a departure point to formulate hypotheses about the relationship between budget institutions, fiscal policy, policy commitment and access to the sovereign debt market. These are the four key variables that help explain the effect of fiscal policy on a government's access to the sovereign debt market.

The variables are instrumental in examining how, why and with what consequences credible fiscal policy commitments translate into public finance capacity. The conceptual model implies that the antecedent variable, budget rules, influences fiscal policy commitment and choice. Policy commitment is linked to the antecedent variable because budget institutions shape fiscal policy commitments. As an intervening variable, policy commitment causally links the independent variable, fiscal policy, and the dependent variable, access to the sovereign debt market.

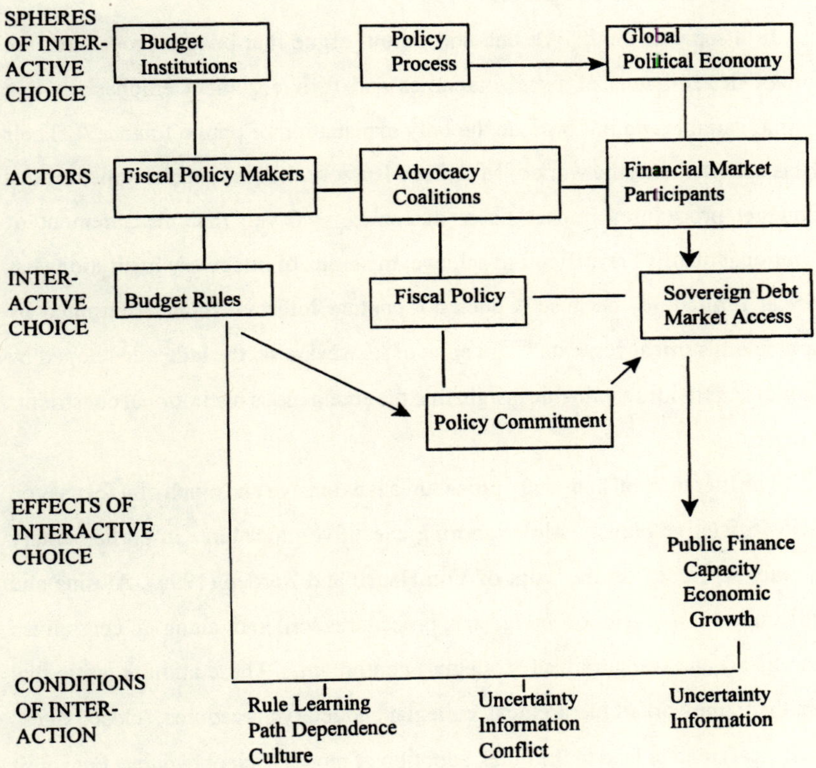

Figure 3.2 A Model of Interactive Institutional Choice

A detailed definition and overview of concepts used to measure the variables in each hypothesis follows.

Antecedent Variable: This variable represents the budget institutions in each country. It consists of the rules and procedures leading to the formulation, approval and implementation of the budget. This variable is measured in accordance with the index of budgetary institutions developed by Alesina *et al.* The data for the construction of this index was collected through a survey of the budget directors of 20 Latin American and Caribbean Countries in 1995.[98]

In a separate study, Alesina and Perotti argue that budget procedures are important determinants of fiscal outcomes and their argument emphasizes that economic variables do not provide the only explanation of public finance.[99] Their analysis complements the work of Miller and Russek who examine how institutions and budget procedures impact fiscal outcomes. Given that measurement of "institutional quality" is difficult to achieve, the index of budgetary institutions has empirical limitations, because it does not capture informal rules determined by cultural and historical contexts.[100] In spite of its weakness, the index developed by Alesina *et al.* provides a valuable insight into the endogenous institutional constraints on budgets.

The literature on budgetary procedures is extensive and much of it focuses on the US legislative branch, while ignoring executive procedures in parliamentary democracies. Based on the work of Von Hagen and Harden (1994), Alesina and Perotti suggest a menu of budgetary procedures ordered along a centralized (hierarchical) and decentralized (collegial) continuum. These authors argue that within the framework of hierarchical/ collegial budgetary procedures, "closed rules" (hierarchical) tend to lead to the quick adoption of more efficient budgets, but admit that with "open rules" (collegial) the power of the agenda setter diminishes, creating a more egalitarian distribution of benefits.

Alesina and Perotti conclude that these different budgetary procedures achieve different goals and respond to different needs, but that ultimately any set of rules should "prohibit the adoption of creative budgeting....the guideline should be greatest possible simplicity, clarity and transparency."[101]

Hierarchical budget institutions are associated with top-down budget processes that largely exclude legislative input and strongly emphasize cabinet or prime minister veto power. Thus, hierarchical institutions fit within the framework of presidential systems, which tend to concentrate power in the executive branch. In contrast, collegial institutions broaden democratic accountability and are inclusive of legislative input.

Alesina and Perotti identify three steps in the budget process including the formulation of a budget proposal within the executive, the presentation and approval by the legislature and the implementation phase by the executive bureaucracy.[102] These authors point out that voting procedures in the first two stages and the degree of transparency of the budget are two critical factors in budget outcomes. Voting procedures direct attention to who has influence in the budget process at any given step of the process and transparency determines whether it is feasible to monitor the budget process.

Transparency can also be explained in terms of efficiency. Budget inefficiencies arise from opaque budget rules. In contrast to transparent rules, opaque budget rules obscure the process by which budgets are formulated, approved and implemented. The work of Von Hagen and Harden contributes to an explanation of budget inefficiencies from a procedural standpoint. These authors argue that "fiscal illusion" and "deficit bias" are the primary sources of budget inefficiencies. They define fiscal illusion as the propensity to ignore marginal costs in the financing of public activities. In turn, deficit bias arises from the tendency to rely on debt financing thus shifting the burden of current expenditures on future taxpayers. In this context, open-ended expenditures dependent on past rather than current political decisions contribute to the negative effects of fiscal illusion and deficit bias.[103]

Independent Variable: Fiscal policy represents an ordinal variable with three values based on three mutually exclusive and jointly exhaustive debt financing categories.[104] Debt financing is divided into three sub-categories, money-financing (senioriage - printing money), loan-financing (commercial loans) and bond-financing (sovereign debt). This ranking order of debt financing mechanisms is developed to match the Miller and Russek financing categories most compatible with economic growth for developing countries. Tax financing mechanisms are not included in the ranking, although Miller and Russek argue that tax-financing strategies can contribute to economic growth in developing countries.[105] The ranking order is as follows: 1= bond-financing (most compatible with economic growth), 2= loan financing (somewhat compatible with economic growth) and 3= money-financing (least compatible with economic growth).

Although fiscal policy changes can result from either domestic or external shocks, the kind of financing approach policy makers choose matters. In a recent study of fiscal structures and economic growth, Miller and Russek find that for developing countries, debt-financed increases in government expenditures retard growth and tax-financed increases stimulate growth, while for developed countries the former increases do not affect growth and the latter increases lower growth.[106] These findings are significant, because they suggest that financing public expenditures through debt or taxes makes a difference in the credibility of fiscal commitments.

Intervening Variable: Policy commitment represents the intervening variable linking the dependent and independent variables. A typology of policy commitments is developed as an integral part of the conceptual model. This typology addresses both the determinants and the characteristics of credible fiscal policy commitments. The concept of policy commitment is qualified resulting in three categories of commitment: incremental, strategic, and partisan. Each category is measured as an ordinal variable and is assigned three values ranking from 1 to 3: 3) = credible policy commitment; 2)= questionable policy commitment and 1) non-credible policy commitment.

We begin by disaggregating fiscal commitments, with the simplifying assumption that all policy commitments are inherently political. Not all policy commitments, however, are created equal. Further, it is assumed that it is possible to classify policy commitments into three broad categories that differ in content, scope, and durability. The definitions for each category represent an oversimplification of the nuances of each 'type' of commitment. The three categories are not mutually exclusive and jointly exhaustive. Nevertheless, some policy commitments may be hybrids sharing characteristics that cut across categories.

Incremental fiscal policy commitments are formed over a decade or more, much in line with Lindblom's expedient model of public policy.[107] These commitments shape legitimate, known and widely accepted fiscal choices that have a broad social and economic reach. Such commitments are usually difficult to unwind, because they become institutionalized. In some cases these commitments become law. Incremental policy commitments are durable and extend across government administrations. These commitments imply rule learning over extended periods of time.

Strategic policy commitments are reactive. These commitments evolve in response to domestic and international events. Strategic commitments are shaped within shorter periods of time and their scope is narrower than that of incremental commitments. Strategic policy commitments impact only certain segments of society or the economy. Strategic policy commitments tend to be contested and can become law but often do not. They are less durable than incremental commitments, because those who oppose these commitments tend to challenge them over time.

Partisan policy commitments are the most contested and relative to incremental and strategic commitments, the least durable. These commitments can be reversed because they are seldom institutionalized. Some examples are commitments made through executive orders or decrees. Such policy commitments can easily be overturned by a change in the government's administration. For example, many economic reforms in Argentina have been implemented through presidential decrees, permitted under the State Reform Law.[108] Despite the legal grounding of these economic reforms, future administrations may encounter political pressure to amend or overhaul partisan policy commitments inherited from President Menem.

From this standpoint, incremental policy commitments are preferable to strategic and partisan policy commitments. Not all incremental fiscal policy commitments, however, are credible to financial market participants. Incremental policy commitments derived from transparent budget rules learned and applied over time are more credible than those commitments derived from budget rules leading to open ended expenditures and other budget inefficiencies.

Dependent Variables: Access to the sovereign debt market is measured in dollars and represents an interval variable. This is a narrow measure of net new issues in the international sovereign debt market. This measure determines the size and the annual percent change in the sovereign debt issues of each country over time. The average maturity, coupon provisions and ratings of sovereign issues are also considered. Access is defined as the actual amount of sovereign debt issued by a government. This definition does not include open lines of credit or potential access, which governments can obtain but do not use.[109]

Public finance capacity is broadly measured in terms of government expenditures as a percent of GDP. This measure acknowledges the inherent limitations of GDP, which ignores unofficial economic activities. Nevertheless, this measure of public finance capacity captures the overall size of a government's share of a national economy. More specifically, growth-oriented expenditures, namely expenditures that can contribute to economic growth, are measured in terms of the sum of health, education, and infrastructure expenditures.

The variables described thus far constitute the main components of the conceptual model from which three hypotheses are drawn. These hypotheses are tested through qualitative and quantitative comparative analysis.

Hypothesis 1. Credible fiscal policy commitments – commitments signaling fiscal restraint to financial market participants– increase access to the sovereign debt market.

Hypothesis 2. Budget institutions and fiscal policy commitment lead to fiscal policy choices that either strengthen or weaken a government's public finance capacity.

Hypothesis 3. Access to the sovereign debt market increases government capacity to finance public expenditures that can contribute to economic growth.

The first hypothesis is tested primarily through qualitative analysis due to the difficulty in quantifying the intervening variable, fiscal policy commitments. Limited quantitative analysis, however, is possible by extending the definition of credible fiscal policy commitment to include two measures of debt management used by credit rating agencies to assess a government's creditworthiness. These measures are the debt ratio and the debt burden ratio. A detailed description of these measures is included in the introduction of Chapter Five.

The second hypothesis is primarily used in the quantitative comparison for two reasons. First, the antecedent variable, budget institutions consists of an index that quantifies ten separate endogenous constraint variables affecting the formulation, approval, and implementation of budgets. The index of budget institutions captures the extent to which budget rules contribute to fiscal restraint and discipline. Second, the independent variable, fiscal policy choice and the dependent variable, public finance capacity are quantifiable variables that can be subjected to quantitative analysis. The limitations of quantitative analysis are reduced by interpretive historical analysis of budget trends. In addition, qualitative analysis of public finance trends provides a richer descriptive texture of fiscal policy choices in each country.

The third hypothesis is primarily used in quantitative comparison. The dependent variable, access to the sovereign debt market becomes the independent variable and is quantified as the actual value of sovereign bonds issued by each government. Government capacity to finance growth-oriented expenditures – public expenditures that can contribute to economic growth – becomes the dependent variable and is measured as the sum of health, education, and infrastructure expenditures.

The conceptual model of institutional choice provides the guidelines to draw hypotheses and examine the relationships between variables. One of the most effective methods for applying a conceptual model is comparison. Comparison can complement theoretical constructs by focusing on a limited number of similar cases that share common variables with the exception of the variable one sets out to explain. Comparison can be both qualitative and quantitative. Following Collier's prescription for combining quantitative and qualitative analytical tools[110]. This study relies on both techniques to identify and compare budgetary institutions and fiscal policy patterns. Comparison is useful to explain how institutional and policy choices affected access to the sovereign debt markets in Argentina, Chile, and Mexico from 1980-1995.

Comparing Cases: Argentina, Chile and Mexico (1980-1995)

As with all social science research, the comparative method faces several problems. Two of these problems are particularly relevant when comparing the institutional and policy choices Argentina, Chile, and Mexico made to gain access to the international sovereign debt markets from 1980-1995. The first problem is that of too many variables and too few cases. This problem can be addressed by either reducing the number of variables or increasing the number of cases. This study is not a comparative analysis of political systems, but rather a comparative analysis of budget rules and fiscal policy choices. Consequently, the number of cases increases from three governments to forty-eight institutional and policy choices. Additionally, the use of data mining in the quantitative comparison identifies the most important variables, targeting fewer explanatory variables.

The second problem is that of measurement. Non-quantifiable variables pose the greatest measurement challenge but even variables that are subject to straightforward quantification can be problematic. For example, in measuring public finance capacity one can use the percent of public expenditures relative to a country's gross domestic product. The problem with gross domestic product is that it does not reflect purchasing power parity nor does it reflect economic activities of the underground economy.[111] Unlike data on unofficial economic activities, data on public expenditures as a percent of gross domestic product is readily available. Clearly, the quality and availability of data determines the quality of any comparative analysis. In spite of its weaknesses, comparison remains central to public policy analysis. The comparative method is an effective tool to examine the causal relationships between institutional and policy choices, policy commitments and access to the sovereign debt markets.

The objective of the quantitative comparative analysis is not to interpret specific historical outcomes in a small number of cases, but rather to produce generalizations about the relationship between the variables. This variable- oriented strategy is supplemented with a limited case-oriented strategy that provides a qualitative supplement to the quantitative analysis.[112] Such analysis is compatible with time-series analysis, which can be linked to historical sequences and outcomes across cases. The objective of the qualitative analysis is to compare trends in budget institutions and fiscal policy choices across all three countries. The analysis relies on secondary data produced by the World Bank, The Inter-American Development Bank, the International Monetary Fund and the Bank for International Settlements. These international financial institutions produce the most standardized data available for cross-national comparisons.

The comparative method sharpens the power of description and allows for the interpretation of the significance of historical outcomes. Comparison helps to formulate hypotheses and construct empirically verifiable and explanatory theory.[113] According to Skocpol and Sommers, the goals of comparison include an examination of covariation among cases for the purpose of causal analysis, the parallel demonstration of theory and the contrast of contexts. The purpose is not necessarily to test theory, but rather to show how a conceptual model can point to causality.[114] These views are consistent with the reasons for using comparison in this study.

The selection of Argentina, Chile and Mexico to compare the institutional, policy and private financing patterns that emerged from 1980- 1995 is based on the fact that these three countries are most similar in terms of their cultures, political change and opening of their economies during this period. These new globally linked countries share a common Hispanic culture and each has experienced political and economic liberalization since 1980. All three cases share the experience of similar structural changes during this period. The timing of structural reforms and the sequence of these reforms, such as financial deregulation, privatization, and trade liberalization differ in each country. These structural changes are not the focus of analysis. Nevertheless, structural reforms provide an important context for explaining the economic and political conditions framing budgetary choices and fiscal policy commitments in each country.

All three countries began the "lost decade" of the 1980s under conditions of declining economic growth, mounting public debt and an increasing loss of investors' confidence, which resulted in the complete lack of access to private market financing. As fiscal crises continued to unfold during the first half of the decade, structural reforms and debt restructuring programs were implemented in all three countries. During the second half of the decade, these policy initiatives led to the slow and partial reentry to private capital markets. By the early 1990s, however, all three countries emerged from their respective economic crises and regained access to private capital markets in general and to the sovereign debt market in particular.

When governments seek private market financing, credible fiscal policy commitments can lead to market access. Nevertheless, what is credible to financial market participants may or may not be desirable to constituents, unions, special interest groups or political coalitions. Budgetary institutions, fiscal policy choices and fiscal policy commitments that bind governments to fiscal restraint can be politically contested, because fiscal policy has distributive and redistributive effects. As Wildavsky points out, "budgets are conflicting commitments."[115] This means that in making fiscal choices, policy makers confront the problem of making commitments that need to be credible to multiple actors. Some actors may be concerned primarily with social equity, while others seek political stability or economic growth.

Fiscal policy choices are reflected in the composition of each government's budget. Budget compositions reflect social needs and demands and point out the political costs of gaining greater public finance capacity. Variables such as expenditures on education, health care, and infrastructure represent indicators of social equity. The comparative analysis of education, health care and infrastructure expenditure patterns allows for an assessment of how policy makers in Argentina, Chile, and Mexico balanced "conflicting commitments" from 1980-1995.

This study focuses on the credibility of fiscal policy commitments relative to a government's access to the sovereign debt market. Consequently, the questions about budgetary institutions, fiscal policy choice and credible fiscal commitment relate mainly to the concerns of economic actors. Questions about budgetary institutions, fiscal choices and credible fiscal commitment, however, are not just questions about balancing budgets, cutting deficits and servicing debt. These questions are inherently political - the answers point in the direction of who gets what, when and how.[116]

This is not a normative analysis of what governments should do about institutional and policy choices, but rather an empirical analysis of how the governments of Argentina, Chile, and Mexico made institutional and policy choices from 1980-1995. This period is best suited for tracing the impact of institutional and fiscal policy choices on private market access. This particular time frame provides a unique window for analyzing the steps by which Argentina, Chile, and Mexico lost access to private credit markets and then gained gradual access to the sovereign debt market.

The current literature on credible commitments recognizes that it takes time for governments to build credibility.[117] Moving from non-credible to questionable and to credible policy commitments, or vice versa, involves a credibility trajectory that changes the terms under which governments can access the sovereign debt markets. The qualitative analysis seeks to identify the political and economic factors accounting for this credibility trajectory.

The quantitative analysis seeks to isolate specific institutional and policy markers that signal a specific kind of commitment and subsequently trigger government access, limited access, or no access to private market financing. Data mining and correlation analysis are complementary approaches used in this quantitative analysis. Data mining methods have been used as business decision-making tools capable of generating predictive models based on patterns and relationships uncovered through data analysis.

The limitations of the predictive power of data mining and some general data limitations need to be considered when applying this method to problems of public decision making. The application of data mining to business decision making generally involves a well-defined and quantifiable target or dependent variable, such as monthly sales volume. Searching for the most significant variables affecting monthly sales from a vast array of independent variables helps to identify data patterns that contributed to monthly sales volume in the past and are likely to contribute to sales in the future.

The application of data mining to examine the relationship between budgetary, financial and institutional variables is limited to an analysis of data patterns. The predictive dimension of data mining tools has limited application for policy analysis. The policy environment is subject to unpredictable political changes not encountered in a business environment. In addition, data mining systems face problems of "noisy" data when many of the attributes of data are inexact and incorrect. Data that is not representative and limited information can also contribute to application problems.[118] Data mining is simply an advanced analytical tool that can complement qualitative policy analysis, it is not a substitute for this kind of analysis.

This chapter began with a theoretical discussion of institutional choice. The next two chapters, test the hypotheses derived from the model through qualitative and quantitative comparison. Chapter 4 focuses on a qualitative analysis of the political and economic context in which policy makers in Argentina, Chile, and Mexico made choices about budget institutions and fiscal policy. Chapter 5 addresses the research questions of this study from a quantitative perspective by testing the hypotheses through data mining techniques and correlation analysis.

Chapter Four
Comparing Cases: Qualitative Analysis

This chapter begins with a comparison of the economic and political contexts in which budget institutions and fiscal policy choices evolved in Argentina, Chile, and Mexico from 1980 to 1995. These contexts are then contrasted to identify how credible fiscal policy commitments signaling fiscal restraint to financial market participants served to increase the access of each government to the international sovereign debt market.

From the 1950s to the early 1980, Latin American governments adopted an interventionist role in the economy, guiding development through import substitution policies, subsidies, and price and wage controls. The failure of these policies to translate into social welfare and economic growth, eventually motivated Argentinean, Chilean and Mexican policy makers to emulate East Asian market-oriented policies. By the mid-1980's, the focus on East Asia created a "new Latin American consensus," which redefined the role of government in promoting economic openness and market mechanisms.[119] This reform consensus did not take place in a political vacuum. The emergence of democracy in Chile and Argentina and the opening of Mexico's political system beyond the confines of the dominant party, the PRI (Partido Revolucionario Institucional) suggest that economic liberalization was facilitated by the changing structures of political authority in each country.

During the late 1980s, policy makers with strong connections to financial conglomerates, the strong support for reform from the private sector, and the neutralization of union reaction characterized the political conditions for privatization and financial deregulation in Argentina .[120] In addition, one could hypothesize that without a significant measure of popular support, the Menem administration would not have been able to carry out market-oriented policies. Union support for Menem as the Peronist candidate boosted popular support and locked in the middle class vote.

In contrast to Argentina, Chile implemented economic policy reforms prior to democratization. The structural factors influencing economic policy choices include a technocratic, executive state, a legitimate, coalitional political system and narrow corporatism.[121] In Mexico, economic crisis paved the way for political reforms. During the late 1980s, the Mexican government confronted public deficits and overcame the challenge of patrimonial and clientelistic structures that had blocked reforms in the past. High levels of cohesion within the Mexican elite allowed policy makers to transform the institutional framework of Mexico's economy "without compromising political stability or regime continuity."[122]

From the mid 1980s to the mid1990s, Latin America in general and Argentina, Chile and Mexico, in particular, launched market- friendly, economic liberalization reforms that facilitated access to international capital markets. Increased market access is reflected in capital flows. From the mid 1980s to 1992, Latin American capital inflows grew from $8 billion to over $53 billion annually. Although Mexico received the largest percentage of these inflows, Argentina and Chile also ranked among the major recipients.[123]

The Politics of Precision

In Argentina, Chile, and Mexico, the retreat of government, privatization, and financial deregulation converged to shrink the size of the public sector, strengthen the role of the private sector and deepen the reach of financial markets. The internal factors influencing policy choices are not far removed from the process of financial globalization. These factors are intimately linked to a question of power that transcends domestic political and economic institutions. Some authors link this question to the 'power of capital'. In this context, capital mobility leads governments to renounce discretionary power, limit intervention, deregulate, and privatize in order to win the trust of international investors.[124]

From this perspective, capital flows and the "Washington consensus" represent external structural and institutional factors influencing economic policy choices in Latin America during the 1980s and 1990s.[125] In addition to capital flows, financial markets themselves are viewed as structural factors influencing policy. For example, Mahon argues that asset markets in Latin America are "virtual Senates," where a narrow, internationally-oriented elite of households and firms is represented and exercises veto power over economic policy.[126] Mahon does not back his claim with empirical evidence of how these "virtual Senates" become the architects of privatization and financial deregulation. He redefines financial market participants as political actors but fails to account for their specific political action.

Financial market participants do not formulate, approve, or implement public policy. They do not have veto power over economic policy but through expectations influence the choices of policy makers. [127] When the economic policy agenda becomes a narrow set of market-oriented policy alternatives that confine governments to a minimal interventionist role, the politics of reform is set in motion. Reform politics can be labeled precision politics. Precision politics refers to the narrow, market- oriented policy path from which policy makers cannot deviate, if they seek private market financing. This path consists of a precise mix of policy initiatives – privatization, financial deregulation, and trade liberalization.

Precision politics involves the implementation of market-oriented policies that reduce economic uncertainty and increase the probability of a convergence of policy credibility, political accountability, and budgetary transparency. Precision politics is real-time politics.[128] Policy choices are transmitted and interpreted instantly across the globe, leaving little room for mistakes in policy implementation.

Precision politics is founded on cooperation and takes place within two spheres of interactive choice, the policy process, and the global political economy. In this process, financial market participants cross the line from global finance to domestic politics, and policy makers cross the line from domestic politics to global finance to form market- friendly advocacy coalitions.[129] Precision politics links policy- makers and financial market participants in parallel games aimed at accessing private capital markets. The parallel market access game positions financial market participants as key evaluators of fiscal policy and policy makers as active financial market participants, through the issuance and active trading of financial debt instruments across the globe.

The surge in global capital mobility, particularly since the early 1990s, has resulted in increasing attention to the contributions of global finance to economic growth. The emerging financial markets of Latin America are a product of what Louis A. Pauly calls the "globalization of finance." This process involves the reduction of controls and taxes on capital movements across national borders, the liberalization of regulatory restrictions within national financial markets, the expansion of off-shore financial markets, and the introduction of new technologies that facilitate and speed up financial intermediation.[130] The liberalization of capital controls has been a center of controversy regarding the policy implications of financial internationalization. Some authors argue that as financial markets continue to become more fully integrated, international constraints will increasingly play a role in shaping and limiting domestic economic policy actions.[131] The underlying assumption behind this claim is that once a government joins the global financial regime, domestic policy options shrink. Many scholars have equated the narrowing of policy options with a loss of economic policy autonomy.[132]

It seems more relevant to relate narrower policy options to a redefinition of the government's role in managing open, globally linked domestic economies. This recognition leads to the acceptance of an alternative argument to the conventional wisdom that global finance reduces a government's policy autonomy. Authors such as Frieden and more recently Garrett acknowledge that policy makers have policy autonomy. Frieden contends that national governments are still able to deploy effective sectoral and macroeconomic policy instruments. In discussing the role of the nation- state, Garrett acknowledges that within the global political economy, governments retain considerable autonomy over policy choices.[133]

Although capital market expectations motivate policy makers to adopt policy initiatives that benefit financial market participants (financial deregulation), these initiatives also benefit governments (lower borrowings costs). The benefits for financial market participants are diversification of risk, greater choice in investment alternatives, and increased sources of revenue.[134]

When governments seek private market financing, credit rating agencies and bond market participants evaluate fiscal performance. In this sense, rather than limit government capacity, these actors may provide performance incentives that strengthen public finance capacity. Credit rating agencies and other financial market participants do not formulate, approve, and implement fiscal policy. Credit rating agencies and financial market participants interpret policy commitments, respond to and anticipate policy actions and evaluate the performance of a country's economy as a function of the government's performance.

Government performance incentives originate in credit ratings and evaluations. The evaluations are used by financial market participants to anticipate future policy changes and are conducted after credit rating agencies (Moody's and Standard and Poor's) assign ratings based on a country's ability to meet debt obligations. Ratings measure economic and political risk and enable bond market participants to determine the relative likelihood that a bond issuer will default on its obligations. Sovereign credit ratings are public report cards on government performance.[135]

From a government issuer's perspective, credit ratings provide incentives to improve performance in order to lower public financing costs. Sovereign credit ratings determine the cost of financing and either facilitate or limit access to international or domestic bond markets. Ratings below investment grade (Moody's Baa3 and Standard and Poor's BBB-) are speculative and mean higher borrowing costs. Speculative grade ratings mean that if the issuer is likely to fulfill obligations now, it is uncertain if obligations will be fulfilled in the future. In contrast, investment grade ratings reflect either strong or adequate payment capacity both in the present and in the future.

Sovereign ratings are important not only because some of the largest issuers of debt instruments are governments, but also because these evaluations impact all public and private borrowers within a country. A provincial government or a private firm located in a given country is seldom, if ever, assigned a credit rating that is higher than that of its national government.[136] Sovereign credit analysis supplements credit ratings and serves to determine a country's ability to generate foreign exchange and willingness to service its foreign currency obligations.[137]

A country's ability to pay can be evaluated through objective and measurable economic factors, but its willingness to pay involves the subjective evaluation of political factors. Political factors include subjective assessments of the political system and its centers of decision making, ideology, ruling and opposition parties, political longevity of the government and mechanisms of succession. Other factors include domestic racial, ethnic and religious stability, labor relations and political involvement of unions, regional stability, and political and economic integration with the rest of the world.[138]

The analysis of economic factors focuses on three areas, namely, assessment of a country's economic conditions, evaluating its foreign trade and current account and analyzing its external debt. The most important ratios in sovereign credit analysis measure the relative size of the debt (External debt/ Current Account Earnings), the debt burden (Debt Service/ Current Account Earnings), the net financing requirement (Current Account Balance/GDP), liquidity (Reserves/ 1Month's Imports) and fiscal discipline (Budget balance/GDP).[139]

Considering the significance of economic and political risk assessments in determining a country's fiscal policy credibility and consequently its sovereign debt rating, some of these variables pose a dilemma for developing countries. On one hand, access to bond financing depends on a country's levels of economic development and per capita income. On the other hand, without access to bond financing, countries may have to rely on money- financed spending, which retards economic growth. From this perspective, some argue that credit ratings and evaluations limit public finance capacity by limiting financing options and blocking entry to the sovereign debt market.[140] This claim, however, cannot be accepted without some important qualifications.

First, one must question, whether the function of credit rating agencies is to keep issuers out of the market or to ensure that accurate risk assessments can be transmitted to investors. The business of credit rating agencies is information. Credit rating agencies identify differences in debt issuers' risk profiles and provide this risk information to investors. Bond investors are interested in having many investment choices across a wide range of maturities, yield structures, and risk profiles to match investment objectives. If only investment grade issuers were allowed to participate in the bond markets, investment choices would be limited. All issuers would have similar risk profiles. Ultimately, under such conditions, there might not be a need for credit ratings and risk evaluations. If only investment grade issuers participate in the bond markets credit rating agencies would be obsolete.

Bond issuance in international markets has become a major avenue for new globally linked countries (GLCs) to finance their external debt.[141] For Argentina, Mexico and to some extent Chile, the rise in international bond issues since 1990 is characteristic of an important financing trend for developing countries. One study of private market financing for developing countries notes that for countries facing debt-servicing problems, normalizing relations with creditors played a crucial role in regaining access to capital markets. All three countries rescheduled private and public debts from 1985 to 1989 paving the way for regaining market access. In addition, other factors facilitating market access for developing countries include "a well established legal and regulatory framework, a transparent and nondistortionary taxation system, a stable domestic financial system, and adequate transportation and telecommunications..."[142]

Regulatory frameworks that are consistent with international standards constitute an integral part of the globalization of finance. In this context, regulatory policy harmonization strengthens domestic institutions through rule learning. In Latin America, the Council of Securities Regulators of the Americas (COSRA), founded in 1992, promotes regional cooperation on standardized financial disclosure, clearance and settlement practices and sharing of price and other regulatory information. Argentina, Chile, and Mexico are members of COSRA and have negotiated several bilateral agreements for consultation and technical assistance in the region.[143] Regional regulatory cooperation suggests that within the framework of the global political economy, rule learning involves policy harmonization between national governments and information sharing between governments and private financial markets.

In addition to the primary international bond market, the secondary market for Latin American bond issues has been expanding.[144] According to an IMF report, Latin American debt accounted for 83 percent of total trading in emerging bond markets during 1995, with Mexican and Argentine debt holding the highest turnover rates.[145] Active secondary bond markets in Latin America largely depend on the willingness of institutional investors to participate in thin and poorly regulated markets. Consequently, Latin American governments have taken steps to improve and modernize the securities trading systems. The objective has been to enhance the "functioning and reliability of markets" through computerized trading systems that promote investor confidence, increase market liquidity, and facilitate market surveillance to limit potential price manipulation.[146]

International bond markets play a significant role in facilitating external financing for Latin America's national governments. International bond placements increase liquidity and broaden the investor base beyond the domestic market. Thus, sovereign credits by Latin American governments are usually denominated in foreign currencies. Risk perceptions in the bond markets are reflected in the maturity structure of new issues and the credit ratings assigned to issuers. In Latin America, the short- term average maturities denote increased risk perceptions.

From 1980 to 1983 Mexico had limited access to the international sovereign debt market, while Chile and Argentina had virtually no access. Access follows parallel paths of no access from 1983 to 1989 for Argentinean, Chilean, and Mexican new bond and note issues. Mexico regains market access in 1989 and is followed by Argentina and to a lesser degree Chile in 1990. While Mexico's access levels off by 1992 and declines by 36 percent between 1992 and 1995, Argentina's new issues surge by 405 percent between 1992 and 1995. In contrast, Chile's access to the international bond market remains fairly constant for the entire period with small incremental jumps in new issues in 1993 and 1995 respectively.

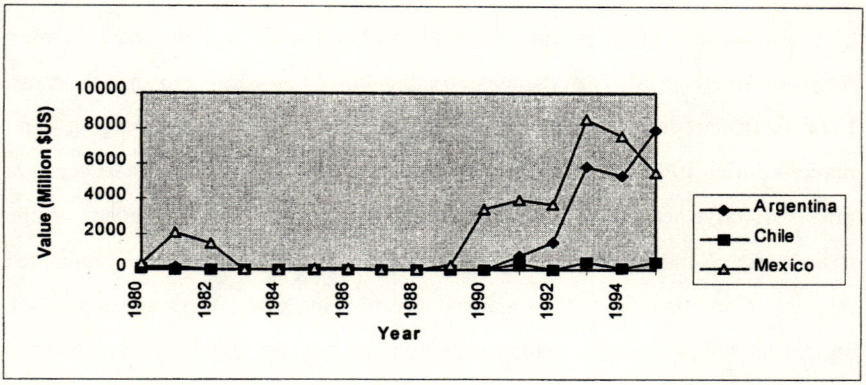

Figure 4.1 Access to the International Bond Market measured in millions of US dollars and representing new bond and note issues denominated in various foreign currencies.[147]

Bond market access, however, has to be qualified in terms of the average maturity and coupons of the announced new bond issues. For example, during the early 1990s, the average maturities for international bonds and notes issued by Argentina, Chile and Mexico ranged from one to four years. It appears that from the standpoint of issue maturities, access to the sovereign market was limited. This limitation appears to be indicative of questionable policy commitments. International bond underwriters and investment bankers engaged in structuring new bond issues for each country were unwilling to extend maturities beyond four years. One possible explanation is that these intermediate maturities were linked to election cycles and thus reflected a political risk premium. Chile's limited presence in the sovereign debt market after nearly a decade of fiscal restraint may be explained by policy makers' financing choices - debt aversion or their preference for tax financing.

Following the 1994 Mexican peso crisis, both the private and public sector bond markets deteriorated in the region. From 1990 to 1995 the average maturity of government bonds in the region dropped from seven to three years. Furthermore, enhancements such as bond-equity conversion options, put options and collateralized guarantees reflect greater uncertainty about solvency, interest rate and foreign exchange conditions.[148] The issuance of enhanced bonds in Latin America increased by 56 percent from 1993 to 1995, suggesting higher risk perceptions on the part of international bond investors and the possibility that Mexico's peso crisis was reflected in the pricing of other international bonds issued in the region.[149] Sovereign credit ratings by Moody's and Standard and Poor's Investor Services for Argentina, Chile and Mexico place Chile as the highest rated government with a ranking of investment grade (Moody's Baa1, S&P BBB+) and Mexico and Argentina with noninvestment grades of Ba2/BB and B1/BB- respectively.[150]

In industrialized countries, roads, schools, bridges, and other infrastructure needs are generally funded through domestic bond markets. In GLCs domestic sovereign debt markets remain rudimentary and international debt markets remain shallow.[151] One problem facing governments in these countries is that infrastructure projects require long term financing. Few institutional investors such as pension plans and insurance companies are willing to accept the financial and political risk inherent in 20 to 30 year sovereign credits from governments lacking the budget rules and incremental policy commitments that signal long term, sustainable fiscal restraint.

This credibility hurdle is reflected in the fact that the average maturity for new bond issues for developing countries remains short. Maturities lengthened from 4 years in 1991 to 7.3 years in 1993 and dropped down to 5 years in 1994. For many developing countries in the Western Hemisphere, average maturities range from 1 to 3 years.[152] Without access to a well-developed sovereign debt market with short, intermediate and long- term maturity structures developing countries are likely to be burdened with higher financing costs. If bonds prove to be a financing source that is compatible with economic growth, delays in the creation of domestic sovereign debt markets will limit financing options and slow down the pace of economic growth for new globally linked countries.

Once governments gain access to the sovereign debt market, international institutional investors are reluctant to participate in markets that lack regulatory transparency.[153] The quality of the regulatory framework is critical in attracting these investors to emerging bond markets. The preference of financial market participants for transparency, financial disclosure, and fiscal restraint influence the budget institutions of governments that seek private market financing. Thus, financial market participants influence rule learning, how budget institutions change and how fiscal policy makers behave. Rule learning suggests that markets and governments engage in precision politics forming advocacy coalitions with the common goal of market access. In Argentina, Chile, and Mexico, precision politics unfolds along the road that leads from economic crisis to reform. A closer examination of the composition of capital flows in Argentina, Chile, and Mexico provides insight as to the ability of each government to increase its public finance capacity through access to the sovereign debt market.

The Road From Crisis to Reform

The Chinese use the same character to depict the words 'crisis' and 'opportunity.' This symmetry of meaning is useful in understanding the relationship between international financial markets and economic policy making in Latin America. In the same way that a crisis can lead to opportunity, Latin America's debt, deficit, and inflation crises of the late 1970s and 1980s turned into portfolio investment opportunities during the 1990s.[154] The combined fiscal and monetary crises became reform catalysts because they triggered market-friendly policy responses designed to reverse the 'lost decade' of the 1980s.

Capital mobility across national borders has intensified in the last twenty years. Latin America has witnessed wide gyrations of capital movements during this period. The 1980s are considered a lost decade due to the region's lack of access to international capital markets resulting from the debt crisis of the preceding decade. This crisis was largely triggered by the oil crisis of the late 1970's, which led to increased levels of bank loans to Latin America's public and private sectors. Up to 1981, international banks were the chief financial intermediaries in the region, but as governments faced increasing difficulties in servicing their external debts, bank financing shifted to official flows. Between 1979 and 1982, domestic capital flight compounded the debt servicing problems.[155]

Between 1984 and 1986, adjustment programs involving reductions in fiscal deficits eased capital flight, but as adjustment programs were abandoned in 1987, capital flight resumed its course in 1988.[156] Adjustment programs were implemented once again and were characterized by reduced inflation and repatriation of domestic capital. Nevertheless, many governments had to rely on debt rescheduling and debt equity swaps to reverse the tide of capital outflows. By the late 1980s, several Latin American countries implemented financial deregulation policies to regain access to capital markets. A combination of economic reforms and debt rescheduling marked the beginning of the new decade and the restoration of Latin America's creditworthiness.

From 1990 to 1994, bond markets replaced international bank creditors as the main sources of private financing in Latin America. The large influx of portfolio investments to Latin America at the turn of the 1990's, signaled a shift from relative capital scarcity to abundance. This shift reflected a vote of confidence in the ability and willingness of governments to sustain the path of economic reforms and pursue prudent macroeconomic policies consistent with capital market expectations. The vote of confidence quickly vanished. In 1994 the Mexican financial and political shock spilled into a regional "tequila effect," reversing the trends of the early 1990s.[157]

In sum, the composition of capital flows to Latin America from roughly 1980 to the mid-1990s can be characterized by changing patterns of private and public financing. These patterns evolve from the shifting configuration of capital flows represented by official creditors, bank loans, bonds, equity, and foreign direct investments.[158] When compared to aggregate trends of capital flows to developing countries, the patterns displayed in Latin America correlate to the overall patterns for developing countries. From 1980 to 1981 portfolio investments are virtually non-existent, while bank loans represent 70 percent of capital flows. But from 1982 to 1988 official creditors increase their presence in Latin America to approximately 40 percent of total capital flows and bank loans shrink to 35 percent. During this period, bonds and equities remain a marginal component of total capital flows. From 1989 to 1991, official creditors maintain a dominant position, commercial bank loans shrink further to less than 25 percent, bonds increase from less than 1 percent in the previous period to more than 15 percent of the total inflows. From 1991-1993, bonds and equities reach almost 40 percent of total capital flows and official creditors shrink to approximately 25 percent.[159]

Over the course of the 1980s and 1990s these changing financing patterns had policy linkages to be examined later in this chapter. For now, we turn to a closer examination of selected capital flow trends in Argentina, Chile, and Mexico.[160] We begin with an overview of selected financial flows and economic policy choices in each country. Argentina liberalized the capital account in 1977, and a substantial increase in capital flows followed. As a result of lax credit, the financial crisis of 1980-81 resulted in extensive private capital outflows that to some extent anticipated the debt crisis of 1982. At this time, the rationing of private credit extended to the public sector and Argentina reverted to a closed economy.[161] The debt crisis of 1982 set the stage for the rise in capital flight and credit rationing of the 1980s, but higher international interest rates also impacted capital flows to and from Argentina. The limited access to private capital markets during the 1982-90 period was counter-balanced by the inflow of public credit, particularly up to 1985.

By 1991, macroeconomic stabilization was implemented through the Convertibility Plan. This plan converged with a reduction of international interest rates, and a reduction of Argentina's external debt, which led to a reduction of credit rationing and a reversal of capital flows. A year later, a key structural reform, privatization, was expanded. With increasing participation by foreign investors in the privatization initiative, the capital flight patterns of the 1980s turned into massive private capital inflows.[162] Privatization represented the cornerstone of Argentina's structural reforms. Financial deregulation initiatives, however, greatly influenced the influx of foreign portfolio investments since 1989.

Chile preceded Argentina with a wide range of financial liberalization measures implemented from 1978 to 1981. In 1980, the complex restrictions on international capital transactions began to be lifted. By 1982, the Central Bank liberalized the capital account and deregulated the foreign exchange market.[163] Nevertheless, from 1982 to 1987, a shortage of foreign exchange constrained Chile's economy and motivated the implementation of policies to rebalance the external and fiscal accounts. By 1989, portfolio investments became a significant component of total capital flows. The 1991 deregulation of capital outflows resulted in a rise of Chilean investments in Latin America, mainly through pension plan investments in Argentina.[164] Chile introduced mandatory savings programs and through the 1980 pension reform, pension plans have become key buyers of Central Bank notes, mortgage bills, corporate and government bonds.[165] By 1985, Chilean pension funds were allowed to invest in shares of privatized joint-stock corporations. The rise in portfolio investments from 1990-1993 stands in sharp contrast to the absence of this type of capital flow prior to 1986. In addition, the rise in bonds and private loans for 1990-93 is accompanied by a slight decline in official loans. These trends reflect Chile's recaptured creditworthiness and correlate to trends in Mexico for the same period.

Mexico represents the most dynamic of the Latin American emerging markets in terms of the scope and magnitude of capital flows during the period studied. As in the case of Chile, the rise in portfolio investment begins in 1989, but 53 percent of the total portfolio investments between 1990 and 1993 take place in the latter year. Based on a recent report from the International Finance Corporation (IFC), the Mexican peso crisis of 1994 had a pronounced impact on portfolio flows to emerging markets. The IFC estimates that portfolio flows to emerging markets dropped from $84 billion in 1993 to $56 billion in 1995 driven by sharp drops in equity flows, reversing the trends set by institutional investors between 1990-1993.[166] These trends translate into a 1,325 percent change between the levels of portfolio investments in Mexico between 1990 and 1993. In addition to these private capital flows, a clear reversal and decline of public loans takes place from 1980 to 1993, while private loans increase by 56 percent between the periods examined, after sharp declines from 1983- 1989. The capital flow trends observed need to be analyzed in the context of two major policy initiatives pursued by Argentina, Chile, and Mexico, namely financial deregulation and privatization. Evidently, economic policy impacts capital flows, but it seems that capital flows, in turn, shape policy.

Policy Choices and Capital Flows

The consensus view in the literature on Latin America's capital movements is that volatility of capital flows can be attributed to exogenous forces such as international interest rates and investor preferences.[167] There is ample empirical evidence documenting how declining capital flows to Latin America during the

1980s coincided with rising current account deficits in industrial countries. Nevertheless, strong arguments are advanced regarding the central role of Latin American policy as a response to shifts in capital flows. Some scholars even claim that policy can create institutions and regimes that are capable of absorbing the shocks of mobile capital. Specifically, during the 1990s, Latin American countries that liberalized their economies aggressively, reduced inflation, and maintained or created open financial systems received larger capital flows than countries that did not pursue these policies. In short, it can be argued that capital flows are a "policy issue."[168]

Within the framework of economic liberalization policies implemented in Latin America since 1980, financial deregulation and privatization seem to play a particularly important role in creating the financial openness favored by international financial market participants. In tracing these linkages, it is important to consider the timing of policy initiatives and capital flows trends in each country.

Policy Initiatives

1980-1982	Argentina	Financial Crisis
	Chile	Privatization of Social Security Financial Crisis
	Mexico	Debt Crisis
1983-1985	Argentina	Rescheduling of Private Debt
	Chile	Second Wave of Privatization (First Wave: 1970s)
	Mexico	Financial Deregulation (exchange controls)
1986-1989	Argentina	Financial Deregulation Privatization Begins
	Chile	Large Divestitures in Public Utilities
	Mexico	Dual Exchange Rate System and Elimination of Credit Controls and Quotas Rescheduling of Public Debt (Brady Plan)

Policy Initiatives (Continued)

1990-1995	Argentina	Rescheduling of Public Debt (Brady Plan)
		Convertibility Plan
		Large Scale Privatizations
	Chile	Privatization Completed
		Deregulation of Capital Outflows
		Capital Controls on Short Term Inflows
	Mexico	Expansion of Privatization
		Elimination of Capital Controls

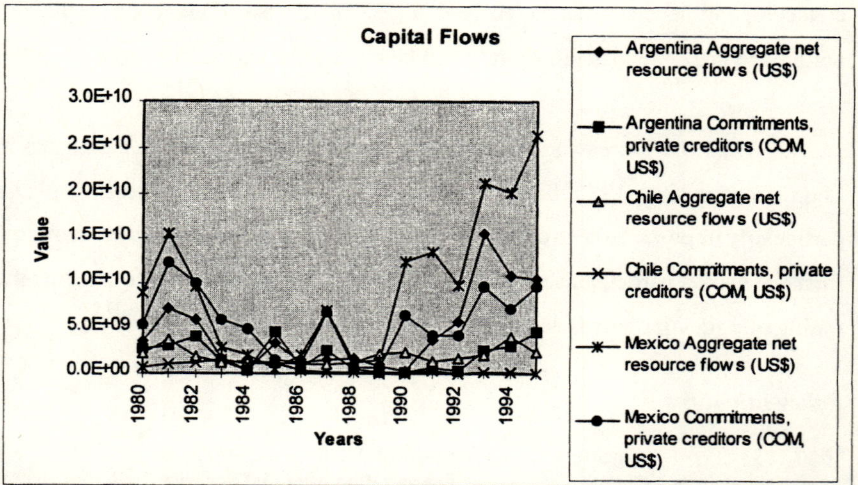

Figure 4.2 Policy Choices and Capital Flows. Policy initiatives in financial deregulation and privatization and trends in capital flows.

Source: Data for this figure is derived from the Global Development Finance data base (1998, CD-ROM) World Bank, Washington DC Capital Flows are divided into three categories: aggregate resource flows, commitments from private creditors and commitments from public creditors. Values range from 0.0.E+00= 0 Billion Dollars to 3.0E+10= 30 Billion Dollars. Aggregate Resource Flows are the sum of long term bond debt plus foreign direct investments, portfolio equity flows and official grants. Commitments from private creditors include bank loans to the government with maturities exceeding one year.

The politics of economic liberalization share a common denominator across all three countries, democratization. The process of political liberalization in each country has distinct characteristics, but all three countries moved along parallel and simultaneous tracks in opening their economic and political systems. The emerging democratic regimes of Argentina, Chile, and Mexico share a legacy of authoritarianism. This legacy is deeply rooted in the military experience of Argentina and Chile during the 1960s and 1970s and the hierarchical political authority, elite cohesion and clientelistic structures of Mexico since the end of the 1920s.[169] The early 1980s marked a political turning point for all three countries. Argentina and Chile returned to democratic rule. Mexico began to loosen the reigns of power held by the PRI, a highly centralized political machine controlled by the government.[170] The political and institutional conditions in all three countries are characterized by weak democracies, strong economic bureaucracies, and emerging private sectors. Weak democracies and strong bureaucracies are mutually reinforcing because political authority is mainly centered in the executive branch. In this context, the executive branch can govern by decree without significant input from the legislative and judiciary branches. Thus, the number of "veto players" is reduced, increasing the possibility of bureaucratic autonomy.[171] This scenario takes place when a strengthened private sector forms alliances with policy makers. Such alliances facilitate the implementation of economic policy and closes off public debate about alternative policy initiatives.

Argentina began 1980 under military rule, but a chain of devaluations initiated in 1981 plus the military defeat against Britain in the Malvinas led to the reinstatement of elections and a constitutional regime in 1983. The newly elected civilian government first focused on reversing the 1982 financial crisis, but by the mid 1980s, the burden of financing public owned enterprises amounted to 90 percent of the external debt. This led to the first attempt to privatize the largest government owned firms, a public utility, and the national airline. The main objective of privatization was to reduce the fiscal deficit, but privatization became an effective vehicle for converting bank debt into claims on real assets. Debt-equity swaps can also be linked to privatization efforts in Chile and Mexico.[172]

During the initial period of Argentinean privatizations, from 1988 to 1991, ten transactions were completed and private capital flows increased slightly. In 1992, twenty- five additional state-owned enterprises were sold and private flows quadrupled from the previous year value and reaching $11.4 billion. In 1989, Argentina began a series of deregulation initiatives including the elimination of ten regulatory agencies, price and wage controls, and exchange controls. In 1989 foreign and national capital began to receive equal treatment and restrictions on buying and selling foreign currencies were lifted. A second phase of financial deregulation was implemented in 1991 including the elimination of transaction taxes in the capital markets, the deregulation of brokerage commissions and the simplification of requirements for the issuance of financial assets.[173] Also in 1991, the Convertibility Plan established a fixed exchange vis a vis the dollar and required that the "monetary base be fully backed by liquid international reserves."[174] Coupled with currency convertibility and monetary stability, the incremental changes in financial deregulation greatly enhanced the international attractiveness of Argentina's emerging financial market. As in the case of privatization, the incremental financial deregulation in Argentina coincides with rising private capital flows.

In Chile, financial deregulation began in 1974 with a lowering of reserve requirements for commercial banks. By 1979, limited capital mobility was allowed and from 1981-1984 Chile implemented a massive rescheduling of private sector debt. In 1981, the government initiated social security reforms that represented a key building block for Chile's privatization initiatives. A voluntary system of individual retirement accounts managed by private investment management companies replaced an insolvent, government administered, pay-as-you-go system. Workers had the choice of remaining with the government plan or shifting to privately managed funds.

A strong regulatory framework was implemented to ensure fiduciary compliance and efficient management of pension funds holding individual retirement accounts. The expansion of individual retirements accounts is reflected in the private savings increase from approximately 4 percent of GDP in 1983 to 14 percent in 1991, at which time private pension fund assets represented 26.5 of Chile's GDP.[175] As in Argentina, Chilean privatization complemented financial deregulation and fueled the rise of Chile's emerging financial markets.

Chile adopted the 1980 Constitution to assure the passage from a military to an authoritarian regime. In accordance with this constitutional framework, the 1988 plebiscite allowed the military to retain power, while retreating gradually from politics. This retreat became a political formality in 1990 when the first democratic government assumed power and faced the challenge of democratization. In 1991, the transition to democracy was barely completed but the lengthy process of privatization, begun under military rule two decades earlier was now completed.[176]

The first phase of Chilean privatization from 1973-81 targeted financial institutions. During the financial crisis of 1982, however, Chile reversed its pioneering divestitures of state-owned enterprises. Banks and other financial intermediaries collapsed due to weak regulatory frameworks that led banks o accumulate large portfolios of non-performing loans. The Chilean government responded to the crisis by resuming temporary control of the failed entities. During 1986 Chile adopted new banking laws establishing a strong regulatory framework and privatized the previously nationalized financial institutions. From 1985-to 1988, divestitures involved large industrial conglomerates and public utilities.[177] The capital flow trends for Chile during the 1980s and 1990s largely reflect these policy reform initiatives.

In contrast to the concentrated privatization and financial deregulation initiatives in Argentina during the late 1980s and early 1990s, Chile's structural and financial reforms stretched over a period of two decades. Consequently, the linkages between policy initiatives and capital flows are less explicit than those identified for Argentina. Nevertheless, the surge in private portfolio investment from 1990 to 1993 follows the same pattern as the rise in capital flows in Argentina. One explanation for the similarities in the capital flow trends for Argentina and Chile in the 1980s and 1990s is that international financial market participants tend to view Mexico as a proxy for other emerging financial markets.[178]

The prominence of Mexico as an emerging financial market can be traced in part to its proximity and economic integration with the US. Furthermore, the impact of NAFTA in opening Mexico's economy through trade liberalization and deregulation played key roles in attracting international capital in the 1990s. In 1982, however, Mexico's debt reached a critical point, triggering the implementation of fiscal and monetary restraints until 1986.[179]

Mexico's financial deregulation can also be traced to the aftermath of the 1982 crisis, when greater flexibility in exchange controls was introduced. In 1987 a dual exchange rate system was implemented and in 1991 capital controls were eliminated. With the elimination of credit controls and quotas in 1988, Mexico launched the creation of new financial instruments to reduce transaction costs and hedge risks. In addition, efforts to strengthen financial intermediaries resulted in a number of reforms between 1989 and 1990. These reforms introduced a number of new participants, such as insurance companies, to the savings and financing process.[180]

Privatization began in 1982, but did not reach any significant expansion until 1989, when large state owned enterprises were auctioned. This delay could be attributed to the lingering effects of protectionist import-substitution policies, dating back to the 1950s, which effectively retarded the development of privately managed domestic industries. Without a competent and efficient pool of private managers, it is impossible to implement privatization. Consequently, Mexican privatization moved gradually from the divestiture of small and medium size public firms between 1983 and 1987 to the sale of large public service monopolies beginning in 1988.[181] From 1985 to 1989 revenues from privatization averaged approximately 0.33 percent of GDP, but in 1990 and 1991 these revenues grew to 4.32 and 14.4 percent of GDP respectively.[182] Private capital flows coincide with the implementation of privatization and financial deregulation initiatives from 1989 to 1993.

Privatization and financial deregulation initiatives in Argentina, Chile, and Mexico from 1985-1995 had direct effects on fiscal performance. Privatization initiatives reduced public expenditures incurred by tax-exempt, state-owned firms and increased revenues by creating private, taxable entities. In many cases, particularly with the sale of highly inefficient firms, (e.g. Aeromexico and all the banks) privatization eliminated the need for the government to bail out firms that were unable to compete and in some cases were at the brink of financial collapse.[183] Financial deregulation initiatives reduced capital and foreign exchange controls attracting another sources of tax revenue: foreign direct investments, bond, and equity portfolio flows and other private capital flows. Deregulation initiatives not only freed capital movements, but regulated them in more efficient ways. These initiatives established new regulatory frameworks (banking laws, private pension management laws) that reduced private bank failures, discouraged private pension fund abuses and significantly reduced the need for costly government bailouts which, prior to financial deregulation initiatives, had translated into public expenditures.[184]

For some scholars the link between financial globalization and the reduction of financial controls appears evident. Haggard and Maxfield explain this relationship from the standpoint of international pressures. Developing country governments reduce financial controls in response to financial market demands. These authors also recognize the importance of domestic economic crises as catalysts for economic liberalization.[185] But explaining economic policy choices from the standpoint of globalization pressures and domestic economic crisis obscures the importance of the institutional factors that facilitate or constrain policy implementation.

Two domestic institutional frameworks influenced economic policy choices in Argentina, Chile, and Mexico: independent central banks and the budget process. The establishment of independent central banks in all three countries effectively served to isolate monetary and exchange rate policy from short-term political whims.[186] The budget process remained politicized in all three countries. Budgeting is centered in the executive branch and legislatures play a weak role in approving budgets capable of constraining executive action. The lack of a rigorous legislative budget oversight process may have created the conditions leading to the lost decade of the 1980s.

The Politics of Budgeting and Conflicting Commitments

National government budgets define one dimension of the relationship between domestic politics and international economies. Although budgets represent administrative plans outlining public receipts and expenditures, these are also political documents that spell out who assumes costs, who receives benefits, and how resources are allocated. Budgets intersect politics and economics, because taxes and fiscal balances can determine the level of economic growth, savings, and investment. Concurrently, national budgets define the range of governmental functions and carve out spheres of political influence. By drawing the boundaries of public policy, national budgets separate private economic activity from public action in some areas and integrate it in others (joint ventures, subsidies, and tax deferrals).

While the political process of formulating and implementing a budget varies across governments, one could argue that for democratic governments the budget represents a tool for public action and accountability, a main avenue for competition among politicians and a blueprint for the implementation of fiscal policy.[187] In mature representative democracies such as the United States, expenditure priorities and revenue projections result from the interaction between the executive and legislative branches of government. In this context, the budget process involves bargaining and negotiation among competing political interests. The allocation of public resources and the distribution of political power are parallel outcomes of the politics of budgeting.

In the context of regime stability, budgets matter because they are linked to economic performance. In a 1993 study of South America, Limongi and Przeworski found that between 1945-1988 the "probability that a democratic regime would survive four or five years of consecutive negative growth was 57 and 50 percent respectively.[188] In representative democracies national budgets shape the political agenda and as such become vital sources of regime stability.

For the emerging democracies of Latin America, the linkage between public finance and regime stability takes on an added significance in light of the recurring cycles of financial crises and policy reform in the region. The rising budget deficits of the early 1980s created a crisis of confidence that triggered capital flight and blocked access to global credit markets for most Latin American governments. Fiscal reforms implemented in the late 1980s and early 1990s contributed to a reversal in these trends. Argentina, Chile, and Mexico are leading reformers in Latin America. In large measure, reforms have contributed to an increase in trade and capital flows. Consequently, in spite of the continuing problems of poverty, corruption, and skewed income distribution, all three countries have achieved "respectability among international investors."[189] By 1993, Mexico's current account deficit had surged to almost 7 percent of GDP and the following year another capital flight crisis engulfed Mexico and swept across the region.[190]

The larger question of whether democracy will grow and mature in Latin America, particularly in Argentina, Chile and Mexico is beyond the scope of this study, but this important question is closely connected to issues of institutional and policy choice.[191] Particularly important is how budget institutions shape fiscal policy in each country. Additionally, it is necessary to identify what policy choices contributed to deficit reduction and fiscal restraint in Argentina, Chile, and Mexico and to determine how these choices influenced each government's access to the sovereign debt. Finally, it is necessary to examine whether this access contributed to an increase of public finance capacity. This comparative study only addresses public finance questions for the period of 1980- 1995, but the combined answers are relevant for questions of democratic sustainability in the region.

The comparison of public finance trends in Argentina, Chile, and Mexico for the 1980-1995 period begins with a brief overview of the literature on budget processes and institutions. This literature establishes a useful analytical framework to compare public finance from an institutional perspective across the three countries. Much of the extensive literature on budget process and the politics of public finance focuses on the United States and comparative and cross-national studies are predominantly directed at OECD countries.[192]

A recent cross-national study of industrialized and developing countries focuses on the effects of national fiscal structures on economic growth. This study concludes that the "method of financing government expenditures plays an important role in determining the effect of that expenditure on economic growth...[and that] different expenditure categories affect growth differently."[193] The study explains how developing countries choosing tax financing over debt financing alternatives achieve higher levels of economic growth. In turn, countries that pursue debt-financed education fare better than countries that issue debt to pay for defense, health, social security, and welfare expenditures. One can conclude that when it comes to economic growth, it matters how or what fiscal policy choices are made and how public expenditures are financed.

It is equally important to consider who makes these choices. In representative democracies, elected officials are accountable for budgetary decisions. Ideally, fiscal choices reflect political commitments to the electorate. In practice, however, the process by which budgets are prepared, approved, and implemented is largely a function of the institutional regime structure. This means that not all elected officials have input into the budget process and that many appointed rather than elected officials are an integral part of the process.[194]

In reviewing the budgeting literature, it is important to identify key factors that combined can explain the differences and similarities of budget institutions and outcomes in Argentina, Chile and Mexico. Three factors can be useful to compare and contrast fiscal policy choices across countries and include a) the method of financing, including tax and debt alternatives, b) budget rules in both the executive and legislative branches and c) level of transparency of the budget.

For most of this century, Argentina, Chile, and Mexico emphasized debt financing and implemented limited tax financing mechanisms. From the late 1980s through the early 1990s, all three countries adopted tax reforms emphasizing an expanded tax base and strong enforcement mechanisms. These tax reforms were in large part induced by IMF conditionality with the purpose of increasing tax revenues, reducing tax evasion, and facilitating the simplification and efficiency of the tax system.[195]

Following the Von Hagen and Harden and Alesina and Perotti typology[196], one can rank budget institutions along a hierarchical/ collegial matrix. Hierarchical budget rules are characterized by centralized executive veto power over the formulation, approval, and implementation of budgets. Furthermore, within the executive branch, budget decisions are highly centralized. Either the President or the

Finance Minister tends to control budget formulation by exercising veto power over spending ministries. Centralized control extends to the approval of budgets through limitations on legislative budget amendments.[197]

In contrast, collegial institutions emphasize democratic rules and accountability at every stage of the budget process. Collegial rules emphasize the prerogatives of spending ministries, legislatures and opposing minorities within legislatures. These rules are characterized by decentralized procedures that shift budget formulation from a President's or Finance Minister's office to the entire Cabinet. Within this framework, finance ministers serve as intermediaries between the cabinet and spending ministries. In terms of budget approval, collegial rules allow for a wide range of legislative budget amendments.[198]

Transparency of a budget refers to the extent to which individual public agencies (spending ministries) exercise discretion over borrowing procedures. Transparency relates to the conditions under which a central government assumes the debt obligations contracted by public agencies. The most transparent rules restrict central governments from assuming the debts of any public agency, at any government level (state, local). The least transparent rules allow central governments to assume such debt obligations and in some cases, such rules stipulate that the central government is only allowed to assume guaranteed debt. When central governments assume the debts of national, state or local public agencies, public liabilities can be hidden from public view – this can be labeled off-balance sheet public accounting. Transparency is closely linked to budget efficiency because the more transparent the budget rules, the less likely it is for governments to: a) favor excessive spending divorced from the cost of financing public activities (fiscal illusion) or b) favor deficit financing at the expense of future taxpayers (deficit bias).[199]

The hierarchical/ collegial framework offers a useful organizing principle to understand budget institutions and processes in Latin America. Given the marginal role of legislatures in the budgetary process, it is necessary to focus on the interactions within the executive branch, namely, between the Finance Ministry and other executive agencies negotiating the formulation, approval, and implementation of the budget. Combining this framework with a matrix of transparent/ opaque budgets provides a more detailed institutional analysis.

The first step in comparing fiscal policy choices is to identify the magnitude and composition of revenues, expenditures and financing methods for each country based on data reported in the IMF, Government Finance Statistics Yearbook. The use of government finance data in conjunction with a qualitative analysis of the financing methods, budget rules and transparency of the budget can yield an overview of public finance trends in each country. We now turn to a comparative analysis of public finance trends in Argentina, Chile, and Mexico.

Public Finance Trends: Argentina

From 1980 to 1995 the salient feature of Argentina's financing methods is a sharp shift from debt financing to tax-financing. From 1980-84 to 1985-89 Argentina increased its debt based financing by 374 percent, while tax based financing for the same period only increased by 97 percent (Table 4.1). A reversal of these trends is evident when comparing the periods 1985-89 to 1990-95: tax based financing grew by 378 percent while debt based financing declined by 36 percent. Another way to show this shift is to consider that from 1980-1989 Argentina financed merely 14 percent of its total expenditures through tax revenues and 50 percent through debt, while from 1990-1995, tax revenues financed 44 percent while debt financed 25 percent of total expenditures (Tables 4.1 and 4.3). These trends can be attributed to the 1990 tax reform implemented by the Menem administration.

Argentina's revenue and expenditures for the period reflect growing fiscal imbalances beginning in 1980 and culminating in 1988. A temporary reversal of deficits in 1991, 1992 and 1993 was over shadowed by persistent deficits in 1990, 1994 and 1995 (Table 4.3). Budget surpluses from 1991-1993 can largely be attributed to tax reforms aimed at increasing public sector revenues and reducing expenditures. The goals of tax reform were only partially achieved. Although tax revenues increased as reflected by the changes in tax- based financing from 1980 to 1995, the combined expenditures for public services, health care, education, social security, and welfare increased by an annual average of 43 percent. Concurrently, total revenues merely increased by an annual average of 27 percent (Tables 4.2, 4.3) while economic affairs and services and interest payment expenditures increased at a 16 percent annual rate (Table 4.2).

These trends point to the fact that increases in tax revenues rather than spending cuts may have contributed to deficit reduction. In fact, between the periods of 1980-85 to 1990-95 each category of social expenditures (public services, health care, social security and welfare) shown on Table 4.2 grew at more than three times the rate of growth shown for total revenues. Education was the only category that did not – the increase in education expenditures during this period was only 76 percent higher than the increases in total revenue for the period. From 1980-84 public services, education, health care, social security and welfare constituted 62 percent of total expenditures. For the periods 1984-89 and 1990-95 these combined expenditures represented 42 and 65 percent of total expenditures (Tables 4.2 and 4.3).

In 1990, the introduction of value added (VAT) taxes and taxes on fixed assets and bank checks were coupled with administrative efforts to improve the collection of taxes. In addition, in 1991, under the "Convertibility Law," institutional reforms were implemented to abolish all exchange and capital controls and eliminate central bank financing of public enterprises, the federal government, or the provinces.[200] These initiatives significantly contributed to the greater efficiency but represented a partial solution to the larger problem of provincial debt financing.

In spite of tax reform initiatives, one of the most salient features of Argentina's fiscal federalism is the process of transferring spending to the provinces without a corresponding increase in their taxing powers. In Argentina, the constitution establishes a federal system of government. Power is heavily concentrated in the executive branch, particularly in the realm of taxing and spending. The result is that provincial and municipal governments are highly dependent on national financing.[201] This financial dependency has produced a rapid rise in intergovernmental transfers, particularly through the federal tax revenue sharing system.

Table 4.1 – Argentina: Cumulative Financing Methods and Period Percent Change (Central Government Budget, Million Pesos).

	1980-84	(%) Change	1985-1989	(%) Change	1990-95
Tax-based financing*	326	(97)	641	(378)	3069
Other non-tax revenue	13	(1592)	220	(581)	1500
Debt-based financing **	588	(374)	2787	(-36)	1768

*Tax-based financing excludes extra-budgetary accounts, social security funds and various budgetary items.
**Includes domestic and foreign financing. (%) represents percent change between periods 1980-84 and 1985-89 and periods 1985-89 and 1990-1995 respectively.

Table 4.2 – Argentina: Composition of Cumulative Major Expenditures by Function and Period Percent Change (Millions of Pesos)

	1980-84	(%) Change	1985-89	(%) Change	1990-95
Public Services	60	(78)	107	(391)	526
Education	98	(58)	155	(189)	449
Health	18	(100)	36	(736)	301
Social Security and Welfare	400	(73)	692	(368)	3242
Economic Affairs and Services	220	(63)	360	(108)	749
Interest Payments	146	(-2)	143	(304)	579

Table 4.3 – Argentina: Cumulative Budget Trends 1980- 1995 and Period Percent Change. (Millions of Pesos)

	1980-84	(%) Change	1985-89	(%) Change	1990-95*
Total Revenue	927	(155)	2367	(109)	4955
Total Expenditure	1299	(332)	5624	(24)	6966
[Overall Deficit]/ Surplus	[-372]	(776)	[-3257]	(-38)	[-2011]

*During the 1990-1995 period only during 1991,1992 and 1993 did Argentina show budget surpluses of 37, 1306 and 160 respectively. In 1990, 1994 and 1995 budget deficits amounted to -245, -416 and -2975 respectively.

Sources for Tables 4.1- 4.3: IMF, Government Finance Statistics Yearbook, 1986, 1991, 1996.

From 1983 to 1992 such transfers increased by 31 percent accounting for 70 percent of total provincial budgets.[202] During the same period, the federal government decentralized fiscal administrative functions in the areas of education, health care, and social welfare reducing its administration of public spending by 10.5 percent. Poorly designed transfers make revenue sharing highly inefficient by limiting the impact of tax reforms and constraining macroeconomic management.[203] Revenue sharing represents a main institutional constraint for Argentina. This system has a negative effect on transparency, because it allows for the national government to assume the non-guaranteed debt of provincial governments. More importantly, transparency is compromised because provincial governments (state and local) have complete borrowing autonomy.[204]

Within the national government, the executive branch controls budget formulation and implementation. Specifically, the Minister of Finance has considerably greater authority than spending ministers regarding the budget.[205] Located within the executive branch, spending ministers oversee agencies with constituencies favoring specific spending programs (health care, education, transportation, welfare, social security, and labor). When it comes to budgeting, spending ministers are like legislators - constituent preferences strongly influence spending choices. In the legislative branch, many small districts characterize proportional representation. Often, these districts have just one representative and show a high degree of party system fragmentation. These institutional characteristics have led some policy analysts to define systems, where presidentialism coexists with proportional representation, as the most inefficient and the most prone to political instability.[206]

The institutional framework of Argentina's political system shapes budgetary inputs. Significant institutional changes have taken place since 1992. The executive branch has increased its controls over spending and taxing while the legislative branch has reduced its veto power over the budget. For example, from 1980 to 1992, Congress could propose budget amendments without any restrictions. Since 1993,

Congress can only propose amendments that do not increase deficits. Furthermore, if Congress rejects a budget, the previous year's budget is enacted.[207]

Greater centralization of budget veto power has rendered Argentina's budget rules more hierarchical, but not necessarily more transparent. The lack of transparency is reflected in the joint inefficiencies of "fiscal illusion" and "deficit bias." The wide gap between Argentina's revenues and expenditures for most of the 1980-1995 period indicates that fiscal policy makers grossly neglected to consider the costs of financing public expenditures. When revenues represent only 71 percent of total expenditures (1980-1984), expenditures are not sustainable. From 1985 to 1989, revenues represent only 42 percent of total expenditures and only 71 percent from 1990-1995 (Table 4.3). Argentina's fiscal choices for all periods reflect a high degree of fiscal inefficiency. In terms of deficit bias, it can be argued that when Congress surrendered its limited veto power to the executive branch in 1993, fiscal choices were removed fully from public scrutiny.

Public Finance Trends: Chile

In contrast to Argentina, Chile's tax-based financing constituted 66 percent of expenditures from 1980-84 and during this period Chile financed only 14 percent of its expenditures through debt. By the first half of the 1990s the percentage of tax financing had increased over 25 percent to account for 83 percent of expenditures, while debt financing declined 35 percent to account for a mere 9 percent (Table 4.4 and 4.5). These choices in the method of financing reflect Chile's greater focus on fiscal discipline.

These choices are also reflected in Chile's composition of major expenditures and budget trends, which only exhibit deficits for the 1980-1984 period (Table 4.6). As in Argentina, Chile's Minister of Finance has the greatest authority within the executive branch regarding budget decisions. Unlike Argentina, Congress can only propose budget amendments with the approval of the executive branch and if Congress rejects a budget, the budget proposed by the executive branch is enacted.[208]

In contrast to Argentina, Chile's total revenue increases for each period exceeded expenditure increases in public services, education and social security and welfare. The exception to this trend of fiscal efficiency is found in health care expenditures which increased by 361 percent between 1980-84 and 1985-89 and 328 percent between 1985-89 and 1990-1995 exceeding increases in total revenue by 49 and 15 percent respectively for each period (Tables 4.5 and 4.6). From 1980-84, public services, education, health care, social security, and welfare represented 70 percent of Chile's public expenditures, for the periods of 1984-89 and 1990-95, these combined expenditures represented 64 percent and 58 percent respectively (Tables 4.5 and 4.6). The privatization of social security largely accounts for this decline. The budget line item for social security reported in the Government Finance Statistics Yearbook includes welfare expenditures and the increases shown for each period reflect increases in welfare spending, rather than social security spending.

Table 4.4 – Chile: Cumulative Financing Methods and Period Percent Changes (Central Government Budget, Billion of Pesos).

	1980-1984	(%) Change	1985-1989	(%) Change	1990-1995
Tax-based financing*	1429	(204)	4349	(334)	18902
Other non-tax revenue	408	(228)	1340	(181)	3772
Debt-based financing**	199	(17)	232	(757)	1990

*Tax-based financing excludes extra-budgetary accounts, social security funds and various budgetary items.
**Includes domestic and foreign financing.

Table 4.5 – Chile: Composition of Cumulative, Major Expenditures by Function and Period Percent Change (Billions of Pesos).

	1980-84	(%) Change	1985-1989	(%) Change	1990-1995
Public Services	246	(26)	309	(169)	834
Education	309	(137)	734	(288)	2855
Health	121	(361)	558	(328)	2393
Social Security and Welfare	834	(146)	2054	(244)	7082
Economic Affairs and Services	200	(246)	693	(338)	3037
Interest Payments	65	(648)	486	(163)	1285

Table 4.6 Chile: Cumulative Budget Trends and Period Percent Change 1980- 1995. (Billions of Pesos).

	1980-1984	(%) Change	1985-1989	(%) Change	1990-1995
Total Revenue	2139	(182)	6037	(278)	22870
Total Expenditures	2156	(165)	5723	(265)	20880
[Overall Deficit]/ Surplus	[-76]	(234)	102	(1850)	1990

Sources for Tables 4.4- 4.6: IMF, Government Finance Yearbook, 1986, 1991, 1996.

Chile's hierarchical budget procedures are considered to be a contributing factor to fiscal restraint. This argument is consistent with Von Hagen and Harden's "structural hypothesis." This hypothesis holds that hierarchical institutions and procedures lead to fiscal responsibility.[209] Alesina, Hausman, Hommes and Stein extend this argument. Their index of budget procedures associates lower primary deficits in Latin America from 1980-1993 with more hierarchical and transparent procedures.[210]

In Chile, the power over the budget is centered in the executive branch. The 1980 constitution prohibits the Central Bank from financing any type of public expenditure with either direct or indirect credits. Congress does not have the power to raise or lower estimated revenues, it can only lower non-permanent expenditures.[211] Given that decisions on fiscal policy are made almost exclusively within the executive branch, members of Congress are not able to engage in "pork-barrel politics," funding projects benefitting the member's own geographic district. Thus, public spending is not directed to constituents' local interests and political competition for resources is limited. Additionally, "the tax structure is not subject to annual discussion or revision."[212]

Chile has also limited its exposure to fiscal instability resulting from the volatility in copper prices. It has established a stabilization fund to smooth out copper tax revenues and avoid public expenditure increases during periods of high copper prices. Unlike Argentina's revenue sharing system, Chile's centralized budget authority promotes fiscal restraint. State and local governments and other local public entities are restricted to spending their own revenue. The national budget authority has to approve all regional and local loan contracts.[213] The constraints on spending imposed by the copper stabilization fund and the limitations on the borrowing autonomy of state and local governments reflect Chile's high level of budget transparency.

In spite of Chile's hierarchical but transparent budget procedures, the level of fiscal flexibility is constrained by the integration of Chile's small open economy into the world economy. With exports accounting for over 30 percent of GDP by 1994, Chile has attempted to reduce its exposure to exchange rate fluctuations by imposing reserve requirements on capital inflows.[214] As Chile becomes more integrated with the world economy, maintaining a balance between fiscal responsibility and fiscal flexibility becomes a major political challenge.

Public Finance Trends: Mexico

A review of Mexico's budgetary trends shows that the widening fiscal deficits of the mid- to late 1980s were reversed in the first half of the 1990's. A heavy reliance on private and public bank loans characterizes Mexico's public financing during the 1980's. From 1980-84, 32 percent of expenditures were financed through public and private loans. During 1985-89, this percentage increased to 36 percent. From 1990-1994 debt financed only 12 percent of Mexico's public expenditures reflecting a growing reliance on tax revenues (Tables 4.7 and 4.9). During 1980-1984, taxes financed 51 percent of expenditures. In contrast by 1990-95 taxes financed 82 percent of public spending (Tables 4.7 and 4.9).

It should be noted that expenditures in all major functional categories, except public debt interest payments, declined during the period 1990-1994 compared to the previous period (Table 4.8). Thus, it could be argued that in Mexico, drastic expenditure reductions, particularly in education, social security and welfare, economic services and interest payments, were an important contributing factor to deficit reduction. A reduction in capital expenditures in economic services, primarily through privatization, also helped to improve public sector accounts.[215] In sum, the combination of higher tax revenues and lower expenditures contributed to Mexico's severe fiscal adjustment.

Fluctuations in fiscal deficits and surpluses can be tied to fluctuations in Mexico's oil export earnings.[216] The wide annual gyrations in revenues and expenditures during the 1980s, however, could also be tied to political trade-offs. When oil prices declined and public spending levels could not be maintained, political expediency replaced fiscal responsibility as a deeper deficit plunged Mexico into fiscal crisis.

Table 4.7 – Mexico: Major Financing Methods and Cumulative Period Percent Change (Millions of Pesos).

	1980-1984	(%) Change	1985-1989	(%) Change	1990-1995
Tax- based financing*	8530	(85)	15754	(299)	62831
Other non-tax revenue	525	(438)	2826	(162)	7422
Debt- based financing**	5281	(111)	11185	(67)	18740

*Tax-based financing excludes extra-budgetary accounts, social security funds and various budgetary items.
**Includes domestic and foreign financing.

Table 4.8 – Mexico: Cumulative Composition of Major Expenditures by Function and Period Percent Change (Millions of Pesos).

	1980-1984	(%) Change	1985-1989	(%) Change	1990-1995
Public Services	2204	(213)	6919	(-10)	6230
Education	2041	(57)	3210	(-19)	2612
Health	231	(89)	438	(-24)	332
Social Security and Welfare	1787	(49)	2672	(-15)	2268
Economic Services	4372	(-2)	4264	(-58)	1768
Public Debt Interest	4522	(293)	17782	(52)	27094

Table 4.9 – Mexico: Cumulative Budget Trends and Period Percent Change 1980-1994 (Millions of Pesos).

	1980-1984	(%) Change	1985-1989	(%) Change	1990-1995
Total Revenue	11085	(93)	21446	(291)	83909
Total expenditure	16523	(89)	31290	(143)	76223
[Overall Deficit] / Surplus	[-5438]	(81)	[-9844]	(178)	7686

Sources for Tables 4.7- 4.9: IMF, Government Finance Statistics Yearbook, 1986, 1991, 1996.

For example, in the late 1980s, social-spending increases in education, health, and infrastructure were designed to maintain the PRI as the dominant ruling party.[217]

Mexico's drastic financial turnaround in the early 1990s took place in the context of formal and informal rules.[218] The Mexican regime is characterized by strong and relatively autonomous government entities that allow for limited input by selected interests through clearly demarcated, corporatist channels. In Mexico, the hierarchical, yet "pluralist" model seems to define budgetary procedures and limit budget transparency. Fiscal reforms implemented since the mid-1980s introduced a number of administrative measures to reduce corruption and tax evasion in the process of fiscal policy implementation. The newly adopted formal budget rules evolved within the corporatist framework of Mexican politics.[219] Since 1991, the highly centralized executive budget process coexists with electoral reforms. Giving more power to opposition parties, these reforms change the balance of power in the legislative branch, thus adding institutional constraints to budget cycles.

When one considers the strengths of a hierarchical model in delivering fiscal responsibility and restraint, one might be inclined to downplay the trade-off between efficient fiscal management and public representation in the allocation of public resources. The most direct implication of the hierarchical model is a reduced level of public representation in the allocation of public resources. In contrast to a closed, hierarchical executive process, a collegial budget process involving both legislative and executive branches favors public debate, enforcement, and accountability. Argentina, Chile, and Mexico managed to reverse budget deficits in the early 1990s, but one needs to question whether the economic benefits of fiscal restraint outweighed the political costs of these policy choices.

The Political Costs and Benefits of Fiscal Restraint

Some scholars have asked why persistent deficits were acceptable for countries such as Australia, New Zealand, Ireland, and South Korea but were unsustainable for Latin American countries, such as Chile and Mexico. One study finds that the most significant measures of current account sustainability include "the size of the export sector, the level of international competitiveness, the level of domestic savings, the composition of external liabilities, the strength of the financial system, ... degree of political stability and fiscal consolidation."[220] These measures suggest that there is more to credibility than institutional and policy choices. The size, openness, and structure of an economy matters. Given these findings and Argentina, Chile, and Mexico's public finance trends from 1980-1995, one could pose a different but related question, namely, are deficit reductions sustainable in these countries? If deficit reductions are sustainable, will these countries be able to establish a track record of fiscal policy credibility to carry them through their next crisis? How do measures of current account sustainability impact credibility?

For each one of these countries, the lost decade of the 1980s was a journey of spiraling deficits. During the mid 1980s, policy makers confronted with repeated cycles of debt and inflation began to implement a wide range of reforms to attack the interrelated problems of debt, adjustment, inflation and development. Deficits were controlled in the mid-1980s by Chile and in the early 1990s by both Argentina and Mexico. Nevertheless, by the end of 1994, Mexico's currency devaluation triggered another financial crisis that impacted all of Latin America and severely affected Argentina and to a lesser degree Chile. In spite of this setback, Argentina, Chile, and Mexico were able to sustain their reform efforts.

A combination of fiscal discipline, public expenditure priorities, and tax reforms enabled each country to improve debt burdens. From 1986 to 1995, Argentina's debt service ratio (Debt Service/Current Account Earnings) declined 58 percent. During the same period, debt ratios for Chile and Mexico declined 48 percent and 52 percent respectively (See Table 4.10). Debt service ratios measure a country's ability to pay interest and principal by comparing total debt service obligations and their relative size to current account earnings.

Mexico's debt ratio (External Debt/Current Account Earnings) increased by 30 percent from 1990 to 1995 (Table 4.11). During this same period, Argentina's debt ratio declined by 8 percent and Chile's debt ratio declined by 27 percent (Table 4.11). Although the ability of these countries to service their debt has improved considerably, due to greater reliance on tax revenues resulting from tax reforms initiatives, increased debt levels have become the norm.[221]

Table 4.10 – Debt Service Ratio - Selected Years (Percent)

	1986	1990	1995
Argentina	82.8	37	34.4
Chile	40.6	26	21.3
Mexico	45.7	21.7	21.6

Source: Inter-American Development Bank, National Accounts Database 1997.

Table 4.11 – Total External Debt to GDP (Percent)

	1986	1990	1995
Argentina	39.9	40.6	37.2
Chile	90.2	55.5	40.7
Mexico	51.7	43.3	56.4

Source: Inter-American Development Bank. National Accounts Database 1997.

The continuing reliance on debt, in spite of the shift from debt to tax financing in each country is evidenced by the rising levels of public debt interest payments in each country's composition of major expenditures (See Tables 4.2, 4.5 and 4.8).

The financing trends in all three countries from 1980 to 1995 suggest that increased reliance on tax financing did not eliminate debt- financing needs. In fact, for Argentina, Chile, and Mexico increases in all major expenditure categories during this period may have contributed to the continuing dependency on debt financing (See Tables 4.1, 4.2, 4.4, 4.5, 4.7, and 4.8).

A comparison of each country's fiscal discipline, public expenditure priorities, debt management, and tax reforms provides a glimpse of the progress in each area. In terms of fiscal discipline, it appears evident that towards the end of the 1980s policy makers began to pay attention to deficits, resulting in substantial fiscal consolidation, which measures deficits as a percent of GDP. Public expenditure priorities vary across each country reflecting policy responses to social needs and demands. Argentina and Chile increased expenditures in public services, education, health care, and social security from 1980 to 1995. In contrast, Mexico increased these expenditures from 1980-1989 and then reduced them from 1990-1994. Clearly, the path of deficit reduction in each country differed, suggesting that in Mexico deficit reductions in the 1990s translated into social spending cuts, while in Argentina and Chile deficit reductions did not adversely affect social spending.[222] Trends in public expenditures and taxes in Argentina, Chile and Mexico from 1980-1995 are somewhat consistent with the findings in a recent study at linking financial deregulation to an increase in corporate taxation, a decrease in individual income taxes, and an increase in government expenditures.[223] For example, while trends in Chile more closely fit Quinn's findings, Mexico experienced higher corporate taxes in the early 1980s and these taxes were cut in 1989-1991 to increase international competitiveness.[224]

In comparing public finance trends in Argentina, Chile, and Mexico from 1980 to 1995, one can conclude that the patterns of revenues and expenditures directly reflect fiscal policy choices – choices about taxing and spending. The conceptual model outlined in Chapter 3, suggested that fiscal policy choices are largely shaped by budget institutions. In Argentina, Chile, and Mexico, these institutions carry a strong authoritarian legacy that shapes budgetary processes and fiscal outcomes. In the three countries, the executive branch plays a pivotal role in all stages of the budget process. In this context, presidential cabinets and Finance Ministers set the budget agenda while legislative branches have limited influence in formulating, approving and implementing budgets.

From 1980-89, Argentina and Mexico relied heavily on debt financing, while Chile emphasized tax-based financing. From 1990-95, both Argentina and Mexico reduced their dependence on debt, while Chile began to increase the issuance of debt to complement tax revenues. The method of financing matters when it comes to fiscal performance. A heavy reliance on debt crowds out private investment.[225] This was evidenced by the higher interest rates resulting from the deficits of the 1980s and early 1990s in all three countries.

Where conflicts are resolved also matters. When it comes to budgetary decisions, conflict resolution at the cabinet level leads to greater fiscal restraint than conflict resolution in the legislative arena. Support for this claim can be found in comparing deficit reductions in Chile and Argentina from 1980-1990. In Chile, the executive branch monopolizes the budget agenda in its formulation, approval, and implementation stages. Chile reversed budget deficits within a period of four years from 1980-1984. In Argentina, the executive controls the process, but the legislature plays a more active role in the approval of budget changes. Budgets can be modified on the initiative of the executive branch with congressional approval.[226] In Argentina, the process of reversing budget deficits lasted from 1980-1990. The hierarchical model in Argentina is the most "collegial" of the three countries, but the added democratic accountability comes at the cost of fiscal restraint.

In Mexico and to some extent in Argentina, hierarchical budget rules did not produce fiscal restraint during the 1980s.[227] This could be attributed to either the influence of informal corporatist rules or the lack of rule transparency. More than likely the combination of these two factors contributed to the lack of fiscal restraint. Informal rules are not conducive to transparency and as a result may hinder the effectiveness of formal budget rules.[228]

In terms of transparency, it appears that Chile has the most transparent budget process. Chile's budgetary rules, norms, and laws delineate clear centers of budgetary authority, leaving little room for political contests in the allocation of resources. In contrast, Mexico's hierarchical model involves less transparency. Mexico's corporatist interests seem to yield political influence on budgetary decisions. The rules of the budgetary process are even less transparent in Argentina, perhaps as a function of some degree of congressional discretion in the approval of budget changes and the weak budgetary constraints on provincial governments.

Although all three countries reversed their budget deficits, their hierarchical approach to budgeting involves a major political trade-off. While removing the budget from public debate may contribute to fiscal restraint, such approach severely undermines democratic principles, namely, the level of public representation in the allocation of public resources.

In the context of Argentina, Chile, and Mexico, however, the pluralist and hierarchical models of policy making seem to coexist. Wiarda points out that in Latin America, "even in democracies, corporatism and organicism often remain present in important institutions and policy processes."[229] The authoritarian legacy in the region is evident in the budgetary process of each country. Perhaps these hierarchical structures explain why from 1980- 1995 an escalation of social demands did not materialize in Argentina, Chile, or Mexico. Rigid decision-making corporatist structures leave little room for public challenges to government policy.

Another explanation for the lack of social demands during this period may be the public's acceptance of market-friendly reforms after four decades of deteriorating living standards. By the 1970s, Latin Americans experienced the most unequal income distribution in the world.[230] As Argentina, Chile and Mexico implemented structural reforms and emerged from the lost decade of the 1980s, several social indicators improved, suggesting that social spending to some degree met social demands.

Fiscal policy choices have an impact on the ability of policy makers to access private markets to finance public expenditures. Fiscal policy choices also have a direct impact on who gets what, when and how. The political costs and benefits of fiscal restraint can best me measured in terms of social impact. To illustrate the social impact of fiscal choices made in Argentina Chile and Mexico from 1980-1995, it is useful to compare public service, health care and education expenditures (Tables 4.2, 4.5 and 4.8).

Although from 1985-89 to 1990-95 Argentina showed a 391 percent change in public services expenditures and Chile showed a 169 percent change (Tables 4.2 and 4.5), the gap between access to safe water in urban and rural areas widened in both countries (Table 4.12).

Table 4.12 – Selected Social Indicators for Argentina, Chile, and Mexico (1980 -1995).

	Argentina		Chile		Mexico	
	1980-85	1990-95	1980-85	1990-95	1980-85	1990-95
Total Population (Million)	30.3	35.2	12.0	14.4	74.8	93.2
Mortality*						
(Infant)	29	22	20	12	43	32
(Under 5)	38	25	37	13	76	36
Life ** Expectancy	68	73	65	75	64	72
Immunization Rates						
Measles +	67	76	92	93	64	90
DPT ++	63	82	91	98	40	92
Access to Safe Water***	55	64	86	85	82	83
Urban	63	73	78	97	95	91
Rural	26	17	28	22	50	62
School**** Enrollment	100	100	94	100	86	92
Illiteracy Rate *****	4	4	7	5	14	10

*Infant Mortality per thousand live births, under age 5 per thousand live births.
**Life expectancy at birth, years for total male and females.
+Measels immunizations, percent under 12 months old, ++DPT, percent under 12 months old.
***Access to safe water, percent of total population including urban and rural.
****Net Primary enrollment rate, percent of school age population, total male and female
*****Illiteracy rate, percent of total population age 15+.

Source: World Bank Social Indicators, Social Indicators Data Sheets for Argentina, Chile and Mexico. 1998 CD-ROM.

From 1985 to 1995, urban residents in Argentina experienced a 16 percent improvement in their access to safe water, while urban residents in Chile experienced a 24 percent improvement. In contrast, during this period, rural residents in Argentina experienced a 34 percent decline in their access to safe water and rural residents in Chile experienced a 21 percent decline (Table 4.12). It is useful to compare trends in access to safe water to public service expenditures to fully assess the effects of fiscal policy choices on social benefits. In both Argentina and Chile, urban expenditures in public services received a higher priority than rural expenditures. Higher levels of expenditures do not always result in higher levels of public services. Between 1985 and 1995, Argentina's public service expenditure percent increases were 131 percent higher than Chile's (Tables 4.2 and 4.5). Yet, Chilean access to safe water for urban residents was 33 percent higher than access for Argentinean urban residents during the same period (Table 4.12).

In contrast to Argentina and Chile, Mexico's public service expenditures from 1980-85 to 1990-95 declined by 10 percent (Table 4.8). During this period, urban residents experienced a 4 percent decline in their access to safe water, while rural residents experienced a 24 percent improvement for the same period. In Argentina and Chile, urban improvements in the access to safe water came at the expense of rural residents. In Mexico, rural improvements in the access to safe water came at the expense of urban residents.[231] Safe water is not just a quality of life issue but a serious economic issue. Healthy individuals are more productive than unhealthy ones. Aggregate data (total access to safe water) obscures the sharp differences in the quality of services delivered to urban and rural residents.

Health indicators such as mortality rate, immunization rates and life expectancy provide a wide lens for examining the improvements in each country from 1985 to 1995, a period when fiscal restraint dictated the allocation of public resources in all three countries. Health care expenditure patterns differ in each country yet remarkably, mortality rates declined and immunization rate and life expectancy rates improved in each country (Tables 4.2, 4.5, 4.8, 4.12).

Argentina shows a 736 percent change increase in health expenditures, the highest of all three countries, from 1985-89 to 1990-95 (Table 4.2). Chile follows with a 328 percent change increase, while Mexico shows a 24 percent change decline in health care expenditures during this period of time (Tables 4.5 and 4.8). Interestingly enough, the highest increases in health care expenditures did not produce the highest improvements in life expectancy. Argentina's life expectancy increased by 7 percent while life expectancy in Chile and Mexico increased 15 and 12 percent respectively (Table 4.12). A similar improvement pattern is found for mortality rates for infants under the age of 5. The improvement in Argentina was 34 percent, in Chile 64 percent and in Mexico 52 percent. The improvement patterns for measles immunizations are 13 percent for Argentina, 1 percent for Chile and 40 percent for Mexico.

As in the case of mortality rates and life expectancy, improvements in immunizations, particularly in Mexico, seem to defy the conventional wisdom that expenditure cuts are necessarily followed by a decline in social indicators. One explanation for this seeming aberration is that expenditure cuts cannot be accurately assessed with aggregate data. For example, it is necessary to examine exactly what programs in health care are cut and what programs are targeted for remaining funds. Clearly, the 24 percent cut in health care expenditures in Mexico did not impact measles immunization programs - specific health programs adversely affected by the budget cuts are not reflected in these figures.

From 1985 to 1995, the percent changes in education expenditures in Argentina and Chile were 189 and 288 percent respectively (tables 4.2 and 4.5) while Mexico cut education expenditures by 19 percent. Improvements in the net primary enrollment rate for the school age population follows the similar patterns to the improvements in infrastructure and health care indicators. In spite of the triple digit increase of expenditures in Argentina and Chile, primary school enrollment remained at 100 percent in Argentina and only improved by 6 percent in Chile, while Mexico's expenditure cuts resulted in a 7 percent improvement in primary school enrollment.[232]

From 1980 to 1995, policy makers in Argentina, Chile, and Mexico made fiscal policy choices affecting the lives of the citizens in each country. Improved social indicators in Argentina, Chile, and Mexico did not translate into social equity defined as the elimination of poverty, equality of opportunity and protection against economic crises during the 1980-1995 period. Nevertheless, improved economic conditions created what Boeninger considers "social peace." Within a democratic context, social peace refers to the acceptance of rules and procedures for settling conflicts over living conditions, social services, wages and social justice at the bargaining table.[233] Although public representation in the allocation of public resources was limited in all three countries, improved living standards may account for public acceptance of social spending choices. Fiscal choices in spending, taxing and financing are not bound only by domestic political expectations. Global capital market expectations also shape fiscal policy choices.

Conclusion

A preliminary examination of the relationship between fiscal policy choices and access to the sovereign debt market suggests that capital market expectations and sovereign credit ratings may provide incentives for governments to make binding commitments of fiscal restraint. Sovereign credit ratings represent public report cards on government performance. In an age of instant communications, public scrutiny influences institutional and policy choices and, in turn, these choices influence the flow of capital to and from any particular financial market. Ultimately, the institutional and fiscal policy choices governments make either facilitate or block access to the sovereign debt market, a major source of public finance capacity.

When institutional and policy choices are credible to financial market participants, policy makers have an opportunity to finance public expenditures through the sovereign debt market. Policy makers can seize this opportunity to finance education, health care and infrastructure investments contributing to economic growth. Furthermore, by financing such long-term investments through sovereign debt, policy makers can reduce dependence on regressive taxes.

In comparing domestic institutional and policy choices within the framework of global finance, the economic and political reforms in each country were examined. The conceptual model emphasized institutional and policy choices as determinants of market access. The qualitative comparative analysis revealed that fiscal choices evolved in the context of structural reforms such as privatization and financial deregulation. Other contextual factors contributing to each government's fiscal policy credibility included a legal, regulatory and tax framework, a stable system of financial intermediation and an improved transportation and communication infrastructure. Measures of fiscal credibility included the size of the export sector, the composition of external liabilities, the degree of political stability, and fiscal consolidation.

These combined factors suggest that there is more to credibility than the choice of budget and fiscal policy choices. From the perspective of financial market participants, the size, openness, and structure of the domestic political economy are important measures of credibility. The next chapter takes these measures into account and shifts to a quantitative comparative analysis of institutional and policy choices in Argentina, Chile and Mexico. The aim is to identify institutional and policy patterns that combined with contextual factors translated into government access to the international bond market.

Chapter Five
Comparing Cases: Quantitative Analysis

This chapter complements the qualitative comparison of the previous chapter through quantitative analysis. The qualitative comparative analysis revealed that the variables in the model may only capture partial relationships. For example, the independent variable, fiscal policy, focuses on debt financing and ignores tax-financing initiatives. The intervening variable, fiscal policy commitment, ignores various measures used by credit rating agencies to assess a government's credible fiscal commitments. Credit rating assessments focus on the openness of the economy and the ability of a government to generate foreign exchange earnings. These measures represent potentially significant factors capable of explaining a government's access to the international debt market.[234] Each one of these measures represents another dimension of policy choice (trade policy, regulatory policy), expanding the scope of policy making beyond fiscal decisions. Additionally, it is important to disaggregate the index of budget institutions (antecedent variable in the model) and consider each of its individual components. The index includes ten variables representing various measures of institutional constraints on budgeting.

Keeping the analysis focused on three countries and extending the number of variables originally proposed in the conceptual model requires a refinement of variables. This study used data mining to filter the most significant predictors of market access from a large set of variables.[235] This technique involves the search for relationships and patterns that exist, but that are hidden among vast amounts of data.[236]

Data mining could be interpreted as a technique allowing data to speak for itself. Yet, as Gerry Stoker asserts, "facts do not speak for themselves and only make sense in the context of a framework of investigation. Ideas about what is important and the way things work structure all observations. Theory and facts are not independent of one another."[237] The model presented in this study provided the theoretical framework guiding the qualitative analysis. Likewise, the model was the point of departure for the data mining analysis. Although it can complement the more comprehensive qualitative analysis, data mining has limited explanatory power and only allows for tentative conclusions.

Data mining begins with research questions and ends with a questioning of results. It extracts information from a large database by identifying non-intuitive relationships between dependent and independent variables. These non-intuitive relationships are the patterns that data mining discovers. The knowledge discovery in databases cycle (KDD) consists of five steps: Data selection, data preprocessing, data transformation, data mining and data interpretation and evaluation. Data selection consists of selection of relevant data to answer the research questions. Data preprocessing involves eliminating missing values to ensure that coded values have uniform meaning. Data transformation involves converting the data into a two-dimensional table and eliminating highly correlated fields to ensure the validity of results.

Data mining involves the application of algorithms to the data. This is accomplished through predictive models. The interpretation and evaluation of data involves questions about the usefulness of the models. The KDD cycle is iterative and allows for the return to previous phases to improve the analysis of data.[238] This analysis was carried out across all three countries to identify what combination of variables converged to facilitate market access and public finance capacity from 1980 through 1993.[239] Data mining analysis was used to test the first and second hypotheses. Multiple regression was used to test the third hypothesis to determine whether access to the sovereign debt market increases a government's capacity to finance growth-oriented expenditures. This chapter begins with a refinement of the variables outlined in Chapter 3.. An overview of the steps used in data mining and the results of the data mining and SPSS analyses complete this chapter.

Refinement of Variables

The qualitative analysis identified multiple factors associated with market access. These factors require the extension and refinement of the antecedent, independent, intervening and dependent variables of the conceptual model introduced in Chapter 3. Independent variables were clustered into nine general categories. Variable clusters represent selected institutional and policy indicators that capture the antecedent, intervening and independent variables in the model.

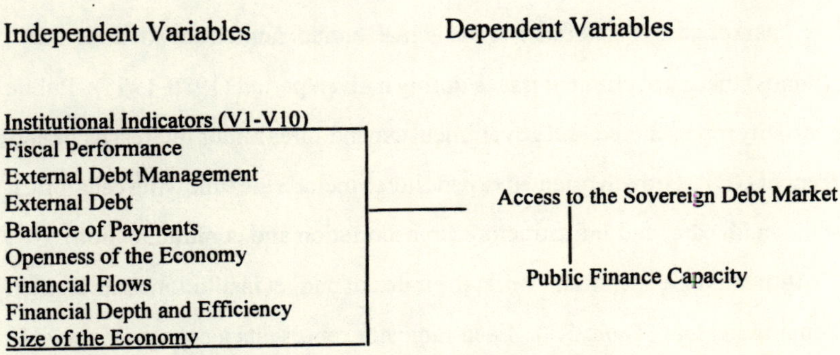

Figure 5.1 Multiple institutional and policy variables.

The institutional indicators represent the antecedent variable (budget institutions) in the conceptual model sketched in chapter three (Figure 3.2). Fiscal performance, external debt management and external debt represent combined dimensions of the independent variable, fiscal policy choice. Fiscal performance, in particular, reflects fiscal policy commitments. Policy choice is expanded to include balance of payments, financial flows, financial depth and efficiency and openness and size of the economy, all indicators that capture choices about trade liberalization, financial deregulation, and privatization.

The institutional indicators include budget institutions, fiscal performance, external debt management, external debt, financial flows, openness of the economy, balance of payments, size of the economy, financial depth and efficiency. The dependent variables include market access and public finance capacity. Market access is measured in terms of newly issued bonds and notes in the international bond market, average interest rate (coupons), and average maturity. Market access is not defined as a government's open lines of credit - the potential access to private credit that a government can obtain. Open lines of credit, potential access, often exceeds the actual levels of sovereign debt market access that governments procure at any given time. Potential market access, however, is difficult to quantify. Therefore, market access is defined as the actual, annual amount of sovereign debt credits (bonds) that a government issues during a given period (1980-1995). Public finance capacity represents central government expenditures minus interest payments as a percent of GDP. Growth oriented expenditures include the following categories: education, health care, and infrastructure (transportation and communication).

Within this extended framework, the index of budget institutions captures ten institutional indicators (Table 5.1). Each indicator represents a constraint variable affecting the formulation, approval, and implementation of the budget.

Table 5.1 – Index of Budget Institutions. [240]

Variable	Description	Value
V1	Macroeconomic constraint on budget	10- important 5- some importance 0- no importance
V2	Standing of Treasury minister vis a vis spending ministers	5- high standing 2.5 - somewhat high standing 0- all ministers on equal footing
V3	Legislative constraints (amendments)	10- amendments cannot increase size of budget 5- Congress can only propose budget size. 0- no constraints
V4	Legislative rejection of budget	10- full executive veto power 5- limited veto power
V5	Borrowing autonomy of government	10- most autonomy 0- no autonomy
V6	Budget modification after legislative approval	10- no modification 5- some modification 0- no constraint
V7	Executive discretion to cut spending after budget is approved	10- only when revenues lower than projected 5- some discretion 0- no discretion
V8	Government assumes other entities' debt	10- no debt assumption 5- only guaranteed debt 0- assumes all debt including non-guaranteed debt
V9	Borrowing autonomy of state and local governments	10- no borrowing autonomy 5-some autonomy 0- no restrictions
V10	Constitutional constraints	10- balance budget rules 5- deficits need to be financed 0- no constraints

Source: Alesina *et al.,* "Budget Institutions and Fiscal Performance In Latin America," 9-15.

Each variable is measured on a scale from 10-0 denoting degrees of either macroeconomic, legislative, or executive constraints on the budget throughout its preparation, approval and implementation. By focusing on executive and legislative constraints, the index highlights important dimensions of transparent, non-transparent, hierarchical and collegial budget institutions. The index captures the extent to which budget rules conform to macroeconomic constraints. The index also captures the extent to which budget rules contribute to fiscal restraint.

Only one variable (V1) measures the degree to which a macroeconomic program imposes macroeconomic constraints on the preparation of the budget by the executive branch. Alesina *et al.* do not distinguish whether such a macroeconomic program originates domestically or originates within an international financial institution such as the IMF (as in the case of structural adjustment programs). The degree to which hierarchical or collegial rules characterize the budget process is measured by the standing of the finance minister vis a vis spending ministers (V2), legislative constraints (V3), legislative rejection of the budget (V4), budget modification after legislative approval (V6) and executive discretion to cut spending after the budget is passed (V7). Two variables capture the degree of budget transparency. These variables are a) a government's track record in assuming guaranteed and non-guaranteed debt originally incurred by other public entities (V8), and b) the national government's level of constraints on local and state governments' borrowing autonomy (V9). The borrowing autonomy of a government (V5), and constitutional constraints on the budget (V10) represent measures of fiscal restraint and discipline.

Alesina *et al.* classify V8 and V9 as indicators of transparency due to the fact that both variables measure disclosure of budgeting information related to the financing relationship between national governments, local and state governments and other entities. Although Alesina *et al.* do not explain why they consider V8 and V9 measures of transparency, one can argue that national governments that either guarantee local and state debt or fail to impose constraints on the level of local and state government borrowing have less transparent budgets than governments that constrain local, state, or other entities' borrowing autonomy. A lack of constraints on local, state or other entities' borrowing autonomy indicates constraints on the disclosure of budget information, particularly as it relates to specific financing arrangements between national, local, and state governments. These arrangements can easily be obscured through off-budget and open-ended expenditures. Hence, a lack of transparency can be considered a source of budget inefficiency.

The intervening variable, fiscal policy commitment was operationalized as an ordinal variable classifying commitment along a continuum from credible to non-credible commitments. Attaching fiscal restraint measures to each commitment category allows for a comparison of policy credibility among cases. In order to quantify credible, questionable and non-credible fiscal policy commitments, the three values assigned to the intervening variable are ranked in terms of two debt management ratios used in sovereign credit analysis. These ratios include the debt ratio (V129) and the debt burden ratio (V102).

Quantitative analysis allows for the measurement of one of the effects of interactive choice, namely public finance capacity. In this context, growth oriented public expenditures are examined in relation to both market access and public finance capacity.[241]

Table 5.2 – Values for Intervening Variable (Fiscal Policy Commitment).

Ratio	Value (percentage)	Credibility Ranking
Debt Ratio	0-100	credible commitment (1)
	100-200	questionable commitment (2)
	over 200	non-credible commitment (3)
Debt Burden Ratio	0-10	credible commitment (1)
	10-20	questionable commitment (2)
	over 25	non-credible commitment (3)

Source: Adapted from "Guide to Evaluating Sovereign Credits." Fixed Income Credit Research (New York: Morgan Stanley, 1992), 160.

The debt ratio measures the size of the external debt relative to the current account earnings (External Debt/Current Account Earnings) and the debt service ratio measures the debt burden (Debt Service/Current Account Earnings). The percent thresholds selected represent rules of thumb applied by credit rating agencies and financial analysts involved in sovereign credit analysis.[242]

Data Mining Steps and Analysis

The hypotheses derived from the conceptual model of institutional choice represented the departure point for the quantitative analysis. These research hypotheses express important relationships between the main variables in the conceptual model and determine the preprocessing of data for data mining.

Data preprocessing is a preliminary step to format all data values according to the specific requirements of data mining techniques. A total of 131 variables were organized into a data set compatible with data mining analysis. To test the hypotheses, the analysis focused on cross-sectional time series data.[243] Three countries and sixteen years produced 48 cases. Each case had 131 yearly observations and provided a total of 6,288 data values. Accounting for the missing data values that were removed, the data set was reduced to 5,502 values. The preprocessing of data involved eliminating missing values in the data, insuring that all coded values had a uniform meaning and that all variables were coded as continuous variables. Once this step was completed, the data was converted into a two-dimensional table and all highly correlated fields were eliminated. Next, the most relevant data mining tools were selected to analyze the data.

Selecting an appropriate model to address the research questions became a critical step, because many data mining tools are designed for very specialized applications.[244] Although there are no specific data mining tools designed to address problems of policy decision making, tools designed to improve business decisions can be valid and useful in the public policy arena. Three tools were selected to test hypotheses 1 and 2: Unica Technologies Model 1, Cognos, and Knowledge Seeker. All tools use industry-accepted algorithms. Model 1 is based on neural network algorithms, which mimic human learning about classification and prediction based on general patterns. Cognos uses a statistical model based on stepwise regression to construct decision trees that identify a sequence of variables with linked patterns. Knowledge Seeker uses rule association algorithms that identify causal relationships.[245]

The selection of data mining tools was based on the tools' flexibility to address general decision making problems. Tools specifically designed to address narrow business applications such as the development of customer profiles were avoided. Once each selected tool was tested, qualitative analysis was applied to determine if the results from each model made sense. The most significant variables identified by each model were compared to the qualitative analysis to determine if the quantitative results matched the qualitative findings.

Additionally, as presented in the next section, the rankings for the most sensitive variables identified by each model were normalized and tested again to compare results across models with a reduced number of variables. Similar variables were identified by all three models but each model assigned a different level of sensitivity to the selected variables suggesting that while the weighting of each variable differed across models, all tests uncovered similar patterns across the relationships among variables.

Data mining models do not measure "significance" as defined in statistical significance but measure the sensitivity of each independent variable relative to each other and to the "target" (e.g. dependent) variable. For example, for Unica Model 1, a neural network model, sensitivity is a factor of the weights attached to each neuron of the hundreds of neural networks created by the model.[246] Neural network algorithms represent complex, multidimensional connections of nodes and branches that mimic human learning process based on artificial intelligence programs. Data mining tools based on neural networks (e.g., Unica Model 1) are the most complex. These tools create various layers of neurons. Through iteration, optimal models are automatically selected. Through a process of elimination the selected models experiment with the optimal numbers of neurons trained to recognize relationship patterns. [247]

Rule induction models like Knowledge Seeker, are based on the repetitive analysis of " if...then" rules. For example, data mining tools based on rule induction programs analyze how separate parts form complex patterns through iterative analysis, which models "what if" factors. In contrast, data mining tools based on decision trees (e.g., Cognos) identify sequences of variables with linked patterns. Decision tree algorithms consist of nodes and branches. Each node is connected to additional branches leading to end-nodes. This structure is similar to the extensive form of games in game theory.

The final step was to validate each model. The detailed steps of how each data mining software tool arrives at the selection of the most significant variables (i.e. "most sensitive variables") is proprietary information for Unica Model 1, Cognos and Knowledge Seeker. The Unica Model 1, Cognos, and Knowledge Seeker uncovered similar sensitivity patterns, in spite of each program's different algorithm structure (e.g., neural networks, decision trees and rule association). This could be attributed to either the importance of the variables or to the standardized set of economic data used to identify patterns across time and across countries. The data mining findings, however, suggest that there is internal validation across all three data mining tools. In fact, some data mining tools validate results automatically. For example, in testing institutional and policy indicators, Unica Model 1 selected four out of 231 available neural network models. Findings presented in tables 5.3, 5.4 and

5.5 reflect the combined results for the top four models selected by this data mining tool. The performance of these models ranks from 80.96 to 80.03 percent. This performance measure represents an internal Model 1 validation measuring the probability that these models are correct.

The entire cycle of data selection, preprocessing, transformation, analysis, interpretation and evaluation focused closely on the research questions - What is the effect of fiscal policy choices on a government's access to the sovereign debt market? How, why, and with what consequences do credible fiscal policy commitments translate into public finance capacity? How does access to the sovereign debt market increase a government's capacity to finance expenditures leading to economic growth?[248]

Quantitative Analysis: Empirical Results

Hypothesis 1(H1): *Credible fiscal policy commitments - commitments signaling fiscal restraint to financial market participants - increase access to the sovereign debt market.* According to the conceptual model, budget institutions represent the antecedent variable, fiscal policy commitments represent the intervening variable, fiscal policy choices are the independent variable, and access to the sovereign debt market represents the dependent variable. In testing this hypothesis, the first step was to rank institutional and policy indicators in order of sensitivity relative to a government's access to the international sovereign debt market. Table 5.3 highlights the most sensitive institutional indicators affecting Argentina, Chile, and Mexico's access to the sovereign debt market from 1980-1993 and Table 5.4 summarizes policy indicators.

Institutional Indicators

Only one variable (V3) measuring legislative constraints received a high sensitivity ranking across two of the three models. This finding suggests that the greater the restrictions on the content of legislative budget amendments (hierarchical budgeting), the greater the government's access to the debt market. V9 (Borrowing autonomy of state and local governments) received the second highest ranking across all three models suggesting that the lower the borrowing autonomy of state and local governments (transparent budgeting), the greater the access of the national government to the debt market. The combined rankings of these two variables confirm the conclusion of Alesina *et al.* about the strong relationship between hierarchy of budget institutions and fiscal restraint.[249] In addition, the significance rankings suggest that transparency in budget institutions is strongly associated with market access.

Cognos excluded three variables (V2, V7 and V8) measuring the standing of the Treasury minister vis a vis spending ministers, spending cuts after the budget is approved, and the extent to which government assumes other entities' debt. V2 and V7 measure the level of hierarchy in the budgeting process and the rankings of these two variables are consistent with the rankings for V3 and V9, high and somewhat high sensitivity respectively. In contrast, V8 measures the degree of transparency in budgeting and its ranking parallels the rankings for V9 under Knowledge Seeker, but shows a somewhat low sensitivity ranking under Unica Model 1.

Table 5.3 – Ranking of Sensitive Institutional Variables Associated with Access to the Sovereign Debt Market.

Tool	**Cognos**	**Knowledge Seeker**	**Unica Model 1*** **
Variable (Ranking)	V3 (1)	V3 (1)	V3 (2)
	V9 (2)	V9 (1)	V9 (2)
	V1 (3)	V1 (1)	V1 (4)
	V4 (3)	V4 (2)	V4 (2)
	V6 (4)	V6 (2)	V6 (2)
		V2 (1)	V2 (2)
		V7 (1)	V7 (2)
		V8(1)	V8 (3)

Notes:

V1	Macroeconomic Constraint	V6	Budget after Legislative Approval
V2	Executive Branch Hierarchy	V7	Executive Discretion to Cut Spending
V3	Legislative Constraints	V8	Government Debt - Public Firms
V4	Legislative Veto Power	V9	Autonomy of State and Local Governments
V5	Borrowing Autonomy	V10	Constitutional Constraints

Ranking codes used in this table are adapted from Cognos, Knowledge Seeker and Model 1 and are measured as 1 (high sensitivity ranges from 90-70); 2 (somewhat high sensitivity ranges from 70-50); 3 (somewhat low sensitivity ranges from 50-30) and 4 (low sensitivity ranges from 30-10). [250]

Source: All data were calculated using Scenario-Cognos 1997, Angoss-Knowledge Seeker 1993 and Unica Technologies- Model 1 1995 data mining software packages.

Macroeconomic constraints in the budget were captured by V1 but the rankings of this variable across models were inconclusive. While Knowledge Seeker attached high sensitivity to this variable, Cognos, and Unica Model 1 attached a somewhat low and low sensitivity respectively to the existence of a macroeconomic program aimed at curbing spending. In contrast, the rankings for V4 (legislative budget rejection) and V6 (modification after congressional budget approval) were consistent across all three models. Cognos attached low sensitivity to both variables and Knowledge Seeker and Model 1 attached a somewhat high sensitivity to these variables.

Automatically excluded variables across all three models include V5 (Central Government Borrowing Autonomy) and V10 (Constitutional Constraints). One possible explanation for the exclusion of these variables is that V5 is captured in the values of V8 and V9, while V10 may be linked to V1 (the existence of a macroeconomic program may coincide with the implementation of balanced budget rules).

Policy Indicators

The quantitative analysis of policy indicators revealed that fiscal policy choices narrowly defined as debt-financing choices cannot be singled out as factors impacting a government's access to the sovereign debt market. After eliminating highly correlated variables with levels of significance between 90 and 100 percent, four sets of independent policy variables emerged as the most significant factors associated with access to the sovereign debt market: fiscal performance, balance of payments, external debt management, and external debt.

GNP growth (V33) is the only variable that receives a high sensitivity rating across all three models. This result seems to confirm the Miller and Russek findings that associate bond financing with economic growth in developing countries.[251] Variables identified across all three data mining tools include: Current Account Balance (V18), Exports (V29), Gross International Reserves (V38), GNP Growth (V33), Aggregate Net Resource Flows (V88) and the Debt Ratio (V129). These variables emerged as either highly sensitive or somewhat highly sensitive with respect to sovereign debt market access.

Cognos identified mobile phones (V54) as having high sensitivity while Unica Model 1 identified the use of IMF credit (V86) and debt buyback (V99) as having a high sensitivity ranking. Knowledge Seeker identified openness of the economy (V3) debt service (V101) and short term debt (V124) as high sensitivity variables.

Table 5.4 – Rankings of Sensitive Policy Variables Associated with Access to the Sovereign Debt Market.

Tool	Cognos	Knowledge Seeker	Unica Model 1
Variable (Ranking)	V18 (2)	V18 (2)	V18 (1)
	V29 (1)	V29 (2)	V29 (2)
	V33 (1)	V33 (1)	V33 (1)
	V38 (1)	V38 (2)	V38 (2)
	V88 (2)	V88 (1)	V88 (2)
	V129 (2)	V129 (1)	V129 (2)
	V77 (3)		V77 (3)
		V124 (1)	V124 (3)
	V3 (2)		
	V54 (1)		
	V82 (2)		
			V86 (1)
			V99 (1)
			V100 (4)
	V101 (2)		
	V102 (2)		

Notes:
The variables used in this analysis were labeled V1 through V129. Each variable is defined according to World Bank databases (Global Development Finance and World Development Indicators, CD-ROm, 1998) as follows:

V18	Current Account Balance (percent of GDP)	V101	Debt Service (US$)
V29	Exports of Goods and Services (BoP current US$)	V102	Debt Burden Ratio
V38	Gross International Reserves (current US$)	V124	Short Term Debt
V54	Mobile Phones (per 1000 people)	V129	Debt ratio
V77	Tax Revenue (percent of GDP)	V3	Openness of Economy[252]
V82	Total Debt Service (percent of GDP)	V33	GNP growth (annual)
V86	Use of IMF Credit (current US$)	V100	Debt Outstanding
V88	Aggregate Net Resource Flows (US$)	V99	Debt buyback

Ranking codes used in this table are adapted from Cognos, Knowledge Seeker and Model 1 and are measured as 1 (high sensitivity ranges from 90-70); 2 (somewhat high sensitivity ranges from 70-50); 3 (somewhat low sensitivity ranges from 50-30) and 4 (low sensitivity ranges from 30-10).

Source: All data were analyzed using Cognos- Scenario 1997, Angoss- Knowledge Seeker 1993 and Unica Technologies- Model 1, 1995 data mining software packages.

Knowledge Seeker and Model 1 identified mobile phones, the use of IMF credit and short- term debt as variables associated with increased market access. These three variables were not captured by hypothesis 1 or by the qualitative analysis. Knowledge Seeker identified additional variables captured either by hypothesis 1 or by the qualitative analysis[253]: debt ratio (102), debt burden ratio (129), debt service (101), debt outstanding (100), total debt service as percent of GDP (82), openness of the economy (V3), and tax revenue (V77).

Of particular interest is the relationship between mobile phones (V54) and market access (V4) identified by Cognos. At first glance, one may doubt the importance of this relationship. On closer examination, however, the relationship suggests that the availability of communication technologies may facilitate access to the international sovereign debt markets. Given that instant communications are one of the transactional pillars of capital markets, the association of mobile phones and market access is hardly surprising. Without communications technology, global capital markets would stop functioning. Bond and other financial market cross-border transactions require the instant flow of information. In fact, discovering the association between communication technology and access to the sovereign debt market validates the definition of globally linked countries (GLCs). Communications technology facilitates capital and trade flows and represents a vital link between open, national economies and global capital markets.

Hypothesis 2 (H2): *budget institutions and fiscal policy commitments lead to fiscal policy choices that can either strengthen or weaken a government's public finance capacity.* In testing this hypothesis, two of the three data mining models reveal similar patterns of institutional indicators emphasizing hierarchy and transparency, while all three models identify similar fiscal policy indicators emphasizing debt management and tax structure. These patterns suggest that public finance capacity (V27), defined as government expenditures as a percent of GDP, increases as a function of a combination of hierarchical and transparent budget institutions, lower debt service burdens and higher tax revenues.

Most of the policy variables identified by all three models fall into the categories of either external debt management or fiscal performance. One interesting exception is equity portfolio investments (V63) identified by Cognos. Equity portfolio investments in Argentina, Chile, and Mexico resulting from the sale of state-owned enterprises are generally associated with a reduction in government expenditures. The strong relationship between equity portfolio investments and public finance capacity suggests that privatization initiatives may be associated with increased public finance capacity in all three countries.

This finding suggests that funds freed up from the sale of state-owned enterprises may not necessarily be deployed to pay down or service public debt. Privatization proceeds may well be deployed to finance increased public expenditures. The use of privatization proceeds to increase public expenditures challenges the conventional efficiency arguments linking privatization to reduced public expenditures as a percent of GDP.

The emphasis on tax revenues as a source of public finance capacity is reinforced by the identification of a strong relationship between portfolio equity flows and public finance capacity. This relationship points to the importance of privatization initiatives in all three countries resulting in an expanded private corporate private sector contributing to the increase in income, profits and capital gains taxes as well as the increase in portfolio equity flows.[254]

Table 5.5 – Rankings of Significant Institutional and Policy Variables Associated with a Government's Public Finance Capacity.

Tool	Cognos	Knowledge Seeker	Unica Model 1
	V77 (2)	V77 (1)	V77 (1)
	V63 (2)	V67 (1)	V67 (2)
	V102 (2)	V75 (1)	V79 (1)
	V74 (2)	V74 (1)	V74 (3)
	V100 (3)	V131 (2)	V131 (3)
	V57 (2)	V57 (1)	V57 (1)
		V109 (1)	V109 (1)
		V80 (1)	V80 (2)
		V1 (1)	V1 (2)
		V3 (1)	V3 (1)
		V4 (1)	V4 (1)
		V5 (1)	V5 (1)
		V9 (1)	V9 (1)

Notes:
Policy Variables:

V77	Tax Revenue as percent of GDP;	V63	Portfolio Investment, Equity;
V67	Quasi-Liquid Liabilities as percent of GDP;	V 75	Social Security Taxes as percent of Current Revenue;
V 79	Taxes on Income, Profits and Capital Gains as percent of Current Revenue ;	V 80	Taxes on International Trade as percent of Current Revenue
V57	Other Taxes as percent of Current Revenue;	V 74	Short -term Debt as percent of Total External Debt;
V 100	Debt Outstanding;	V 102	Debt Service/ Exports of Goods and Services = Debt Burden Ratio;
V 109	Interest Payments/GNP;	V 131	Total Debt Service Paid.

Institutional Variables:

V 1	Macroeconomic Constraints on the Budget
V 3	Legislative Constraints on the Budget
V 4	Legislative Rejection of Budget
V 5	Borrowing Autonomy of Government
V9	Borrowing Autonomy of State and Local Governments

Ranking codes used in this table are adapted from Cognos, Knowledge Seeker and Model 1 and are measured as 1 (high sensitivity ranges from 90-70); 2 (somewhat high sensitivity ranges from 70-50); 3 (somewhat low sensitivity ranges from 50-30) and 4 (low sensitivity ranges from 30-10).

Source: All data were analyzed using Cognos 1997, Knowledge Seeker 1993 and Unica Model 1 1995 data mining software packages.

In testing institutional and policy variables associated with public finance capacity, data mining tools seem to place greater emphasis on policy variables than institutional variables. For example, Cognos filters out all institutional variables and Knowledge Seeker and Model 1 only identify five institutional variables out of ten. Institutional transparency (V9) and hierarchy (V4, V5) as well as macroeconomic (V1) and legislative constraints (V3 and V4) appear to be highly sensitive to market access.

The data mining findings suggest that while transparent and hierarchical budget institutions may be associated with fiscal policy choices, these choices are more about tax-financing than about debt financing alternatives. Tax financing showed a robust relationship to public finance capacity in the data mining tests, suggesting that from 1980 to 1993 Argentina, Chile and Mexico's increased public finance capacities were a function of tax financing rather than a function of debt financing choices. Increased public finance capacity, however, as evidenced by budget trends in all three countries, did translate into higher infrastructure expenditures for Argentina and Chile (Tables 4.2 and 4.5) but not for Mexico (Table 4.8). Yet increased public finance capacity seems to be associated with higher health care expenditures (Tables 4.2, 4.5 and 4.8) and subsequent lower infant mortality rates (Table 4.12) in all three countries.

Hypothesis 3 (H3): *access to the sovereign debt market increases a government's capacity to finance public expenditures that can contribute to economic growth.* The limited number of variables used to test hypothesis 3 was not sufficient to get accurate data mining patterns. Consequently, SPSS correlation analysis was used to test the third hypothesis. In testing this hypothesis, the first step was to sum education, health care, and infrastructure expenditures for each country, for each year from 1980 through 1993. This calculation resulted in V115 as the dependent variable, labeled as growth-oriented expenditures.[255]

In determining what independent variables to add to the linear multiple regression model, the first choice was include the theory-derived variable, V4 (Access to the Sovereign Debt Market). The theoretical model developed in chapter three of this study expressed the relationship between access to the sovereign debt market and public finance capacity (Figure 3.2). This relationship was expressed in linear and simple terms. Complex public policy questions, however, are seldom explained by a single cause. Consequently, the multiple regression model incorporates variables that could provide alternative explanations to increases in a government's capacity to finance education, health care and infrastructure expenditures. Given that domestic, foreign, private and public sources of financing can contribute to increases in public expenditures, eleven additional variables representing each one of these four general categories were selected.[256]

Five assumptions inform the linear regression model. First, the independent variables and the dependent variable have a linear relationship. Second, the dependent variable is a continuous variable. Third, the independent variables are not highly correlated with themselves. Fourth, the variation in the difference between the actual and the predicted values are the same for all values of Y meaning that the differences show homoscedasticity. Fifth, successive observations of the dependent variable are uncorrelated. SPSS generates an equation that is useful to explain the strength and importance of the relationship between all independent variables and the dependent variable. This equation is the basis of the statistical model used in Model 1:

$$Y = \beta_o + \beta_1 X_1 + \beta_2 X_2 + \dots\dots\dots + \beta_{12} X_{12} + e$$

Therefore: growth-oriented expenditures (V115) = $\beta_o + \beta_1$ market access (V4) + β_2 exports of goods and services as percentage of GDP (V28) + β_3 tax revenues as percent of GDP (V77)..... $+\beta_{12}$ use of IMF credit (V83) + ε where Y is the dependent variable (growth-oriented expenditures), $X_1, ..., X_{12}$ are the independent (predictor) variables, β_0 represents the intercept (constant) coefficient, $\beta_1 .... \beta_{12}$ represent the slope coefficients and ε represents the errors in the model. SPSS uses the method of least squares to estimate the slope and the intercept.

In evaluating individual regression coefficients, the objective is to determine if there is statistical evidence that variables $X_1, X_2, ..., X_{12}$ have an influence on the dependent variable, Y. For example, one might want to know whether growth oriented expenditures increase when access to the sovereign debt market increases. The relationship between growth-oriented expenditures and the following independent variables ($X_1, X_2, X_3, ..., X_9$) is expected to be positive – meaning that growth-oriented expenditures increase when each one of these variables increases: access to the sovereign debt market (V4), exports of goods and services as a percentage of GDP(28), domestic financing as percent of GDP (V23), financing from abroad as percent of GDP (V31), net foreign direct investments (V32), gross national savings as percent of GDP(39), tax revenues as percent of GDP (V77), average maturity of official debt (93), and average maturity of private sector debt (V94). The null and alternative hypotheses for each one of the corresponding coefficients ($\beta_1, \beta_2, \beta_3, ..., \beta_9$) are defined as follows:

$$Ho: \beta_{1,2,3,...,}\beta_9 \leq 0$$

$$Ha: \beta_{1,2,3,...,}\beta_9 > 0$$

In contrast, it is expected that the relationship between growth-oriented expenditures and the following independent variables (X_{10}, X_{11}, X_{12}) is negative – meaning that growth-oriented expenditures increase when these variables decrease: domestic credit provided by banking sector as percentage of GDP (V22), interest rate spread (V48), and use of IMF credit (V86). The null and alternative hypotheses for each one of the corresponding coefficients ($\beta_{10}, \beta_{11}, \beta_{12}$) are defined as follows:

$$Ho: \beta_{10},\ \beta_{11}, \beta_{12} \geq 0$$

$$Ha: \beta_{10},\ \beta_{11}, \beta_{12} < 0$$

The summary for Model 1 suggests that with an R-square of .844, the combined variables explain approximately 84 percent of the variability of growth oriented expenditures. However, one needs to be cautious about relying on a high value of R (multiple R, a simple correlation between the dependent and the independent variables) or a high R-square value (the coefficient of determination measuring the proportion of the total variation of the dependent variable accounted for by the independent variables).

First, models with these many variables may be overfitted. More variables do not necessarily result in a better model. Although the SPSS method of variable selection is based on stepwise selection, thus automatically addressing the problem of multicollinearity, the problems of autocorrelation and heteroscedasticity could still be present.[257] Second, although Model 1 has a high R-square, a non-linear regression model may be more appropriate for addressing complex public policy problems. One of the assumptions of this estimated multiple regression model is that the coefficients are linear. In the real world, few relationships among public policy variables are linear. As such, non-linear multiple regression model may be more suitable.

An analysis of the coefficients summary for Model 1 (Table 5.6) provides greater insight as to the relative importance of each variable in explaining growth-oriented expenditures. Simply comparing the *Beta* coefficients does not yield a useful assessment of the importance of each independent variable. "Even if the independent variables are all measured in the same units, a comparison of their size may not be revealing."[258] The SPSS applications guide recommends that "the probabilities (percentiles of the *t* distribution reported in the column labeled *Sig.*) should not be used for a formal test regarding the importance of each variable."[259] The guide goes on to suggest that these probabilities are not appropriate when one looks for the strongest or weakest variable. For such an analysis, SPSS recommends using *t* values. The *t* statistic provides a measure of the relative importance of each variable in the model. Assuming a two-tailed test, the rule of thumb for *t* values greater than 1.96 suggests that we can be 95 percent certain that the coefficient is not equal to zero. In other words, *t* values greater than 1.96 are usually statistically significant at the 95 percent confidence level.[260]

Given that t- statistics greater than +2 or below -2 denote useful predictors, only three variables in Model 1 (Table 5.6) seem to be useful predictors of growth-oriented expenditures: sovereign debt market access (V4), exports of goods and services (V28) and use of IMF credit (V86). As expected, the correlation between sovereign debt market access and growth oriented expenditures is positive and strong (2.648). Likewise, the correlation between exports of goods and services and growth oriented expenditures is also positive and strong (4.392). Exports of goods and services is clearly a stronger predictor; market access is more marginal. In contrast, the correlation between use of IMF credit and growth oriented expenditures is negative and strong (-3.564).

These relationships make sense because one expects that governments gain greater financing flexibility when they are able to access the sovereign debt market and to generate export revenues. Concurrently, governments capable of reducing their dependence on lenders of last resort, such as the IMF, are more likely to have greater flexibility in making expenditure choices. Governments that rely on IMF credit are subject to strict conditions that constrain their fiscal choices. Furthermore, the use of IMF credit may place limitations on access to the sovereign debt market.

Table 5.6 – SPSS Model 1

Variables Entered/Removed

Model	Variables Entered	Variables Removed	Method
1	V93, V28, V32, V48, V23, V22, V94, V77, V31, V39, V4, V86		Enter

a All requested variables entered, b Dependent Variable: V115

Model Summary

Model	R	R Square	Adjusted R Square	Std. Error of the Estimate
1	.919	.844	.755	174559.383

a Predictors: (Constant), V93, V28, V32, V48, V23, V22, V94, V77, V31, V39, V4, V86

Coefficients

		Unstandardized Coefficients		Standardized Coefficients	t	Sig
Model		B	Std. Error	Beta		
1	(Constant)	179876.03	401171.151		.448	.658
	V28	2.516E-04	.000	1.018	4.392	.000
	V23	-4766.345	9355.583	-.063	-.509	.616
	V22	-1941.173	1807.491	-.132	-1.074	.295
	V4	183.072	69.147	1.011	2.648	.015
	V31	25.935	52.669	.100	.492	.628
	V32	-560.365	6340.308	-.012	-.088	.930
	V39	4562.391	6277.982	.228	.727	.475
	V48	-3.710E-05	.000	-.201	-.967	.344
	V77	-4.451E-06	.000	-.086	-.342	.735
	V86	-2.822E-05	.000	-1.851	-3.564	.002
	V94	-1.424E-06	.000	-.013	-.064	.950
	V93	2.089E-05	.000	.089	.529	.602

Dependent Variable: V115

Note: Access to the sovereign debt market (V4); tax revenues as a percentage of GDP (V77), exports of goods and services as a percentage of GDP (V28); domestic financing as a percentage of GDP (V23); average maturity of private sector debt (V94); net foreign direct investment (32); average maturity of official debt (93); interest rate spread -lending rate minus deposit rate (48); domestic credit provided by banking sector as percentage of GDP (V22), financing from abroad as percent of GDP(31); gross national savings as percent of GDP(39) and use of IMF credit (V86). SPSS output tables showing listed of .000. have actual values of less than 0.0005.

Source: All data were analyzed using the Statistical Package for Social Sciences, SPSS 8.0 for Windows 98. Note that a complete list of the description for each variable in this table can be found in Appendix 3.

For example, use of IMF credit signals the inability (or unwillingness) of a government to stand on its own creditworthiness and may result in lower credit ratings and higher costs of issuing sovereign debt.

None of the remaining nine variables in Model 1 have *t* values below - 2 or above +2. For example, the tax revenues as a percent of GDP (V77) variable shows a very low *t* value of -.342 suggesting no statistical difference from zero. This means that tax revenues were not predictors of higher education, health care and infrastructure expenditures in Argentina, Chile and Mexico from 1980-1995. This finding is not surprising, given the higher dependence on debt financing over tax financing in all three countries during this period. All of the weak variables have some missing data values, so it is beneficial to exclude them from the regression model. [261]

Automatic stepwise procedures cannot exclude all the variables that are not useful in predicting growth-oriented expenditures. Consequently, the next step in the analysis involves building a model with the three most important independent variables identified in Model 1. In evaluating individual regression coefficients, the objective is to determine if there is statistical evidence that variables X_1, X_2, and X_3 have an influence on the dependent variable, Y.

For example, one might want to know whether growth oriented expenditures increase when access to the sovereign debt market increases. In this case, the alternative hypothesis is that the coefficient is positive. The null hypothesis is that the coefficient is less or equal to zero. One might also want to know whether growth oriented expenditures increase when exports of goods and services increase. In this case the alternative hypothesis is that the coefficient is positive and the null hypothesis is that the coefficient is less or equal to zero. Lastly, one might want to know whether growth-oriented expenditures decrease when the use of IMF credit increases. In this case, the alternative hypothesis is that the coefficient is negative and the null hypothesis is that the coefficient is greater than or equal to zero. In defining the alternative and null hypotheses for each coefficient three hypotheses can be tested.

For access to the sovereign debt market (V4):	$H_o: \beta_1 \leq 0$	$H_a: \beta_1 > 0$
For exports of goods and services (V28):	$H_o: \beta_2 \leq 0$	$H_a: \beta_2 > 0$
For use of IMF credit (V86):	$H_o: \beta_3 \geq 0$	$H_a: \beta_3 < 0$

Table 5.7 – SPSS Model 2

Variables Entered/Removed

Model	Variables Entered	Variables Removed	Method
2	V86, V4, V28		Enter

a All requested variables entered. b Dependent Variable: V115

Model Summary

Model	R	R Square	Adjusted R Square	Std. Error of the Estimate
2	.882	.778	.757	171751.985

a Predictors: (Constant), V86, V4, V28

Coefficients

Model		Unstandardized Coefficients B	Std. Error	Standardized Coefficients Beta	t	Sig.
2	(Constant)	174342.033	49894.571		3.494	.001
	V4	131.690	22.586	.728	5.831	.000
	V28	3.355E-04	.000	1.357	8.052	.000
	V86	-2.723E-05	.000	-1.786	-9.629	.000

a Dependent Variable: V115

Note: Access to the sovereign debt market (V4); exports of goods and services as a percentage of GDP (V28); use of IMF credit (V86). SPSS output tables showing listed values of .000. have actual values of less than 0.0005.

Source: All data were analyzed using the Statistical Package for Social Sciences , SPSS 8.0 for Windows 98. Note that a complete list of the description for each variable in this table can be found in Appendix 3.

As expected, Model 2 has a lower R square of .778 suggesting that market access, exports of goods and services and use of IMF credit explain approximately 78 percent of the variability of growth oriented expenditures. Model 2 suggests that there is a strong, linear relationship between the dependent and the independent variables because R-square is not zero or very small. In this model, the direction of the relationships remains the same, positive for market access and exports of goods and services and negative for use of IMF credit (Table 5.7). The coefficients indicate that the regression equation for Model 2 is:

growth oriented expenditures $= 174342.033 + 131.690X_1 + 3.355E\text{-}04X_2 - 2.723E\text{-}05X_3$.

The market access coefficient (V4) of 131.690 suggests that for any given values for exports and use of IMF credit, growth oriented expenditures increase by 131.690 units for every unit increase in market access ($US). The export coefficient (V28) indicates that growth-oriented expenditures increase by 3.3555E-04 units for every unit increase in exports (percentage of GDP). In contrast, the IMF coefficient (V86) indicates that for every unit increase in the use of IMF credit, growth oriented expenditures decrease by 2.723E-05 units ($US).

In terms of market access (V4), the corresponding *t* value for V4 is 5.831, well above the guideline for a useful predictor. The corresponding p-value is very small (< 0.0005)[262] suggesting that it is almost impossible for the market access coefficient to be equal to or smaller than zero. For this reason, we can agree with the alternative hypothesis and reject the null hypothesis. The *t* value for exports of goods and services (V28) is well above the guideline for strong variables at 8.052 and the p-value suggests that it is almost impossible for the export coefficient to be equal to or smaller than zero. Likewise, we can agree with the alternative hypothesis and reject the null hypothesis. The *t* value for the use of IMF credit is -9.629 and also meets the criteria for a strong variable. The corresponding p-value suggests that it is almost impossible for the use of IMF coefficient to be equal to or greater than zero. For this reason, we can agree with the alternative hypothesis and reject the null hypothesis. All three p- values suggest that the regression coefficients for market access, exports of goods and services and use of IMF credit are not zero. Therefore, these three independent variables constitute significant predictors. Focusing on market access, the value of less than .0005 in the p-value column labeled *Sig.*, represents the two-tailed probability of the *t* value greater than 5.831 or less than -5.831. The p-values for exports and use of IMF credit are both less than .0005. The p-values for all three variables are statistically very significant. Model 2 suggests that higher access to the sovereign debt market, higher exports and lower use of IMF credit increases the capacity of governments to finance education, health care and infrastructure (communications and transportation) expenditures.[263]

Focusing solely on the relationship between growth-oriented expenditures and access to the sovereign debt market, the final step is to build a simple regression model. The regression equation is $Y = \beta_0 + \beta_1 X_1$, where : Y represents the dependent variable (growth-oriented expenditures), β_0 is the intercept, β_1 is the slope of the regression line (the average change in Y for each change of one unit in the independent variable X), and X represents the values of the independent variable. As in Models 1 and 2, the relationship between growth-oriented expenditures and access to the sovereign debt market is expected to be positive.

Table 5.8 – SPSS Model 3

Model Summary

Model	R	R Square	Adjusted R Square	Std. Error of the Estimate
3	.319	.102	.074	335037.009

a Predictors: (Constant), V4

Coefficients

Model		Unstandardized Coefficients		Standardized Coefficients	t	Sig.
		B	Std. Error	Beta		
3	(Constant)	63100.440	63002.363		1.002	.324
	V4	57.642	29.838	.319	1.932	.062

a Dependent Variable: V115

Source: All data were analyzed using the Statistical Package for the Social Sciences, SPSS 8.0 for Windows 98.

With an R-square of .102, market access explains only 10 percent of the variability in growth-oriented expenditures. This suggests that by itself, the relationship between growth-oriented expenditures and market access is weak. In contrast, Model 2 showed a positive and strong influence of increasing market access and exports to achieve higher levels of growth-oriented expenditures. The results for this simple regression model seem to point towards spurious correlation between the dependent and the independent variable. Moreover, these results highlight both the data and regression technique limitations.

Table 5.9 – Summary Results for Models 1,2 and 3.

	R	R square	Adjusted R square	Std. Error of the Estimate
1	.919	.844	.755	174559.308
2	.882	.776	.757	171751.986
3	.319	.102	.074	335037.009

Source: All data were analyzed using the Statistical Package for the Social Sciences, SPSS 8.0 for Windows 98.

First, data are seldom perfect. In this case, the dependent variable (V115) exhibits missing values and the independent variable (V4) has a very high standard deviation (square root of variance), its zero values are followed by some very high values.[264] Second, the relationship between growth-oriented expenditures and access to the sovereign debt market might be expressed more effectively in non-linear terms. For example, either a logarithmic transformation or a polynomial regression approach would address the nonlinear problem.[265]

Multiple linear regression is a useful technique but when applied to complex public policy problems, linear regression has limitations in identifying meaningful relationships. Indeed, policy outcomes can seldom be attributed to a single cause. Furthermore, policy outcomes are seldom a linear function of one or many explanatory variables. Although non-linear multiple regression analysis is beyond the scope of this study, it may be a more useful technique to address the problem at hand. Nevertheless, the findings of the linear statistical analysis allows one to infer that governments able to access the sovereign debt market, able to generate higher export revenues and able to reduce dependence on lenders of last resort, such as the IMF, may enjoy greater financial flexibility. This flexibility may or may not translate into higher education, health care and infrastructure expenditures. The level of growth-oriented expenditures ultimately depends on the spending choices of policy makers. Access to private capital markets may not be a direct source of financing for education, health care and infrastructure expenditures. Yet market access may contribute to the financing flexibility of a government, thus enabling policy makers to have a broader range of choices to finance growth.[266]

Conclusion

The data mining and regression analyses partially support the three hypotheses. In testing all three hypotheses, five variables either matched the factors in the conceptual model of institutional choice or matched the factors reported in the comparative analysis chapter. These variables were transparency and hierarchy of budget institutions, fiscal performance, trade balance, and openness of the economy.[267] Access to the sovereign debt market in all three countries is associated with multiple institutional and policy factors: greater transparency of budget institutions, higher export revenues, higher international reserves and lower debt ratios (Tables 5.3 and 5.4).

The importance of transparent budget institutions is in itself an interesting finding because it points to rule learning as an important condition of market access. Given that transparency – the full disclosure of information – is one of the three pillars of international capital markets, it stands to reason that governments that adopt transparent budget rules gain a comparative advantage over governments that chose opaque budget rules when competing for private financing.[268]

For H1, the analysis suggests that credible fiscal commitments signaling fiscal restraint are strongly associated with market access. The debt burden ratio as a measure of fiscal restraint shows a strong relationship with market access. The relationship between credible fiscal policy commitments and access to the sovereign debt market seems important. However, only the debt ratio appears to account for this relationship (Table 5.4). The absence of the debt burden ratio as a significant measure of credible fiscal policy commitments suggests that debt structure may be less important than the level of debt relative to GNP in establishing credibility. Credible fiscal policy commitments, however, only tell part of the story of market access. Trade policy seems to play a significant role in facilitating a government's access to private market financing. These partial findings suggest that export revenues contribute to a government's ability to service its foreign debt. Although credible fiscal commitments seem to matter, ignoring export revenues renders an incomplete explanation of market access. Credible fiscal policy commitments only capture the willingness of a government to service its external debt obligations. Without the ability to do so, it is doubtful that governments can gain access to private market financing.

Additionally, aggregate net resource flows appear to show an important relationship with sovereign debt market access (Table 5.4). These results suggest that policy commitments that are credible to bond market participants are equally credible to equity and other financial market participants. This credibility seems to extend to long-term, foreign direct investors leading to capital inflows across many categories of capital flows (equity and bond portfolio flows and foreign direct investments).

Support for H2 needs to be qualified. Data mining tests suggest that hierarchical budget institutions centered in the executive branch, macroeconomic budget constraints and transparent budget rules are strongly related to increases in public finance capacity (Table 5.5). In the conceptual model, fiscal policy choices represent a narrow definition of debt-financing choices. This definition ignores tax initiatives.

The data mining models associate increases in public finance capacity with debt management indicators such as short term debt as a percent of GDP and interest payments as a percent of GDP. This suggests that debt management plays an important role in shaping a government's public finance capacity. Nevertheless, debt-financing indicators only tell part of the story. Tax financing indicators, such as taxes as a percent of GDP, suggest a robust relationship between tax revenues and public finance capacity (Table 5.5). As in the case of H1, support for H2 is only partial because H2 only captures the debt-financing dimension of the relationship between fiscal policy choices and public finance capacity. The tax-financing dimension emerges as significant in relation to public finance capacity but was not originally captured by H2.

In testing H3, the objective was to examine the effects of market access on the ability of a government to finance growth-oriented expenditures. This hypothesis is partially supported, as one finds a moderate relationship between increases in growth oriented expenditures and market access (Table 5.8). Market access alone does not seem to account for a government's higher capacity to finance expenditures that can contribute to economic growth.

Access to the sovereign debt market, however, becomes a strong explanation for growth-oriented expenditures when combined with export revenues and low or no use of IMF credit (Table 5.7). Access to private capital markets may not be a direct source of financing for education, health care and infrastructure expenditures. Yet market access may contribute to the financing flexibility of a government, thus enabling policy makers to have a broader range of choices to finance growth.

When combined with export revenues and a low or no use of IMF credit, access to the sovereign debt market seems to be strongly related to the increased capacity of Argentina, Chile and Mexico to finance education, health care and communications and transportation infrastructure from 1980 to 1995. In contrast, the weak relationship between domestic financing and increases in education, health care and infrastructure expenditures raises new questions about the effects of weak financial intermediation infrastructures on economic growth and development (Table 5.6). Specifically, one could examine the potential costs and benefits of reducing the dependency of governments on global financing. One alternative might be to pool domestic financing resources across national borders and establish regional bond markets to finance long term growth in Latin America.

The most significant conclusion of this chapter is that a government's budget institutions, fiscal policy choices and commitments need to be qualified in the context of the global political economy. The importance of transparent budget institutions as a threshold for fiscal credibility seems to run parallel to the global information standards of global capital markets. Transparent budget rules are compatible with transparent financial market rules.

Another important finding is that fiscal policy matters not just in terms of debt-financing choices but more importantly in terms of tax choices. For governments, tax revenues are the equivalent of what corporate earnings represent for private firms - a source of present and future cash flow that determines the ability to service debt. In addition, export earnings seem to position governments to compete for private market financing.

Unlike corporate creditors who can be taken to court for failing to service their debt, governments have to be credible in their ability and willingness to meet debt obligations. This is where the puzzle of credible fiscal policy commitments is partially solved by focusing on a government's willingness to pay.

Willingness to pay was partially measured through a government's debt management practices in terms of the debt and debt burden ratios. The findings show that the debt ratio seems to exhibit a stronger relationship to sovereign debt market access than the debt burden ratio. The debt ratio and the debt burden ratio represent narrow, quantitative measures of fiscal policy commitment. As such, both ratios assess a government's willingness to pay. The debt and debt burden ratios only capture past willingness in aggregate form. Present and future willingness of individual policy makers to make binding commitments to meet their government's debt obligations remains elusive.

Governments able to access the sovereign debt market, able to generate higher export revenues and able to reduce dependence on lenders of last resort, such as the IMF, may enjoy greater financial flexibility. This flexibility may or may not translate into higher education, health care, and infrastructure expenditures. The level of growth-oriented expenditures ultimately depends on the spending choices of policy makers.

In summary, these results have important implications for the three hypotheses derived from the conceptual model of institutional choice. First, it is imperative to avoid the error of inferring characteristics of the individual behavior of policy makers and financial market participants from the analysis of aggregate data. For example, it would be a mistake to infer that from 1980 to 1995 policy makers in Argentina, Chile, and Mexico chose hierarchical and transparent budget institutions solely to gain access to the sovereign debt market.

Second, correlation does not mean causation. It would also be a mistake to infer those budget institutions and fiscal policy choices caused Argentina, Chile, and Mexico to gain access to private market financing. Nevertheless, the partial findings in this study suggest that important and interesting relationships exist between institutional and policy choices, policy commitments, access to the sovereign debt market, and public finance capacity. These findings point in the direction of strong association but not causation. Additionally, it is prudent to avoid inferring that these findings have predictive power. Whether one can generalize from the experience of Argentina, Chile, and Mexico to predict how institutional and policy choices and commitments will affect future access of governments to the sovereign debt market remains uncertain. Nevertheless, preliminary analysis of the 2002 financial crisis in Argentina suggests that continued weak budgetary constraints on provincial governments compromised the transparency of budget institutions, possibly leading to this country's renewed inability to access private capital markets.

The partial findings in this chapter have not proven that institutional and policy choices and credible commitments cause access to the sovereign debt market. Nor have these findings fully explained how, why and with what consequences access to the sovereign debt market strengthens a government's public finance capacity and whether such access and subsequent public finance capacity increases a government's capacity to finance human and infrastructure capital expenditures that contribute to economic growth. The next chapter closes the gap between the research questions and these partial findings by interpreting the combined quantitative and qualitative analyses of this study.

Chapter Six
Summary of Findings

During the last decade, international sovereign debt markets have become one of the primary engines of public finance for developing countries. In the context of the global economy, national policy makers retain institutional and policy autonomy – as long as they do not seek private market financing. Governments choosing to finance public expenditures through international private capital markets have to abide by the rules of global finance: credibility, transparency, and accountability. Governments accessing sovereign debt markets increase their capacity to finance public expenditures leading to growth.

The depoliticization of monetary policy solves one dimension of credibility. Credible monetary policy is rooted in central bank independence. Yet credible monetary policy is not sufficient to secure access to private market financing. Unlike monetary policy, fiscal policy is not removable from the political arena. Taxing and spending choices are at the very core of "who gets what, when, and how." These choices are politically motivated and determine the extent to which governments are willing and able to service their debt obligations.

During the period 1980-1995, fiscal policy makers in Argentina, Chile, and Mexico made choices about budget institutions and fiscal policy following a highly centralized, hierarchical decision making model. These choices were made within the context of simultaneous political and economic transitions from authoritarian to democratic rule and from closed economies characterized by import substitution industrialization to open economies characterized by trade liberalization, privatization, and financial deregulation.

Domestic fiscal policy commitments evolve from budget institutions. When fiscal policy commitments result in fiscal policy choices that are credible to international sovereign debt market participants governments are able to issue sovereign debt, an important source of public finance capacity. In turn, the ability to borrow through the international sovereign debt market empowers governments to finance human capital investments leading to growth. To better understand the linkages between budget institutions, the domestic policy process, and the international political economy the analysis relied on concepts derived from neoclassical political economy.

The theoretical framework derived from Sabatier's advocacy coalition framework, a theory of interactive choice, and a theory of institutions that combine historical and economic concepts. These three theoretical approaches link policy makers, financial market participants, policy and institutional choices. In addition, theories of political economy capture the political and economic context in which these choices are made.

Separately, each theoretical approach explains how the policy process works, why decisions are made, or why institutions matter. Jointly, these approaches provide a more complete explanation of the interaction of public and private actors and the effects of their interactive choices. This innovative combination of theoretical approaches resulted in a conceptual framework of institutional choice consisting of three spheres of interactive choice: budget institutions, policy process, and political economy.

In chapter three, a model of institutional choice was formalized. Budget institutions, the policy process, and the political economy represent spheres of interaction. Fiscal policy makers and financial market participants represent the actors who form advocacy coalitions aimed at gaining government access to the international sovereign debt markets. Budget rules, fiscal policy, policy commitments and sovereign debt market access constitute the main elements of interactive choice. The effects of interactive choice were defined as public finance capacity and economic growth. The conditions of interaction included rule learning, path dependence, uncertainty, information, and conflict.

Assuming that political behavior results from bounded rational, strategic choices that satisfy policy makers' objectives, rule learning represents a central theoretical concept. Rule learning captures how and to what extent budget rules change over time (path dependence), how uncertainty constrains choice and how information and conflict shape institutional choice.

The process of rule learning depends on who learns and how domestic politics affect the learning process. Policy makers who are willing and able to learn and apply transparent budget rules face lower borrowing costs and greater access to the international sovereign debt market. Global communications technology accelerates the diffusion of information and technical knowledge and in so doing expands the scope and depth of rule learning across national borders.[269]

For governments seeking access to private market financing, rule learning may be more important than policy learning. Without transparent budget rules, policy makers can adopt fiscal policies signaling fiscal restraint that are credible on a temporary basis. Without an institutional infrastructure that makes transparent budget rules difficult to violate, building a reputation for sustainable and credible fiscal policy is difficult to achieve. Sustainable fiscal policy credibility requires institutional credibility.

A key argument related to rule learning is that budget rules shape fiscal policy commitments because rules delimit who makes budget choices, in what sequence choices are made and where budget conflicts are resolved. Another argument is that fiscal policy commitments influence the decisions of financial market participants who provide access to the sovereign debt market. Financial market participants do not formulate, approve or implement fiscal policy. Through their expectations, financial market participants influence the choices of policy makers who seek access to international private market financing.

The process by which fiscal policy makers and financial market participants form market-friendly advocacy coalitions can be labeled precision politics. Precision politics involves the implementation of economic policies that reduce uncertainty and increase the probability of policy credibility, political accountability, and budgetary transparency.[270] This interactive process is characterized by a common goal of sovereign debt market access and shared benefits. For policy makers, access to the international sovereign debt market can lower public financing costs, providing greater flexibility for financing human capital and infrastructure expenditures. In turn, these expenditures can contribute to economic growth. For financial market participants, a government's access to the international sovereign debt market translates into greater diversification of investment risks, greater choice of investment alternatives and increased sources of revenue.

Once the theoretical model of institutional choice was outlined, an overview of the qualitative and quantitative comparison of budget institutions and fiscal policy choices of Argentina, Chile, and Mexico from 1980-1995 was presented. The strengths and weaknesses of the comparative method were summarized and the goals of combining qualitative and quantitative comparison were sketched in this chapter. The selection of Argentina, Chile, and Mexico to compare the institutional, policy and private financing patterns that emerged from 1980-1995 was based on the fact that these countries were most similar in terms of their socio-economic and political contexts during this period.

The selected cases share similar and simultaneous processes of political liberalization and the accelerating opening of their economies since the mid- 1980s. All three countries began the "lost decade" of the 1980s under conditions of declining economic growth, mounting public debt, and increasing loss of investors' confidence. These combined trends blocked access to international private market financing. By the early 1990s, all three countries emerged from their respective economic crises and regained access to international private market financing in general and the private sovereign debt market in particular. Unfortunately, Argentina is witnessing a reversal to the conditions prevalent during the lost decade of the 1980s as its latest financial crisis unfolds in 2002.

Chapter four described how bond issuance in international markets has become a major avenue for Argentina, Chile, and Mexico to finance public expenditures. In industrialized countries, roads, schools, and other human capital and infrastructure needs are financed through domestic bond markets. In Argentina, Chile, and Mexico domestic sovereign debt markets remain rudimentary and international sovereign debt markets remain shallow.[271] One problem facing these governments is that infrastructure requires long term financing. Few institutional investors such as pension plans, mutual funds, and insurance companies are willing to accept the financial and political risks inherent in 20 to 30 year sovereign debt credits (bonds) issued by governments lacking the institutional infrastructure to support policy commitments that signal a long term ability and willingness to honor debt obligations.

This credibility hurdle is reflected in the fact that the average maturity for new bond issues in Latin America remains short – below three years.[272] National governments in the region including Argentina, Chile, and Mexico have not been able to borrow on an intermediate and long-term basis. This is the equivalent of living from paycheck to paycheck while assuming daily debt obligations.

Governments that are not able to issue intermediate and long term bonds represent a questionable credit risk and are caught in the contradictions of short term financing.

When governments can qualify only for short term debt instruments to finance long term expenditures, debt financing options shrink. One alternative is to pay off short-term debt with the proceeds of new issues. Another alternative is to monetize the debt by printing money. Both debt management strategies serve to perpetuate questionable financial credibility. In sum, the higher the level of short-term debt, the more entrenched a government becomes in short term debt rollovers and other inefficient financing mechanisms. The more a government relies on such questionable debt financing mechanisms, the further away it moves from private long- term financing.

Once governments gain access to international sovereign markets, the regulatory hurdles posed by weak national regulatory frameworks limit the participation of investors in these markets. Consequently, Latin American governments including Argentina, Chile, and Mexico have promoted regional regulatory policy harmonization to strengthen their own domestic financial institutions. Membership of all three countries in the Council of Securities Regulators of the Americas (COSRA) in 1992 contributed to this effort. The objective was to create regional regulatory frameworks consistent with international standards and to cooperate in a) establishing standardized financial disclosure, clearance and settlement practices and b) sharing price and other regulatory information.[273] Argentina, Chile, and Mexico's membership in COSRA coincided with higher levels of market access for all three countries. This finding suggests that cross-national comparison and international macro-level analysis need to be discussed in the context of regional economic relations because regional economies often link the domestic and the international economies.

The objectives of cooperative, regional regulatory initiatives are consistent with financial market rules, namely transparency, credibility and accountability. Regional regulatory cooperation suggests that within the framework of the global political economy, policy makers are engaging in "shared learning" of financial rules bolstering the opportunity of individual governments to gain and sustain access to the international financial markets.[274]

In comparing public finance trends in Argentina, Chile, and Mexico from 1980-1995, one can conclude that economic and political reforms in each country may have contributed to higher levels of policy credibility during this period. Reforms shifting emphasis from import substitution industrialization policies to market friendly privatization and financial deregulation initiatives signaled to international financial market participants the willingness of policy makers to open their economies to capital flows. Capital mobility is essential for the functioning of financial markets. Reform initiatives in all three countries paved the way for each government to gain access to private market financing.

Concurrently, a shift from military to democratic rule in Argentina and Chile and the loosening of the political power reigns held by the PRI for over seven decades constituted important credibility benchmarks for international financial market participants.[275] In this context, political liberalization in all three countries signaled the willingness of policy makers to open the political process to competition and public scrutiny. Financial market participants interpreted this signal as complementary to the opening of competitive markets in the region.

The comparative analysis in chapter four revealed additional factors contributing to each government's policy credibility: a legal, regulatory and tax collection framework. The size of the export sector, the composition of external liabilities, fiscal consolidation, and the degree of political stability enhanced fiscal credibility. Chapter five took these measures into account and focused on quantitative tools of analysis to compare budget institutions and fiscal policy choices in Argentina, Chile, and Mexico.

In chapter five, three hypotheses derived from the conceptual model were tested through data mining techniques and SPSS regression analysis. Data mining served as a filter allowing for the analysis of institutional and policy variables proposed in the theoretical framework. The entire cycle of data selection, preprocessing, analysis and evaluation focused closely on the research questions – What is the effect of fiscal policy choices on a government's access to the sovereign debt market? How, why, and with what consequences do credible fiscal policy commitments translate into public finance capacity? How does access to the sovereign debt market increase a government's capacity to finance expenditures leading to economic growth?

The comparative analysis of chapter four suggested that the variables identified in the theoretical model only captured one narrow dimension of the relationship between policy commitments and market access. Chapter four demonstrated that policy initiatives beyond fiscal choices need to be considered as part of a broader policy mix that contributes to market access. Data mining was used to test two hypotheses and to filter the most important explanatory variables out of a total of 131 institutional and policy variables. Regression analysis was used to test one hypothesis. The quantitative analysis was carried out recognizing the limitations of aggregate cross-country data produced by the IMF, IDB, World Bank and Bank for International Settlements.

In testing the hypothesis that *credible fiscal policy commitments – commitments signaling fiscal restraint to financial market participants – increase access to the sovereign debt market,* the first step was to test each of the ten indicators included in the IDB index of Latin American budget institutions. The second step was to test policy variables. The data mining results suggested that the following institutional and policy variables are the most sensitive to market access:

a) Transparent budget institutions. The greater the transparency of budget institutions measured as low borrowing autonomy of state and local governments the greater the access to the international sovereign debt markets.

b) Export revenue. Higher export revenues result in higher access to the international sovereign debt market.

c) Debt ratio. The lower the ratio of total debt to exports of goods and services, the higher the access to the sovereign debt market.

These findings confirmed that credible fiscal policy commitments signaling fiscal restraint increase access to the sovereign debt market. Furthermore, these findings suggest a strong association between transparent budget institutions and credible fiscal policy commitments. More importantly, however, these findings suggest that exports, a country's significant source of revenues, cannot be ignored in assessing how and why governments gain access to the sovereign debt market.[276]

In testing the hypothesis that *budget institutions and fiscal policy commitments lead to fiscal policy choices that can either strengthen or weaken a government's public finance capacity,* data mining results emphasized the sensitivity of transparent institutions, lower debt burdens and higher tax revenues as determinants of increased public finance capacity. In addition to institutional transparency (measured as a low level of borrowing autonomy by state and local governments) measures indicating hierarchical decision-making for budgets (low levels of legislative constraints on the budget, limits on the ability of legislatures to reject budgets proposed by the executive branch) appear to be associated with higher levels of public finance capacity. Institutional transparency and hierarchy emerged as important variables relative to increased public finance capacity.

In testing whether *access to the sovereign debt market increases a government's capacity to finance public expenditures that can contribute to economic growth* regression analysis demonstrated a positive and robust relationship between sovereign debt market access, increased export revenues and increases in education, health care and infrastructure expenditures. In contrast, use of IMF credit showed a negative and robust relationship with growth-oriented expenditures.

On the surface, these findings are relevant because sovereign debt represents a form of long term financing that along with export revenues increases a government's flexibility to finance growth. Furthermore, reliance on IMF credit imposes constraints on a government's fiscal choices and limits financing flexibility. Upon closer examination, however, it is important to consider the differences in levels of growth- oriented expenditures in each country. Consistent with the social indicator trends presented in chapter four, higher public finance capacity translated into higher health care expenditures than education or infrastructure expenditures.

Combining the findings of both the quantitative and the qualitative analyses is more meaningful than considering these findings in isolation from one another. When one considers that short-term financing has characterized the patterns of sovereign debt market access for Argentina, Chile, and Mexico, it is important to take this characteristic into account. Education and infrastructure represent long-term public investments, while some health care programs can more easily be financed through short-term financing mechanisms (e.g., short-term immunization programs). Thus, it is not surprising that all three countries experienced higher levels of health care expenditures and subsequent improvements in health indicators (e.g. lower mortality rates, longer life expectancy) than improvements in education or infrastructure development.[277]

The combined findings from the qualitative and quantitative analysis can be summarized in terms of a path leading from institutional and policy choices to public finance capacity.

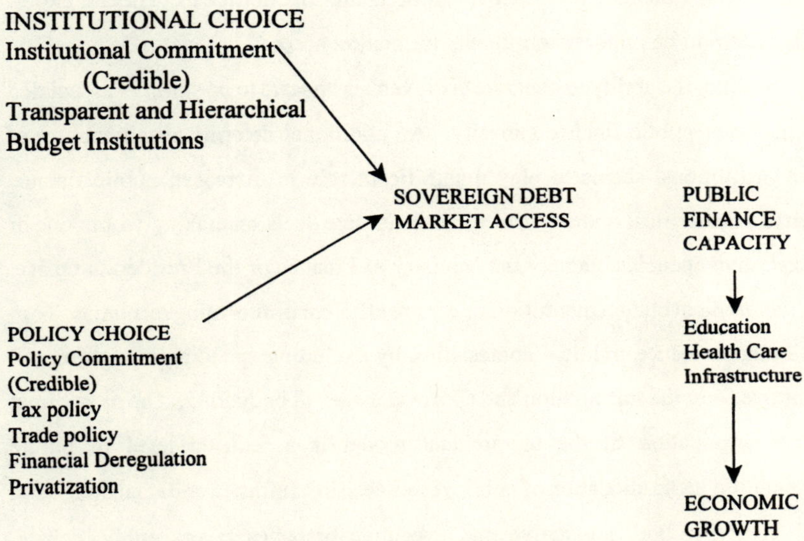

Figure 6.1 The Path of Institutional and Policy Choices

This path suggests that when institutional and policy commitments are credible to financial market participants, governments can gain access to the sovereign debt market. Access, in turn, can contribute to the strengthening of public finance capacity providing greater flexibility to finance human capital expenditures such as education and health care as well as the development of infrastructure. In sum, the combined qualitative and statistical findings of this study point to three main conclusions about the effects of budget institutions and fiscal policy choices of Argentina, Chile, and Mexico from 1980-1995. First, credible fiscal policy commitments leading to greater sovereign debt market access were not just grounded in policy makers' earned reputation for sound fiscal policy – a policy producing low debt and debt burden ratios and high tax revenues. A history of fiscal restraint combined with transparent budget institutions and the ability to generate export earnings seem to be major determinants for market access.

Second, the ability to generate tax revenues appears to be strongly associated with increased public finance capacity. An additional determinant, hierarchy of budget institutions, seems to play a significant role in increased public finance capacity. Hierarchical budget institutions centralize decision making within one or two executive agencies, namely the Ministry of Finance or the President's Office. Thus, hierarchical budget institutions are more efficient in allocating resources. Top-down budgets reduce political contestation by excluding spending ministries and legislatures from the formulation and approval stages of budgeting. The most direct negative implication of the hierarchical model is a reduced level of public representation in the allocation of public resources. In contrast, a collegial budgeting model involving both legislative and executive branches favors public debate, enforcement, and accountability.

Third, access to the sovereign debt market seemed to increase the capacity in all three governments to finance education, health care, and infrastructure. Yet while contributing to improvements in economic and social indicators from 1980-1995, increased human capital investments did not reduce the long-standing inequalities in education, health care and infrastructure access in all three countries. Two main factors might account for the gaps in equitable growth in education, health care, and infrastructure in Argentina, Chile, and Mexico from 1980-1995. First, hierarchical budget institutions produced greater efficiency but not necessarily greater equity. Second, access to the sovereign debt market remained limited in terms of the short-term maturity of the bonds and notes issued by all three governments in the international sovereign debt markets. What do these findings suggest? What institutional and policy lessons could be drawn from the experiences of Argentina, Chile and Mexico? How do these findings change existing knowledge and hypotheses?

Beyond Credible Fiscal Commitments: Credible Institutional Choice

This study demonstrated how, why, and with what consequences budget institutions and fiscal policy choices impact the ability of governments to access the international sovereign debt market. The analysis focused on the institutional and policy choices of Argentina, Chile, and Mexico and how and why these choices affected the ability of each government to access the international sovereign debt market. The findings show a close relationship between market access and an increased capacity to finance human capital and infrastructure investments. These findings suggested that institutional choices cannot be ignored when assessing policy choices. Thus, the conventional separation of institutional and policy analysis is inadequate for explaining the institutional and policy mix adopted by governments that are able to issue sovereign debt. Furthermore, the findings suggested that sovereign debt can indeed enhance the ability of governments to finance human and capital expenditures contributing to long term growth.

The research questions were partially answered through qualitative and statistical analysis but the findings raise many new questions. For example, one might ask how international sovereign debt markets affect the ability of emerging democracies to become more transparent, credible, and accountable to their own citizens. Ultimately, the path by which sovereign debt markets influence budget institutions and fiscal choices may contribute to the broadening of government accountability in Argentina, Chile, and Mexico.

Sovereign debt markets are economic institutions with well defined, formal rules for underwriting debt, assessing corporate and sovereign risks, forming expectations, trading fixed income instruments and protecting property rights. The interests of debtholders are inherently represented in the process by which bond market participants transfer their preferences to government policy makers. In this context, the sovereign debt market, with its emphasis on transparency and disclosure of financial information, could open a window for public scrutiny of government budgets.

Transparent budget rules ensure government accountability towards lenders but financial accountability may well serve the broader interests of policy makers. The intrinsic value of being credible to voters is greater in democratic societies, but all governments regardless of regime structure depend on credibility for their sustained survival.[278] Public knowledge of who gets what, when and how may motivate policy makers in Argentina, Chile, and Mexico to pay closer attention to how they make and keep promises. Credible fiscal policy commitments, particularly those commitments that are credible to international financial market participants ultimately have to be desirable to voters.

This study has not focused on the ability of democratic governments to access private market financing. The research findings, however, lead to new questions, which constitute the first step of a larger research agenda aimed at understanding the relationship between credible democracy and credible institutional and policy commitments. Specifically, one might ask how the choice of budget institutions and fiscal policy commitments affect the ability of democratic governments to finance equitable growth. In the short run, fiscal policy commitments that signal fiscal restraint can be conducive to greater access to the international sovereign debt markets. In the long run, fiscal policy commitments that are only credible to international financial market participants may not be sustained without the support of domestic constituencies.

Fiscal policy commitments that result in increased market access and public finance capacity without corresponding improvement in education, health care, and infrastructure conditions may not be credible to voters. When fiscal commitments are credible to financial market participants, governments gain access to private market financing. This access, in turn, expands the capacity of governments to finance human capital and infrastructure expenditures that contribute to economic growth. Yet from 1980-1995, increases in market access and finance capacity in Argentina, Chile, and Mexico did not result in equitable growth.

The path to equitable growth in these and other Latin American countries is likely to be paved with credible, transparent budget rules and credible fiscal policy commitments, commitments that ultimately are believable to both citizens and financial market participants. In this context, rule learning may involve continued emphasis on efficiency, greater emphasis on transparent institutions and less emphasis on hierarchical institutions. This implies that moving from hierarchical to collegial budget institutions in Argentina, Chile, and Mexico would not necessarily reduce efficiency. In fact, budget rules that introduce local and sectoral incentives to increase efficiency may accomplish the dual objectives of greater efficiency and equity.[279] More transparent and collegial budget rules may pave the way for greater public debate and fiscal accountability. While removing the budget from public debate may contribute to fiscal discipline, such approach severely undermines the level of public representation in the allocation of public resources. Beyond the effects of greater finance capacity and access to private market financing, an institutional choice for collegial budget rules may foster democratic consolidation and stability in the region.[280]

Contributions and Suggestions for Linking Theory and Practice

In an age of instant global communications, drawing institutional and policy lessons across national and regional borders is not only feasible but necessary to harness shared experiences and achieve common regional goals. Recommending specific institutional and policy choices to access private market financing is beyond the scope of this study. Informing theory through the analysis of practice, however, was an objective from the outset of this study.

The theoretical framework developed in chapter three brought together seemingly distant theoretical approaches in political science. The study of interactive choice forged the synthesis of advocacy coalition theory, game theory, economic and historical institutionalisms. Furthermore, this study positioned these combined theoretical approaches in the context of neoclassical political economy. The rationale for such an innovative approach was grounded in the assumption that one cannot separate budget institutions from the public policy process and the political economy (both domestic and international).

The main theoretical contribution of this study was to develop an adaptable framework suitable to study a wide spectrum of public policy choices and their respective institutional choices. For example, the model of interactive choice could be applied to study the effects of public policy choices in the fields of trade, the environment, criminal justice, education, health, and welfare.[281] Increasingly, public policy problems transcend domestic borders. These problems are two-dimensional and involve both domestic and international actors and spheres of interaction. The model of interactive choice offers a theoretical point of departure to address questions about institutional and policy choices.

The methodological contribution of this study is found in the application of data mining techniques to answer questions of institutional and policy choice using time series, aggregate data. The conventional use of data mining techniques has concentrated on the fields of business, astronomy, finance, and health care. Data mining has been applied to solve decision-making problems involving large quantities of data in each of these fields. The objective has been to identify patterns of association across multiple variables. Applying data mining techniques to public decision making might contribute to filtering the most relevant variables in complex public policy problems.

Multiple causes and multiple effects characterize the policy process. Data mining may allow policy analysts and researchers to examine policy patterns and extract the most significant causes and effects of public policy choices. Consequently, the use and refinements of data mining techniques (e.g. allowing for a smaller data base, creating standards for applying tools across different software packages) could make an important contribution to social science research applications.[282]

As policy makers continue to confront the vexing questions of financing growth through private capital markets, the findings of this study may be useful to policy practitioners. From 1995 to the end of the 20th century access to the international sovereign debt market in Argentina, Chile, and Mexico followed a similar pattern to that of the period covered in this study – an ongoing closing and reopening of markets. This pattern continues to this day. International bond placements for each country have fluctuated primarily as a result of higher interest rates and higher commodity (e.g. oil and copper) prices in the region. In 1998, Latin American exports were curtailed as a result of the Asian financial crisis and the financial turmoil of Russia and the Commonwealth of Independent States (CIS) countries. These developments confirm one of the findings in this study: export earnings have a direct impact on a government's credibility and investors' confidence. A proposal advanced by investment bankers at Lazard Freres & Cie in Paris suggests that the G-7 nations could close the credibility gap of Latin American government borrowers by providing them with guarantees for export earnings. These guarantees would, in effect, increase investors' confidence in the ability of Latin American governments to keep their economies growing.[283]

In the coming decades, policy makers in Latin America and other regions of the world will continue to face the challenges of financing growth. Access to the international sovereign debt market increases the ability of governments to rely on long term debt financing and reduces the need for tax financing. In Latin America, a reduced need to tax translates into lower consumption taxes, a regressive form of taxation, which disproportionally hurts the poor. Thus, in the long run, bond financing may contribute to the reduction of income inequality in Latin America.

Directions for Future Research

The findings of this study raise the question of whether the explanations offered can be generalized and whether the findings apply to other cases. Three possible future research directions may answer these questions. First, empirical evidence on how financial market participants respond to policy choices, shows that "market discipline" is unevenly distributed between industrialized and developing countries. One question to consider in the future is why industrialized countries are able to sustain deeper deficits for longer periods than developing or newly industrialized countries.[284] More importantly, why can these governments continue to enjoy access to the international sovereign debt market in spite of a lack of credible fiscal policies? Why are financial market participants more tolerant of deeper deficits in industrialized countries? What determines the difference in credibility standards for industrialized and developing countries - ability or willingness to pay?

Second, one might ask why credible fiscal and trade policies matter less than credible budget institutions. This question may lead to a more thorough analysis of the effects of political coalitions in the formation of credible budget rules. Coalitional analysis could combine the analytic tools of game theory with a narrative approach recognizing context and accounting for specific outcomes. Furthermore, such analysis could be carried out on a cross-regional basis. Electoral rules in Argentina, Chile, and Mexico may have contributed, at least in part, to the adoption of hierarchical budget rules. Electoral rules influence the distribution of power between the executive and the legislative branches and may be linked to rules that limit the number of budget veto players. Hierarchical budget institutions lead to fiscal choices that circumvent public debate, favor political expediency, and undermine democratic values. Do these outcomes apply specifically to Latin America or could one find similar outcomes across regions where emerging democratic regimes struggle to gain policy credibility with domestic constituencies and international market participants?

Third, recognizing that budgetary choices are inherently political but have economic consequences (i.e. government access to private market financing) another research direction could be pursued. This study documented that despite the surge of capital flows to Argentina, Chile, and Mexico since the early 1990's, the structure of government bond debt issued in international markets remained short term. When governments are only able to issue short term debt, their long term solvency and their ability to service debt obligations is seriously questioned. In turn, this lack of fiscal credibility carries higher borrowing costs and limited financing alternatives to pay for public expenditures.

One alternative to financing public expenditures through international private capital markets is to develop regional sovereign debt markets. In Latin America, the small size of domestic economies and the lack of a diversified export base could contribute to the lack of deep, domestic financial markets. Existing patterns of regional trade and legal cooperation could serve as a point of departure for regional financial cooperation.[285] Why would economies of scale resulting from the establishment of regional sovereign debt markets strengthen existing regional trade and investment relations? How could cooperative financial relations within the region lead to stronger ties between domestic and global economies? How can the pooling of regional financial resources contribute to stronger investment and trade ties and possibly to a shared goal of equitable growth? Are there regional financial lessons that policy makers in Latin America and other developing regions could learn from similar regional efforts within the European community?

Globally linked countries face multiple economic, political and social challenges. Institutional and policy lessons from around the globe may serve to mitigate the impact of some of these challenges. Access to private market financing does not solve all economic, political and social problems, but such access can increase public finance capacity. Crafting a credible policy mix backed by transparent budget rules helps policy makers gain access to the sovereign debt market but does not guarantee long term financing.

Ultimately, securing long term financing is a necessary step toward creating the conditions conducive to economic growth and political stability. Policy makers who are able and willing to learn how to empower their governments to finance education, health care and infrastructure development will have a competitive edge over policy makers who neglect human capital investments. After all, educated, healthy and mobile individuals able to connect to their communities, their nations, and the world are the most valuable resources to sustain governments and markets.

For Latin America and other regions of the world, sovereign debt markets provide policy makers with greater flexibility to finance long term human capital investments. A choice to finance growth through private markets requires institutional and policy commitments that are credible to financial market participants. Such a choice can empower governments to become credible and accountable not just to financial market participants but to their own citizens.

In an age of instant communications, policy makers learn the market rules of credibility, transparency, and accountability arriving at a common understanding of new institutional and policy solutions. Learning across national borders not only leads to change in individual beliefs but to an awareness of global interdependence. Within an interdependent global political economy, credibility, transparency, and accountability are not just rules confined to the international financial markets. Financial and democratic credibility, transparency, and accountability are not incompatible; they are two sides of the same coin. When institutional and policy choices that are credible to financial market participants become desirable for citizens, policy makers can begin to pave the way for equitable growth.

Appendix 1 – Selected Capital Flows

(World Debt Tables Extracts. 1996. www.worldbank.org/html/extb/WDT95EN).

Table 1 – Selected Capital Flows for Argentina 1980-1993 (millions $US)

	PRIVATE		PUBLIC	
	Capital Flows	Bonds and Loans	Capital Flows	Bonds and Loans
1980	-743	3,886	2,997	1,016
1981	-3,469	3,112	4,624	2,695
1982	-4,017	-521	209	481
1983	-2514	-1,831	2,403	2,249
1984	-1,558	-2,674	2,205	2,210
1985	-894	-1,733	1,291	1,098
1986	420	-459	364	318
1987	-695	-24	833	421
1988	393	-228	-202	-305
1989	-5,242	111	-351	-391
1990	-1,361	92	251	255
1991	2,821	345	753	647
1992	11,355	611	-157	55
1993	11,707	3,318	3,522	3,567

Source: Adapted from Ffrench-Davis and Griffth-Jones, *Coping with Capital Surges,* 1995, 154-55.

Table 2. – Selected Capital Flows for Chile 1980-1993 (millions $US)

	1980-82	1983-85	1986-89	1990-93
Portfolio Investment	0	0	87	1,549
Medium/ long term capital	2,080	1,438	-3,629	-333
Public (official) loans	80	445	2,368	2,106
Private (bank) loans	3,176	1,021	66	1,085
Bonds	41	0	0	644
Foreign debt conversions	0	-85	-6,109	-2,124

Source: Adapted from Ffench -Davis and Griffith-Jones, *Coping with Capital* Surges, 1995, 103-103.

Table 3. – Selected Capital Flows for Mexico 1980-1993 (millions $US)

	1980-1982	1983-85	1986-89	1990-93
Portfolio Investment	0	0	493	53,849
Public loans	29,565	6,670	3,660	3,247
Private loans	16,365	-6,327	-6,873	25,534

Source: Adapted from Ffrench-Davis and Griffith-Jones, *Coping with Capital Surges*, 1995, 198-99.

Appendix 2. – The Data Set

Three kinds of data inform this study. First, budgetary data related to debt financing for Argentina, Chile and Mexico are available through the IMF, World Bank and the individual Finance Ministries of each country in the form of statistical data bases. Second, financial flows data pertaining to the sovereign debt market are available through the International Finance Corporation in the form of an emerging markets database and the World Economic Outlook database available through the IMF. In addition, credit assessment and evaluation data was collected from the two major international sovereign credit rating agencies, namely Moody's Investors Service and Standard and Poors. Financial flows data is quantitative and credit assessment and evaluation data is both quantitative and qualitative. Third, qualitative data on budget institutions is available through the Inter-American Development Bank (IADB) and is based on a survey of Finance Ministries throughout Latin America. A summary of independent and dependent variables follows:

Independent Variables : Selected Indicators:

1. External Debt Management:	Present value of Debt (% of GNP)
	Total Debt Service
	Public and Publicly Guaranteed Debt
	Short term Debt Outstanding
2. External Debt:	Total External Debt
	Long term Debt
	Public and Publicly Guaranteed Debt
	Private Non-Guaranteed Debt

	Use of IMF Credit
3. Openness of the Economy:	Trade as % of GNP
	Trade in Goods
	Gross Private Capital Flows (Aggregate Resource Flows)
	Gross Foreign Direct Investments
4. Balance of Payments:	Exports and Imports
	Net Income
	Net Current Transfers
	Current Account Balance
	Gross International Reserves
5. Size of the Economy:	Population
	Population Density
	Land Area
	GNP
	GNP per capita
6. Financial Depth and Efficiency:	
	Domestic Credit (Banking Sector)
	Liquid Liabilities
	Quasi Liquid Liabilities
	Interest rate spread
	Spread over Libor
7. Institutional Indicators:	V1 through V10
8. Fiscal Performance:	Current Revenue
	Total Expenditure
	Overall Budget Deficit (incl. grants)
	Financing from Abroad
	Domestic Financing
	Debt and Interest Payments
	Central Government Expenditures as % of GDP
9. Financial Flows:	Net Private Capital Flows
	Foreign Direct Investments

Portfolio Investment Flows

Bank and Trade Related Lending

Dependent variables: selected indicators

1. Access	(BIS data for Argentina, Chile and Mexico)
	For all other countries use:
	PPG, Bonds (AMT,US) Source: GDF dataset
2. Public Finance Capacity	
Central Government Expenditures:	Goods and Services
(as percent of Total Expenditures)	Wages and Salaries
	Interest payments
	Education
	Health Care
	Infrastructure (Transportation, Communications)
Central Government Revenues:	Taxes on Income, profits and Capital Gains
	Social Security taxes
	Taxes on Goods and Services
	Taxes on International trade
	Other Taxes
	Non-tax Revenue

Appendix 3 – Codes for Institutional and Policy Variables

Codes for Institutional Variables

V1Macroeconomic Constraint	V6Budget after Legislative Approval
V2Executive Branch Hierarchy	V7Executive Discretion to Cut Spending
V3Legislative Constraints	V8Government Debt Guarantee - Public Firms
V4Legislative Veto Power	V9Autonomy of State and Local Governments
V5Borrowing Autonomy	V10Constitutional Constraints

Codes for Selected Policy Variables used in data mining and SPSS analyses

V16	Total Central Government Debt as percent of GDP
V18	Current Account Balance (percent of GDP)
V19	Current Account Balance
V22	Domestic Credit as percent of GDP
V23	Total Domestic Financing as percent of GDP
V28	Exports of Goods and Services as percent of GDP
V29	Exports of Goods and Services (BoP current US$)
V31	Financing from Abroad as percent of GDP
V32	Net Foreign Direct Investment
V33	GNP growth (annual)
V38	Gross International Reserves (current US$)
V39	Gross National Savings as percent of GDP
V40	Gross private Capital Flows as percent of GDP
V41	Health care (Percent of population with access)
V47	Interest Payments as percent of Total Expenditure
V48	Interest Rate Spread (Lending rate minus Deposit Rate)
V54	Mobile Phones (per 1000 people)
V55	Infant Mortality rate per 1000 Live Births
V57	Other Taxes as percent of Current Revenue
V63	Portfolio Investment, Equity
V67	Quasi-Liquid Liabilities as percent of GDP
V68	Percent of Total Roads Paved

V70	Sanitation as percent of Population with Access
V74	Short -term Debt as percent of Total External Debt
V75	Social Security Taxes as percent of Current Revenue
V76	Subsidies and other Current Transfers as percent of Total Expenditures
V77	Tax Revenue (percent of GDP)
V79	Taxes on Income, Profits and Capital Gains as percent of Current Revenue
V80	Taxes on International Trade as percent of Current Revenue
V82	Total Debt Service (percent of GDP)
V86	Use of IMF Credit (current US$)
V88	Aggregate Net Resource Flows (US$)
V90	Average Official Interest Rate
V93	Average Maturity Official (Years)
V94	Average Maturity Private (Years)
V98	Current Account Balance (US$)
V99	Debt buyback
V100	Debt Outstanding
V101	Debt Service (US$)
V102	Debt Service/ Exports of Goods and Services = Debt Burden Ratio
V109	Interest Payments/GNP
V124	Short Term Debt
V129	Debt ratio

Endnotes

1. International Monetary Fund, *Determinants and Consequences of International Capital Flows.* International Monetary Fund (Washington DC: International Monetary Fund 1991), 16. This volume by Morris Goldstein, Donald J. Mathieson, and Timothy Lane examines the role of governments and financial markets in the context of international capital flows.

2. For a theoretical discussion of budgetary institutions see Alberto Alesina and Roberto Perotti, "Budget Deficits and Budget Institutions," (Washington DC: International Monetary Fund, 1996); Von Hagen J. and I. J. Harden, "National Budget Process and Fiscal Performance, " unpublished and Alberto Alesina and Guido Tabellini, "A Positive Theory of Fiscal Deficits and Government Debt," *Review of Economic Studies* 57 (1990): 403-414.

3. Alberto Alesina, Ricardo Hausmann, Rudolf Hommes and Ernesto Stein, "Budget Institutions and Fiscal Performance in Latin America," (Washington DC: Inter-American Development Bank, 1996), 5-9. These authors coin the terms "hierarchical" and "collegial" to distinguish between budget institutions that emphasize either the executive or the legislative branches of government in the process of formulating, approving and implementing national budgets.

4. The term 'information standard' is used here to emphasize the importance of information for the efficient operation of global capital markets. The term is also used to contrast the contemporary global monetary system with the pre-Bretton Woods 'gold standard' system.

5. The international sovereign debt market is the market where governments issue notes and bonds denominated in various currencies. The instant price transmission of economic information through government bonds for developing countries takes place because these financial instruments are traded in liquid, real-time, secondary markets. It can be argued that for the same reasons, stock prices instantly transmit economic information and are considered key measures of economic activity. For example, in the United States stock prices are one of the twelve key variables that make up the index of leading economic indicators. In contrast to government bonds, private and official loans to developing countries are not traded in secondary markets. Consequently, these loans are not priced as marketable securities, there is no market value for these loans. One cannot purchase or sell these loans unless the creditor and borrower agree to restructure and securitize these loans by converting them to bonds. This was exactly what took place through the Brady Plan in Latin America in the late 1980s. For a detailed discussion of public debt management and government bond and loan markets in developing countries see George Macesich, *Transformation and Emerging Markets* (Westport, Connecticut: Praeger, 1996).

[6] See H. Clyde Reeves, *Measuring Fiscal Capacity* (Boston, MA: Oegleschlager, Gunn and Hain, 1986), 89-91.

[7] The focus of this study is on international sovereign debt markets because domestic sovereign debt markets in Latin America only began to emerge in the mid 1990s. Data on these markets is very fragmented. In response to a written inquiry, staff from the International Finance Corporation (IFC) informed me that the IFC plans on conducting a survey of domestic bond markets in Latin America in 1999.

[8] World Bank, Global Development Finance on-line database summary, 1998; available at www.worldbank.org.

[9] Richard Cantor and Frank Packer, "Determinants and Impact of Sovereign Credit Ratings," Research Paper 9608, *Economic Policy Review* (October, 1996): 49.

[10] This definition is compatible with Campos and Pradhan's model of what constitutes an effective public expenditure management system. Under such a system expenditure outcomes are characterized by "fiscal discipline, strategic prioritization of expenditures across programs and projects and technical efficiency in the use of budgetary resources to achieve outputs at the lowest possible cost." For a detailed discussion of this analytical model see Ed Campos and Sanjay Pradhan, "Budgetary Institutions and Expenditure Outcomes" *Policy Research Paper* 1646, (Washington DC: The World Bank, September 1996), 3-4.

[11] Financial market participants in this context include bond underwriters, financial analysts, credit rating agencies, bond portfolio managers and bond investors.

[12] Alesina, Hommes, Hausman and Stein, 2-4.

[13] See James N. Rosenau and Mary Durfee, *Thinking Theory Thoroughly: Coherent Approaches to an Incoherent World* (Boulder: Westview Press, 1995) for a comprehensive discussion of how complex global phenomena have to be understood in terms of both order and uncertainty.

[14] Campos and Pradhan, 5. These authors argue that the openness of financial markets imposes fiscal discipline on governments due to the threat of instant capital flight when policy makers fail to maintain fiscal discipline. They contend that "open financial markets make it politically costly for [governments] to run large deficits."

[15] It should be noted that this dual exchange rate system is an oversimplification. In actuality, since the collapse of the Bretton Woods system in 1973, there have been multiple

exchange rate regimes, including crawling pegs, adjustable regimes and target zones. For a detailed analysis of the wide range of exchange rate regime options see Barry Eichengreen, *International Monetary Arrangements for the 21st Century* (Washington DC: The Brookings Institution, 1994).

16. Federal Reserve. *FRBSF Weekly Letter* (San Francisco: 1995), 2.

17. John T. Kontopoulos, "Fiscal Policy and Electoral Competition," Ph.D. dissertation, Columbia University (Ann Arbor, MI: UMI Dissertation Services), 1997, 140. This dissertation uses an econometric model to examine the effects of fiscal policy on a cross-national basis using a sample of thirty-eight countries.

18. Adam S. Posen, "Monetary Realism: Central Banks and the Political Economy of Disinflation" (Ph.D. dissertation., Harvard University, 1997), 5-8. Posen re-examines the consensus view that links central bank independence and credible monetary policy commitments. His pluralist critique of the institutional model inserts politics into the monetary policy equation. He dismisses "institutional solutions" as unrealistic interpretations of the pulling and tugging of interest group politics. In contrast to this view, an extensive literature links credible commitments in monetary policy to central bank independence. For additional discussion see Alex Cukierman, *Central Bank Strategy, Credibility and Independence* (Cambridge: MIT press, 1992); Sylvia Maxfield, "Financial Incentives and Central Bank Authority in Industrialized Nations," *World Politics* 46 (1994); Carl Walsh, "Optimal Contracts for Central Bankers," *American Economic Review* 85 (1995); and William T. Bernhard, "A Political Explanation of Variations in Central Bank Independence," *American Political Science Review* 92 (1998).

19. A draft research proposal prepared by Keefer and Stasavage reviews the literature suggesting that fiscal delegation of spending authority and fixed fiscal rules, such as stringent spending limits solve credibility problems. The authors propose to identify the conditions under which delegation and fixed policy rules improve policy credibility. See Philip Keefer and David Stasavage in "Delegation, Credibility and Efficiency – the Role of Agency Independence and Fixed Policy Rules in Policy Making," *Draft Research Proposal* (Washington DC: The World Bank, April 1998), 4-12.

20. William Mitchell, "Fiscal Behavior of the Modern Democratic State: Public Choice Perspectives and Contributions," cited in *Political Economy: Recent Views*, ed., Larry Wade (Boston: Kluwer-Nijhoff, 1983), 69-72.

21. See Aaron Wildavsky, *The New Politics of the Budgetary Process, Second Edition* (New York: Harper Collins Publisher, 1992). This author argues that budgeting lies "at the heart" of the political process.

[22] See Harold Lasswell, *Politics: Who gets What, When and How* (New York: St. Martin Press, 1988) cited in Stella Theodoulou and Matthew A. Cahn, eds., *Public Policy – The Essential Readings* (Englewoods Cliffs, New Jersey: Prentice Hall, 1995), 8.

[23] David Collier, "The Comparative Method" in A. Finifter, ed. *Political Science: the State of the Discipline* (Washington DC: American Political Science Association, 1993), 111.

[24] For an extensive analysis of comparative approaches see chapters 3 and 4 of Charles C. Ragin, *The Comparative Method: Moving Beyond Qualitative and Quantitative Strategies* (Berkeley, California: University of California Press, 1987).

[25] David Collier, 105.

[26] Peter Hall and Rosemary C.R. Taylor, "Political Science and the Three New Institutionalisms, *Political Science* 44 (1996): 955-6. These authors review the evolution of the historical, sociological and economic institutional approaches and argue that they are complementary. Their argument is a point of departure to combine the selected approaches.

[27] Eduardo Lora, "What Makes Reforms Likely? Timing and Sequencing of Reforms in Latin America." (Washington DC: Inter-American Development Bank, Working Paper Series 424, 2000), 17.

[28] Data mining techniques used in this study include cluster, rule induction and decision tree algorithms designed to identify patterns and relationships across multiple economic, institutional and social indicators. I am grateful to Dr. Bernard Carey of the Center for Data Insight at Northern Arizona University for making this state of the art, data mining research laboratory available. For more detail on these techniques, see Chapter Five.

[29] Fiscal policy choices are measured through performance indicators derived from the Government Finance Statistics Yearbook database provided by the Finance Department of the IMF (Washington DC, 1998). These indicators include total revenue and expenditures, overall deficit/ surplus/, total outstanding debt by type of debt holder, financing by type of debt holder, intergovernmental transfer payments and extra-budgetary revenues and expenditures. Openness of the economy is derived from the sum of net resource flows, exports of goods and services and imports of goods and services /GNP. Debt indicators are selected from the *Global Development Finance* time series database (Washington DC: The World Bank, 1998). These indicators are expressed in percentages and include: total debt stock/exports of goods and services, total debt stock/GNP, total debt service paid/ exports of goods and services, interest payments/exports of goods and services, interest payments/ GNP, international reserves/total debt stock , and short-term debt/ total debt stock.

[30]. Social development indicators are selected from the *World Development Indicators* database (Washington DC: World Bank, 1998).

[31]. See Brian Pollins, "Global Capital: Two Financial Booms Compared", unpublished paper, 1993. Pollins compares the surges in global capital flows from 1870-1914 and from 1973-1991.

[32]. These assumptions complement the concept of bounded rationality developed by Herbert Simon. Rational actors are not only bounded by time, limited information and their own cognitive limitations to process information but are bounded by the formal rules that they chose to impose on themselves.

[33]. This assumption that formal political (budget) and economic (market access) rules, along with bounded rationality constrain the choice of rational policy makers enables one to reconcile formal institutions as determinants of political and economic interaction with the autonomy and agency of individual actors.

[34]. Bo Rothstein, "Political Institutions: An Overview," in Robert Goodin and Hans Dieter Klingemann, eds., *A New Handbook of Political Science* (Oxford: Oxford University Press, 1996) , 139-144. Rothstein identifies several trends that contribute to an increased focus on institutional analysis, namely, a surge of interest in institutions across disciplines (economics, history, sociology and anthropology) and across subfields in political science, the discovery of culture in organizational theory, a renewed interest in "bringing the state back in" by scholars like Skocpol, Evans, Migdal and Rueschemeyer, a surge in interest of regimes by international relations scholars such as Krasner, the failure of convergence theory to predict that developing and industrialized countries would converge in their economic development paths, the fall of Soviet communism, the third wave of democratization documented by Huntington and Chull Shin, and the discovery that Arrow's impossibility theorem of cyclical majorities did not hold in empirical studies of the US Congress.

[35]. North, Douglass C., "Economic Performance through Time" in *Empirical Studies in Institutional Change*, eds., L.J.Alston, T. Eggertsson and D. North (Cambridge, UK: Cambridge University Press, 1996), 353.

[36]. For a detailed review of various definitions of institutions see Hans Keman, "Public Institutions and Public Governance" in *Institutions and Political Choice: On the Limits of Rationality*, eds., R. Czada, A. Heretier and H. Keman (Amsterdam: VU University Press, 1996) 112.

[37] Rothstein, 146-47.

[38] The role of veto players and the sequence of policy action is examined by Geoffrey Garrett and Peter Lange, "Internationalization, Institutions and Political Change," in Robert O. Keohane and Helen V. Milner, eds., *Internationalization and Domestic Politics* (Cambridge: Cambridge University Press, 1996) , 48-75. These authors adopt Tsebelis' argument suggesting that veto players are institutional actors whose assent is required for a policy change. For further details see George Tsebelis, "Decision-Making in Political Systems," *British Journal of Political Science* 25 (1995): 289-325.

[39] See Walter W. Powell and Paul J. DiMaggio, eds., *The New Institutionalism in Organizational Analysis* (Chicago: The University of Chicago Press, 1991) and James G. March and Johan P. Olsen , "The New Institutionalism: Organizational Factors in Political Life, *American Political Science Review* 78 (1984): 734-49. The Powell and Di Maggio volume is a collection of theoretical and empirical essays that reject economic, rational choice explanations of institutions in favor of cultural explanations. March and Olsen's influential article calls for a political theory of organization.

[40] Social norms can influence preferences and constrain action. Preferences, however are not synonymous with action. For example, social taboos may deal out harsh penalties for a given action. Furthermore, cultural factors such as formal or informal education may lead to a moral judgment about a given action. In this regard, education may alter some individual preferences to the extent that the action will not be considered. Other individuals may consider the given action, but penalties may deter the action. Yet other individuals will engage in the given action. For a discussion of how institutions influence preferences, see Samuel Bowles, "Endogeneous Consequences of Markets and Other Economic Institutions, *Journal of Economic Literature* 36 (1998): 75-111.

[41] Daniel Mc Cool, *Public Policy, Theories, Models and Concepts* (Englewoods Cliffs, New Jersey: Prentice Hall, 1995) , 69, citing Carl Friedrich, *Constitutional Government and Politics* (New York, 1939), 16-18.

[42] For representative works by historical institutionalists see Steinmo, Sven, Kathleen Thelen and Frank Longstreth, eds., *Structuring Politics: Historical Institutionalism in Comparative Analysis* (Cambridge: Cambridge University Press, 1992).

[43] See Oliver E. Williamson, "Credible Commitments, "*American Economic Review* 73 (1983): 519-540.

[44] Gary Miller, "The Impact of Economics on Contemporary Political Science," *Journal of Economic Literature* 35 (1997) :1195. For the critics of North's historical and economic institutionalism, the constitutional constraint explanation implies that these constraints emanate from the people. Critics would claim, however, that this explanation hides the actual source of constraint which is power from above (as in the case of the International Monetary Fund). My own interpretation of North's explanation is that constitutional commitments represent institutional choices that reflect the preferences of policy makers limited by bounded rationality, culture and society. These institutional choices reflect the preferences of policy makers and those of their constituents. My interpretation rejects the argument that exogenous international financial institutions such as the IMF dictate endogenous constitutional commitments. In many countries, constitutional commitments are non-existent – constitutions are merely pieces of paper void of any political meaning. The IMF has no legal jurisdiction nor the political power to impose the adoption of constitutional commitments on any sovereign state.

[45] Douglass C. North and Barry B. Weingast, "The Evolution of Modern Institutions of Growth," in *Empirical Studies in Institutional Change*, eds. Lee Alston, Thrainn Eggertsson and Douglass North (Cambridge: Cambridge University Press, 1996) , 129-135.

[46] See Brian Levy and Pablo T. Spiller, ed., *Regulations, Institutions and Commitment* (Cambridge: Cambridge University Press, 1996).

[47] Eric Patashnik, "The Contractual Nature of Budgeting: A Transaction Cost Perspective on the Design of Budget Institutions," *Policy Sciences* 29 (1996): 195.

[48] This study assumes that two political values and goals are implicit in fiscal policy commitments that are credible to financial market participants: political accountability and centralization of budgetary decision making authority. These two political values complement two economic values held by financial market participants, namely transparency and efficiency. Political values that parallel economic values reflecting policy makers' willingness to pay, become credible to financial market participants who provide private financing for governments.

[49] In contrast to open, interdependent economies, politics within each nation- state remain closed. The rules of the game, the institutions of each national political unit, remain nation-specific. This is not to say that all politics is local. The politics of budgeting in particular is played out on a global stage when governments seek financing in the international bond markets.

[50] Shaun Hargreaves Heap et al., *The Theory of Choice, A Critical Guide,* Third Edition (Oxford: Blackwell, 1997) , 138-140.

[51] *Ibid.*, xi.

[52] This argument is elaborated by Timothy Sinclair in " Economic and Financial Analysis Considered as Knowledge Dynamics of Global Governance," (York University, Political Science Department). Unpublished paper presented at the International Studies Association in Chicago, 1995.

[53] Stephen Haggard and Sylvia Maxfield, "The Political Economy of Financial Internationalization in the Developing World," *International Organization* 50 (1996): 62. These authors argue that as global financial markets become integrated, international constraints will play an increasing role in shaping and limiting domestic policy actions.

[54] International bond financing can provide governments with predictable, long- term fixed rates that enable policy makers to plan infrastructure and human capital expenditures. The ability to plan a long- term investment horizon allows policy makers to match revenues and expenditures efficiently. The advantages of bond financing over short term loans or notes are particularly striking when governments are able to lower their borrowing costs by receiving high credit ratings. For an in depth analysis of this subject, see Frank J. Fabozzi, *Bond Markets, Analysis and Strategies*, Second Edition (Englewood Cliffs, NJ: Prentice Hall), 1993.

[55] Carporaso and Levine, 96.

[56] Eric A. Nordlinger, *On the Autonomy of the Democratic State* (Cambridge, Mass.: Harvard University Press, 1981) 11, quoted in Carporaso and Levine, *op.cit.*, 184.

[57] For a classic treatment of the problems of measurement in comparative analysis, see Adam Przeworski and Henry Teune, *The Logic of Comparative Social Inquiry* (New York: John Wiley and Sons, 1970) , 91-112.

[58] Power is a contested concept in political science. One way, and not necessarily the only way, to examine the vast literature on power is to group it along a continuum consisting of three dimensions. The first dimension of power is a relational, pluralist definition of the power to influence decisions or outcomes (Dahl). The second dimension relates to the concept of non-decision making, the power to define policy agendas (Schattschneider). The third dimension of power represents the power to manipulate preferences (Bachrach, Baratz, Gaventa, Lukes, Manley). The first two dimensions can be interpreted as "power to" while the third dimension of power is the "power over." All three dimensions of power share a common assumption of goal attainment. For an overview of the literature on power see David Marsh and Gerry Stoker, *Theory and Methods in Political Science* (New York: St.Martin's Press, 1995).

[59] See Eric A. Nordlinger, *On the Autonomy of the Democratic State* (Cambridge, Mass.: Harvard University Press, 1981).

[60] Rosenau and Durfee, 3-7.

[61] Sabatier's framework fits within the broad literature addressing policy process – how policy is made. I use some elements of game theory to address interactive choice. Game theory is considered an important rational choice tool to explain policy process. In addition, I combine two institutional approaches that explain the policy process. For a detailed discussion of these and other theoretical approaches used to study public policy see Sabatier, *op. cit.;* Doron Gideon, "The State of the Discipline," *Policy Studies Review* 11 (1992): 303-309; Stella Z. Theodoulou and Matthew A. Cahn, *op.cit.*

[62] Sabatier, 131.

[63] Sabatier, 131.

[64] For a comprehensive review of the theoretical and empirical literature on the equality-efficiency debate see Louis Putterman, John E. Roemer and Joaquim Silvestre, "Does Egalitarianism Have a Future?," *Journal of Economic Literature* 36 (1998): 861-902. The authors present trade-offs on a time horizon (from short to long term) and political and economic dimensions matrix. Yet they limit their review to studies focusing on economic variables, acknowledging that an analysis of the philosophical dimensions of equity remains rudimentary in the economic literature. Putterman, Roemer and Silvestre conclude that explanations of the negative relationship between inequality and growth tend to oversimplify democratic politics.

[65] John Sheahan and Enrique V. Iglesias, " Kinds and Causes of Inequality in Latin America," in *Beyond Trade Offs: Market Reform and Equitable Growth in Latin America,* eds., Nancy Birdsall, Carol Graham and Richard H. Sabot (Washington DC Brookings Institution Press, 1998), 12. This volume includes various essays sharing the common theme that economic strategies and social policies combined can produce egalitarian growth. The key to this equitable growth formula lies in human capital investment, macroeconomic and institutional reforms.

[66] Loren A. King, "Economic Growth and Basic Human Needs," *International Studies Quarterly* 42 (1998): 394.

[67] Sabatier, 149.

[68] *Ibid.,* 151.

[69] Choosing social welfare over fiscal discipline may impose costs on the few for the benefit of the many. Choosing fiscal discipline over social welfare may impose costs on the many for the benefit of the few. The aim of this study is not to determine what choice policy makers should make nor to determine the trade-offs between equity and growth. Rather, the aim is much narrower and designed to examine what institutional and policy choices policy makers do make when they decide to finance public expenditures through the international sovereign debt market.

[70] James D. Morrow, *Game Theory for Political Scientists* (Princeton, New Jersey: Princeton University Press, 1994), 51.

[71] *Ibid.*, 53.

[72] For detailed discussions on how to specify a game see James D. Morrow, *Game Theory for Political Scientists,* 51-72 and see Shaun Hargreaves et al., *The Theory of Choice, A Critical Guide,* 93-99.

[73] Morrow, 3-7.

[74] Hargreaves Heap *et al.,* 17.

[75] Patashnik, 190-191. Transaction cost theory recognizes the costs of negotiating, monitoring and enforcing agreements. Therefore, it can be useful to explain budgeting institutions and choices. In conjunction with the concept of bounded rationality, transaction cost theory helps to explain constraints on choice.

[76] Hargreaves Heap *et al.*, 17-21.

[77] Hall and Taylor, *op.cit.,* 955-957. This article notes that Garrett and Weingast, Scharf and Bates are incorporating culture and beliefs into their institutional models. These scholars represent the economic institutionalist perspective and are adopting sociological approaches to explain institutions.

[78] Historical institutionalism refers to the works of Steinmo and Weir, Orloff and Skocpol. For greater detail see Sven Steinmo *et al., Structuring Politics: Historical Institutionalism in Comparative Analysis* (New York: Cambridge University Press, 1992).

[79] Douglass North in *Institutions, Institutional Change and Economic Performance* (Cambridge: Cambridge University Press, 1990). In this seminal work, North argues that

history matters and that institutions connect the past, present and future. In this context, the role of institutions is to reduce uncertainty and structure human interaction. Although North does not address conflict, he views cooperation as a key problem. One of the most comprehensive treatments of institutional analysis is the work of Furubotn and Richter. The introductory chapter of this extensive volume addresses the connection of political, historical and economic variables in creating institutional stability. See Eirik G. Furubotn and Rudolf Richter, *Institutions and Economic Theory: The Contributions of the New Institutional Economics* (Ann Arbor, Michigan: The University of Michigan Press, 1997), 2-37.

80. Hall and Taylor provide an extensive summary of the strengths and weaknesses of each institutional approach presented here, but I only detail selected strengths relevant to a model of institutional choice. For more detail see Hall and Taylor, *op.cit.*, in "Political Science and the Three Institutionalisms."

81. For a succinct description of the features of the dominant culture of Latin America see Charles Wagley, "A Framework for Latin American Culture," in *Political and Social Change in Latin America,* ed., Howard J. Wiarda (Boulder, Co.: Westview Press, 1992) 25-31. In this short essay, Wagley shows how the hierarchical political values of Latin American elite classes have been transferred to all social class strata.

82. The following simplifying assumptions link advocacy coalition, game theory and the three institutionalisms: 1) Policy makers and financial market participants are rational, forward looking actors, but their rational expectations coexist with adaptive expectations (learning from past experience); 2) Strategic calculation takes place within a cultural and historic context; 3) Institutional and policy choices are constrained by information, time, bounded rationality, conflicting commitments and uncertainty; 3) These constraints shape the nature of interactive choices and influence the scope of rule and policy learning.

83. For a more detailed discussion of these theoretical approaches and selected components see the works of Paul Sabatier, James D. Morrow and Peter A. Hall and Rosemary C.R. Taylor cited in this chapter.

84. I am grateful to Dr. Dan Cothran, who suggested that I think in terms of concentric circles when organizing the literature review. I followed this suggestion and adapted the idea to illustrate the institutional, policy process and political economy spheres of interaction between policy makers and financial market participants.

85. For a detailed discussion of effective ways to think theoretically see James Roseneau and Mary Durfee, 1-8 and 177-190.

[86] Max Weber, "The Meaning of Ethical Neutrality," in *The Methodology of the Social Sciences,* trans., Edward Shils and Henry Finch (Glencoe, Illinois: The Free Press, 1949) , 32-33.

[87] R. Hague, M. Harrop and S. Breslin, *Comparative Government and Politics* (London: MacMillan, 1992), 39-40.

[88] For a detailed review of the linkage between history and the evolution of institutions see case studies in Brian Levy and Pablo Spiller, eds., *Regulations, Institutions and Commitment- Comparative Studies of Telecommunications* (Cambridge, UK: Cambridge University Press, 1996). In addition see Howard J. Wiarda, "Social Change, Political Development and the Latin American Tradition,"in Howard J.Wiarda, ed. *Politics and Social Change in Latin America* (Boulder, CO: Westview Press, 1992) 1-22. This essay highlights the historical context in which Latin American political institutions evolved. These institutions are deeply rooted in medieval Iberian culture and civilization characterized by an authoritarian, absolutist, hierarchical and organic structure of political authority.

[89] I adopt North's definition of path dependence: "the consequence of small event and chance circumstances that, once they prevail, lead to one particular path." See Douglass C. North, *Institutions, Institutional Change and Economic Performance,"* (Cambridge: Cambridge University Press, 1990), 94.

[90] In view of the rapid globalization of public finance, the term "newly industrialized country, (NIC)" does not capture the linkages between the domestic politics of budgeting and global finance. For countries that seek financing in the global debt markets a term such as "globally linked country (GLC)"is more appropiate. This label denotes that a country has an open economy and that its economic policies - fiscal, monetary, trade and investment - converge with the policies of other countries with similar, open economies.

[91] Herbert Simon's concept of bounded rationality and transaction cost theory complement each other in defining the limits to rational, self-interested behavior. Bounded rationality and transaction costs inform my definition of rational policy makers. What I attempt to convey here is that there are limits to rationality. The most recent institutional literature acknowledges these limits. For extensive theoretical discussions see R. Czada, A.Heritier and H. Keman, eds., *Institutions and Political Choice- on the Limits of Rationality* (Amsterdam: VU University Press, 1996).

[92] Sabatier, 139.

[93] One interpretation of parallel interactive policy choices can be found in the literature on cross-border epistemic global finance communities. These communities are linked through

knowledge-based expert consensus. For a brief summary of this literature see Peter Dombrowski, "Haute Finance and High Theory: Recent Scholarship on Global Financial Relations," *Mershon International Studies Review* 42 (1998): 18.

94. In the context of this discussion, rational expectations means that policy makers weigh all the possible responses to policy choices by financial market participants.

95. Stanley Fisher, *Rational Expectations and Economic Policy*. (Chicago: The University of Chicago Press, 1980) , 9-11. For a detailed discussion of the political factors that impact economic actor's expectations about policy shifts see Robert Perry and John Robertson, "Political Markets, Bond Markets and the Effects of Uncertainty: A Cross-National Analysis," *International Studies Quarterly* 42 (1998): 134-135. These authors argue that the main determinants of policy risk are the fractionalization of congressional seats and votes, party volatility, seat and vote polarization and ideological volatility.

96. Beth Simmons, *Who Adjusts? Domestic Sources of Economic Policy* (Princeton: Princeton University Press, 1994), 10-11.

97. For detailed a discussion of adaptive expectations, see James D. Gwartney and Richard L. Stroup, *Economics, Private and Public Choice,* 4th Edition (Washington DC: Harcourt Brace Janovich, 1987), 324-325.

98. Alesina *et al., op. cit.*, 9-10. I am grateful to Ernesto Stein of the Inter-American Development Bank and co-author of the study. Mr. Stein made the entire 20 country dataset of Latin American budget institutions available to me. The index is divided into ten variables representing constraint measures on the formulation, approval and implementation of a budget. A detailed explanation of each component of the index is presented in Chapter Five. Table 5.1 summarizes each variable in the index providing a description and range of values. (Chapter 5).

99. Alesina and Perotti, "Budget Deficits and Budget Institutions," 4-5.

100. Philip Keefer and Stephen Knack, "Why Don't Poor Countries Catch up? A Cross-National Test of An Institutional Explanation," *Economic Inquiry* 35 (1997): 592-93.

101. Alesina and Perotti, 24.

102. *Ibid.*, 5.

103. Jurgen Von Hagen and I.J. Harden, "National Budget Process and Fiscal Performance," Unpublished Manuscript, 1994, 323.

104. These categories are mutually exclusive and jointly exhaustive because each depends on a different source of financing. Money-financing is based on a direct official funding source, a country's own central bank. Loan financing depends on private bank financing and bond financing depends on private capital market financing.

105. Stephen Miller and Frank S. Russek, "Fiscal Structures and Economic Growth: International Evidence," *Economic Inquiry* 35 (1997): 607-613.

106. *Ibid.,* 603. Miller and Russek ignore the problem of commitment, but point out that different results between developed and developing countries may reflect the effects of money-financed and bond-financed spending increases. These authors assume that developing countries mainly print money or rely on subsidized credit markets to finance expenditures and industrialized countries finance expenditures through bond issues. They attribute this debt financing difference to different levels of economic growth between the two groups of countries and suggest that money- financed spending retards economic growth, while bond-financing does not. This argument assumes that bonds are a long term financing alternative to pay for education or infrastructure and that governments mainly rely on short term loans to finance consumption. The argument does not seem to hold when notes are used as a short term financing alternative. As short term instruments, notes should also retard growth when used to finance consumption.

107. See Charles Lindblom, "The Science of Muddling Through," *Public Administration Review* 19 (1959): 79-88 cited in Stella Z. Theodolou and Matthew A. Cahn, 113-127.

108. Levy and Spiller, 209.

109. The term "market access" is used widely to refer to a government's ability to issue sovereign debt. The term is defined narrowly as actual access, excluding potential access because it is impossible to measure access in terms of open lines of credit. For example see Pedro Pou, "What Lessons Can Be Learned from the Recent Financial Crisis?" in *Maintaining Financial Stability in the Global Economy,* Federal Reserve Bank of Kansas City (Jackson Hole, Wyoming, 1997) , 147.

110. David Collier, "The Comparative Method,"*op. cit.,* 116. This essay suggests that quantitative techniques are now available for application to small number of cases and that such techniques could be linked to comparative historical analysis and broad qualitative comparison. Also see Sidney Tarrow, "Bridging the Quantitative-Qualitative Divide in Political Science," *American Political Science Review,* 89 (1995): 471-476

111. Purchasing power parity measures gross domestic product taking into account price differentials between countries. The underground economy consists of all economic activity concealed from the government to avoid taxation and regulation. This part of the economy

is impossible to measure accurately.

112. Charles C. Ragin, *The Comparative Method, Moving Beyond Qualitative and Quantitative Strategies* (Berkeley: University of California Press, 1987), 16-18.

113. These goals of comparison represent the respective views of Collier, Ragin and Sartori who argue that we compare in order to control, such as we do when we use the statistical or the experimental method. In addition, comparison is necessary because the experimental method is not feasible for the social sciences. For an additional discussion on comparison see Giovanni Sartori, "Comparing and Miscomparing," *Journal of Theoretical Politics* 3 (1991): 243- 257.

114. Theda Skocpol and Margaret Sommers, "The Uses of Comparative History in Macrosocial Inquiry" in *Social Revolutions in The Modern World,* Theda Skocpol (Cambridge: Cambridge University Press, 1994), 72-3.

115. Aaron Wildavsky, *op.cit.,* 111-115

116. The conceptual model recognizes the conflictual nature of budget commitments. Conflict, narrowly defined as conflict over budget commitments, represents one of the conditions of interaction.

117. Philip Keefer and David Stasavage, "Delegation, Credibility and Efficiency–The Role of Agency Independence and Fixed Policy Rules in Policy Making," Draft Research Proposal, Unpublished (World Bank and Oxford University, April 1998), 12-15.

118. For a discussion of the limitations of data mining see Kenneth Collier, Bernard Carey, Ellen Grusy, Curt Marjaniemi and Donald Sutter, "A Perspective on Data Mining - White Paper," (Flagsatff, AZ: Center for Data Insight, July 1998), 8.

119. Sebastian Edwards, *Crisis and Reform in Latin America* (New York: Oxford University Press, 1995), 41.

120. William Smith, Carlos Acuna and Eduardo Gamarra, eds., *Democracy, Markets and Structural Reform in Latin America* (Miami: Miami University Press, 1994) , 51-56. The authors contend that in an effort to get the middle class vote Menem reached agreements with unions to curtail strikes and mobilization. Union officials had little choice but to accept Menem's terms (union support for neoliberalism) because they would not support Menem's opponent, an anti-corporatist candidate. In accepting the agreements, union officials were rewarded with government appointments. Unions opposing Menem were assured of political isolation and reduced benefits for members. This "carrot and stick" strategy was effective in neutralizing union reaction to the swift economic measures

introduced by Menem once in office.

121. *Ibid.*, 232 -233.

122. *Ibid.*, 266. See also, Dan A. Cothran, *Political Stability and Democracy in Mexico, the "Perfect Dictatorship,"* (Westport, Connecticut: Praeger, 1994), 1-16. The author presents the sources of Mexico's political stability. According to Cothran these sources include the *institutionalization* of the regime, *effective* economic growth, *adaptability* of the regime in responding to social demands, the *cohesion of political elites,* Mexico's *location* and the *use of coercion (emphasis in original).*

123. Michael Mussa and Morris Goldstein, "The Integration of World Capital Markets," in *Changing Capital Markets: Implications for Monetary Policy,"* Proceedings of symposium sponsored by the Federal Reserve Bank of Kansas City (Jackson Hole, Wyoming: Federal Reserve Bank, 1993), 285.

124. For example, see James Mahon, *Mobile Capital and Latin American Development* (University Park, PA: The Pennsylvania University Press, 1996), 158.

125. "Washington consensus" is a phrase coined by Williamson referring to ten market-oriented policy initiatives, some of which include privatization, trade liberalization and financial deregulation. For details see John Williamson, *Latin American Adjustment: How Much has Happened?,"* (Washington DC: Institute for International Economics, 1990), 41.

126. *Ibid.*, 230.

127. One needs to recognize, however, that during times of fiscal uncertainty in developing countries, international financial market participants rely on the official veto power of the IMF to assess the ability and willingness of policy makers to service their debt obligations. In this context, the IMF evaluations of credit risk contribute to financial market participants' expectations.

128. The concept of real-time is used in the financial markets to denote the instant price transmission of financial market transactions across the globe. This concept can be applied to policy choices (political transactions) to denote their instant transmission and interpretation across the global political economy.

129. Policy makers and financial market participants who form market-friendly advocacy coalitions share the common goal of market access. The mutual benefits of this alliance are increased public finance capacity for governments and increased revenues for financial market participants. These revenues include underwriting and transaction fees and investment returns.

130. Louis W. Pauly, "Capital Mobility, State Autonomy and Political Legitimacy," *Journal of International Affairs* 48 (1995): 369.

131. Stephen Haggard and Sylvia Maxfield, "The Political Economy of Financial Internationalization in the Developing World," *op. cit.,* 62.

132. See Haggard and Maxfield, 1996; Ilene Grabel, "Marketing to the Third World: The Contradictions of Portfolio Investment in the Global Economy," *World Development* 24 (1996): 1761-1776; Eric Helleiner, "From Bretton Woods to Global Finance," in *Political Economy and the Changing Global Order,* eds. Richard Stubbs and Geoffrey Underhill (New York: St. Martin Press, 1994).

133. See Jeffry A. Frieden , "Invested Interests: The Politics of National Economic Policies in a World of Global Finance," *International Organization* 45 (1991): 451. Also see Geoffrey Garrett, *Partisan Politics in the Global Economy* (Cambridge: Cambridge University Press, 1998), 12.

134. The benefits for governments are greater access to private market financing and greater public finance capacity. The costs for financial market participants are a miscalculation of a government's ability to pay and misplaced trust in the willingness of policy makers to be bound by their commitments. Both of these costs lead to financial loss. The costs for policy makers are the politics and economic trade-offs between achieving market reforms and equitable growth.

135. I label sovereign credit ratings as "public report cards on government performance" because unlike credit assessments by banks, the information contained in credit rating reports is readily available and widely distributed to the public.

136. Cantor and Packar, 39.

137. Aida Der Hovanessian, "Guide to Evaluating Sovereign Credits," Morgan Stanley, Fixed Income Credit Research Department (New York: Morgan Stanley, 1992), 162.

138. *Ibid.,* 163.

139. *Ibid.,* 164.

140. For a discussion of credit rating agencies as "gate keepers" to the financial markets, see Timothy Sinclair, "Economic and Financial Analysis Considered as Knowledge Dynamics of Global Governance," 22-23.

141. The effects of establishing a well-functioning sovereign debt market have been studied by economists (Corrigan, Dornbush) and economic historians (North and Weingast). For example, according to Corrigan, a well functioning government securities market serves three main functions. First, it provides a private market mechanism to finance public deficits. Second, it facilitates a more effective approach to monetary policy by strengthening the central bank's balance sheet. This is due to the reduced likelihood of monetizing the debt (printing money) when a private market alternative is available. Third, it provides the foundation upon which other elements of the capital markets can be developed. Corrigan contends, however, that without a secondary market for government debt securities, it is very difficult to design sovereign debt instruments that will attract investors. Without this infrastructure which provides liquidity by enabling the central bank and other market participants to readily exchange sovereign debt securities, it is also difficult to keep the central bank from financing deficits or allocating credit. See Gerald Corrigan, "Central Banks and the Financial System" in *Central Banking Issues in Emerging Market Economies* (Kansas City: The Federal Reserve Bank of Kansas City, 1990) , 33. For additional analysis of the effects of government debt markets see Rudiger Dornbush, ed. *Policy Making in the Open Economy: Concepts and Cases in Economic Performance* (New York: Oxford University Press, 1993). For a historical perspective on how the emergence of England's government debt in the seventeenth century contributed to the financing of public expenditures see Douglass C. North and Barry Weingast, "Constitutions and Commitment: The Evolution of Institutions Governing Public Choice in Seventeenth Century England," in *Empirical Studies in Institutional Change,* eds., Lee J. Alston, Thrainn Eggersson and Douglass North, 134-165.

142. International Monetary Fund, "Private Market Financing for Developing Countries," (Washington DC: IMF, 1995), 16.

143. *Ibid.,* 150.

144. The primary bond market refers to new issues and the secondary market refers to bonds and notes that trade once they are issued.

145. International Monetary Fund, "International Capital Markets: Developments, Prospects and Key Policy Issues," (Washington DC: IMF, 1996), 99.

146. IMF, Private Market Financing, 32.

147. Bank for International Settlements, Monetary and Economic Department, I am grateful to Mr. Denis Petre from the International Financial Statistics Division who made the data for this chart available to me.

[148] These enhancements constitute risk management features that enable investors to reduce financial, interest rate and currency risks when investing in international bond markets.

[149] IMF, *Private Market Financing, op.cit.*, 31.

[150] *Ibid.*, 23.

[151] In contrast to deep, liquid bond markets, which are characterized by a wide range of short, intermediate and long term maturities across the entire yield curve, shallow bond markets are illiquid, characterized by short term issues, often denominated in foreign currencies.

[152] IMF, "Private Market Financing for Developing Countries," 19. For an additional discussion of the multiple reasons for the short duration of emerging country debt see Frederic S. Mishkin, "The Causes and Propagation of Financial Instability: Lessons for Policymakers," in *Maintaining Financial Stability in a Global Economy* (Kansas City: The Federal Reserve Bank, 1997), 55-61.

[153] See Mussa and Goldstein (1993) for a detailed discussion of the general characteristics of global capital flows including the participation of institutional investors such as pension plans, insurance companies and mutual funds.

[154] Portfolio investments include both fixed income (bonds) and equity (stocks) instruments that represent financial claims with relatively high degrees of price risk. These instruments are issued in primary capital markets and traded in secondary capital markets. Capital markets, in general, facilitate the transfer of funds between savers and borrowers. Secondary markets, in particular allow investors to change the liquidity, risk and composition of their portfolios. For a detailed analysis of how capital markets enhance the economic development of a country see Frank Fabozzi and Irving Pollack, *The Handbook of Fixed Income Securities,* Second Edition (Homewood, IL: Dow Jones -Irwing Press, 1987).

[155] Morris Goldstein, Donald Mathieson and Timothy Lane, "Determinants and Systemic Consequences of Capital Flows," Occasional Paper 77 (Washington DC: IMF, 1991) , 11. It should be noted that the shift from bank to official financing involved the bailout of public as well as private sector debt. As government deficit financing led to higher interest rates, private firms found it increasingly difficult to borrow through private credit markets, and had to rely on official financing. Ironically, the effect of unsustainable public debt led the private sector to depend on public subsidies to finance private operations.

[156] Liliana Rojas Suarez, "Risk and Capital Flight in Developing Countries," Occasional Paper 78 (Washington DC: IMF, 1991), 84.

[157] For an updated analysis of financial integration in Latin America see Alberto Carrasquilla, "Financial Integration: Opportunities and Risks," *Latin American Economic Policies* 4 (Washington DC: Inter-American Development Bank, 1998), 3-5.

[158] During this period, the changing patterns of public and private financing also evolved as a result of policy and institutional choices in each country. Thus, it could be argued that the capital flow patterns were shaped by economic as well as political factors. For further details on political factors, see *Policy Choices and Capital Flows,* the next section of this study beginning on page 136.

[159] Ricardo Hausmann and Liliana Rojas Suarez, *Volatile Capital Flows: Taming Their Impact in Latin America* (Washington DC: Inter-American Development Bank, 1996), 12-13.

[160] Primary data on capital flows varies according to each country and can be extracted from balance of payments, international finance and world debt statistics published by the IMF and the World Bank. Line items from the current and the capital accounts represent capital inflows, and various measures of capital flight have been developed to depict capital outflows. These measures vary according to many definitions of capital flight. Broad capital flight measures include changes in debt, net foreign direct investment, current account surplus and change in reserves. Narrow interpretations of capital flight calculate private short term capital outflows and errors and omissions. See Benu Varman-Schneider, *Capital Flight from Developing Countries* (Boulder: Westview Press, 1991); John T. Cuddington, "Capital Flight: Estimates, Issues and Explanations 58 *Princeton Studies of International Finance* (Princeton: Princeton University Press, 1986) and Liliana Rojas - Suarez, "Risk and Capital Flight in Developing Countries," *Occasional Paper* 77 (Washington DC: International Monetary Fund, 1991). In addition, capital flow data on Latin America is available from the Statistical Abstract of Latin America and other secondary sources. Tables 1, 2 and 3 in Appendix 1 are based on secondary sources.

[161] Jose Maria Fanelli and Jose Luis Machinea, "Capital Movements in Argentina," in *Coping with Capital Surges,* eds. Ricardo Ffrench Davis and Stephanie Griffith-Jones (Boulder, CO: Lynne Rienner Publishers, 1995), 150.

[162] Edwards, 218-220.

[163] Raul Laban and Felipe B. Larrain, "The Chilean Experience with Capital Mobility," in *The Chilean Economy: Policy Lessons and Challenges,* eds. Barry Bosworth, Rudiger Dornbush and Raul Laban (Washington DC: The Brookings Institution, 1994), 158.

[164] Ricardo Ffrench-Davis, Manuel Agosin and Andras Uthoff, "Capital Movements, Export Strategy and Macroeconomic Stability in Chile," in *Coping with Capital Surges*, 113.

165. *Ibid.*, 131.

166. World Debt Tables Extracts 1996, 1-4. Equity flows refer to the stock portion of portfolio investments, one of the major categories of private capital flows. Other capital flow categories include bond portfolio flows (fixed income securities), foreign direct investments (FDI - long term investments in plant and equipment), commodity and currency transactions (short term flows) and derivatives (short term flows based on derivative instruments of stocks, bonds, commodities and currencies).

167. For example see Mussa and Goldstein 1993; Edwards 1995; Ffrench-Davis 1995; Goldstein, Mathieson and Lane 1991.

168. Housmann and Rojas Suarez, 2-4.

169. For example, Guillermo O'Donnell develops a theory of bureaucratic authoritarianism that explains the relationship between the private and public sectors and in this context examines Argentina during the 1960s and 1970s. See Guillmo A. O'Donnell, *Bureaucratic Authoritarianism:Argentina 1966-1973, in Comparative Perspective.* Translated by James McGuire in collaboration with Rae Flory (1988). In another related work, Philippe Schmitter's most recent work on corporatism focuses on its declining influence as a result of policies aimed at international competition. See Philippe C. Schmitter, "Corporatism is Dead! Long Live Corporatism!"*Government and Opposition* 24 (1989): 54-73.

170. Smith, Acuna and Gamarra, 269

171. Geoffrey Garrett and Peter Lange, "Internationalization, Institutions and Political Change," in *Internationalization and Domestic Politics,* eds., Robert O. Keohane and Helen V. Milner (Cambridge: Cambridge University Press, 1996), 66-67.

172. Roy Culpepper, "The Role of the American Investors" in *Coping with Capital Surges*, 8.

173. Felipe De la Balze, *Remaking the Argentine Economy* (New York: Council on Foreign Relations Press, 1995), 101-102.

174. Edwards, 218.

175. *Ibid.*, 217 and 231.

176. Smith *et al.*, 221-233. According to Manuel Antonio Garreton, the democratization process began with the defeat of the military dictatorship of Pinochet in 1988. By 1990 the

election of Alwyn resulted in the first civilian democratic government in seventeen years. The transition from military to civilian rule, however, left many political issues unresolved: a human rights problem inherited from the military regime, strong non-democratic opposition from pro-Pinochet groups and constitutional powers of the military. During the early 1990s these issues effectively constrained the consolidation of democracy in Chile.

177. Edwards, 186-191.

178. IMF, "Private Market Financing," 3.

179. In August of 1982 Mexico announced that it was unable to service its debt and the following month President Lopez Portillo, nearing the end of his term in office, nationalized the banks and announced that Mexico would stop principal payments on its external debt until 1984. With the inauguration of President de la Madrid in December of 1982, the IMF approved a $US 4 billion loan to Mexico, while the government began to renegotiate its bank debt obligations. The IMF bailout reduced the risk of a Mexican default, which would have threatened the entire international credit system. For a political analysis of the positive correlation between economic crises and presidential transitions in Mexico see Dan A. Cothran, *Political Stability and Democracy in Mexico,* 116-126. For an economic analysis see Sebastian Edwards, *Crises and Reform in Latin America,* 17-32.

180. IMF, *Private Market Financing, op. cit.,* 86.

181. The Mexican privatization program began slowly in 1983 with the sale of smaller size manufacturing firms. These smaller sales, continued until 1987, when the state-owned airline, Aeromexico went bankrupt. In 1988, The Mexican government began to sell large public monopolies, including Telmex, the state-owned telephone company, two airlines and eighteen banks. From the outset, the objective of the Mexican privatization program was to reduce the size of government and to expand ownership. The program was designed in consultation with labor unions and the private sector. In fact, between 1984 and 1991, labor unions purchased controlling interests in sixteen companies. In addition, labor unions bought large blocks of discounted shares of the largest companies, including Telmex. Most banks were purchased by Mexican industrial conglomerates. Prior to privatization, Mexican banks were considered highly inefficient by international standards, so that extensive regulatory reforms had to follow privatization. Some authors attribute the political support of Mexican privatization to the program's design - the joint agreement of government, labor unions and the private sector. For a more detail see Sebastian Edwards, *op cit.,* 183-199. Also see, Manuel Sanchez, " Entorno Macroeconomico Frente al Tratado de Libre Comercio" in Manuel Sanchez, ed., *Mexico y el Tratado Trilateral de Libre Comercio* (Mexico City: ITAM and McGraw-Hill, 1992).

[182]. Pedro Aspe, *Economic Transformation the Mexican Way* (Cambridge: The MIT Press, 1993), 219.

[183]. Critics of privatization may argue that the divestiture of profitable, state-owned firms deny governments a source of revenue. However, in the case of Argentina, Chile and Mexico, the state-owned firms sold were in extremely poor financial condition. In Argentina, the financing requirements of state owned firms accounted for over 50 percent of the total nonfinancial public sector deficit. These firms generated losses rather than revenues for Argentina's government. In Chile, the story of state-owned firms was similar to that of Argentina. Most privatized Chilean firms faced serious financial difficulty, having incurred large losses. Many had extensive productivity problems. In Chile, the cost of restructuring the privatized firms exceeded buyers' expectations, leading to continuing losses after privatization. The story in Mexico includes state-owned firms that went bankrupt prior to privatization (e.g. Aeromexico in 1987). See Arnold Harberger, "Observations on the Chilean Economy," *Economic Development and Cultural Change* 33 (1985): 451-62; Sebastian Edwards, *op. cit.*, 194; and Javier Gavito Mohar, Sergio Sanchez Garcia and Ignacio Lagarreta, "Los Servicios Financieros y el Acuerdo de Libre Comercio: Bancos y Casa de Bolsa," in *Mexico y el Tratado Trilateral de Libre Comercio, op. cit.*

[184]. For an extensive analysis of the effects of privatization and financial deregulation in Latin America see Sebastian Edwards, *op.cit.*, 170-183.

[185]. Haggard and Maxfield, 40-41.

[186]. Edwards, 308.

[187]. Frank Magill, ed., *Survey of Social Science, Government and Politics Series* (Pasadena, CA: Salem Press, 1996), 158-9. For an alternative perspective see Stephen Gill who is a critic of what he calls "the new constitutionalism," an international governance framework that separates economic policies from broad political accountability in order to make governments more responsive to the "discipline of the market" and less responsive to popular, democratic forces and processes. In the context of Gill's argument, the sovereign debt market is the epitome of the new constitutionalism. His argument is earnest but incomplete. Gill's Gramscian, structural perspective fails to capture the influential role of interactive choice (bounded rationality and rational expectations) shaping the behavior of policymakers and financial market participants. For further details on Gill's arguments see "European Governance and New Constitutionalism: Economic and Monetary Union and Alternatives to Disciplinary Neoliberalism in Europe," *New Political Economy* 3 (1998): 5-25.

[188]. Adam Przeworski, Fernando Limongi *et al., "What Makes Democracies Endure?"* in Juan Linz and Alfred Stepan, *Problems of Democratic Transition and Consolidation*

(Baltimore: The Johns Hopkins University Press, 1996) , 79. For an additional discussion of the correlation between economic performance and democratic regime stability see Samuel P. Huntington, "Democracy for the Long Haul," in *Consolidating the Third Wave Democracies,* eds. Larry Diamond, Marc F. Plattner, Yuan-han Chu and Hug-mao Tien (Baltimore: The John Hopkins University Press, 1997) , 5-13.

189. See George Macesich, *Transformation and Emerging Markets,* (Westport, Connecticut: Praeger, 1996), 36.

190. Jose Angel Gurria, "Capital Flows: The Mexican Case," in *Coping with Capital Surges,* eds. Ffrench-Davis and Griffith Jones, *op.cit.,* 218-220. The author contends that the 1994 crisis was triggered by a chain of effects starting with domestic demand for foreign capital (due to low domestic savings) which resulted in an appreciation of the Mexican peso and the subsequent restrictive monetary policy implemented to offset the expansive effects of capital inflows. Once Mexico devalued its currency by 40 percent in December of 1994 capital flight (which had begun in 1993 due in part to higher interest rates in the United States) intensified.

191. For a discussion of the relationship between economic policy and regime stability in Mexico, see Dan A. Cothran, "Mexican Economic and Fiscal Policies to Sustain Political Stability," *Public Budgeting and Finance*, Winter (1994): 98-119 and *Political Stability and Democracy in Mexico, the "Perfect Dictatorship."*

192. For US studies see A.Wildawsky, *The New Politics of the Budgetary Process* and A. Alesina and H. Rosenthal, *Partisan Politics, Divided Government and The Economy* (Cambridge: Cambridge University Press, 1995). For comparative and cross-national studies see J. Huber, "Restrictive Legislative Procedures in France and in the United States," *American Political Science Review* (1992):67-80; N. Roubini and J. Sachs, "Government Spending and Budget Deficits in the Industrialized Countries," *Economic Policy* 8 (1989): 99-132. Some cross-national studies cover developing countries (Miller and Russek 997; Keefer and Knack 1997) and few studies concentrate on comparing Latin American countries exclusively (Lopez Murphy 1995; Edwards 1995).

193. Miller and Russek, 612.

194. International empirical studies on the effects of budget rules on fiscal policy are very limited as discussed by Keefer and Stasavage but the empirical literature on fiscal rules adopted by US states finds that fiscal policy rules are more effective when they are constitutionally grounded and enforced by elected rather than appointed officials. These findings suggest that a) constitutionally grounded rules that limit borrowing and deficit spending are less likely to be changed by current policy makers who may have incentives to renege on policy commitments and future policy makers with different policy preferences

and b) when budget rules are enforced by elected officials, voters hold greater leverage on the fiscal choices of policymakers by forcing them to be accountable. The Keefer and Stasavage paper briefly mentions "delegation" of budget preparation, which can better be defined as centralization of budget authority within a finance ministry. This paper, however, does not focus on fiscal policy credibility focusing instead, as most of the literature on credibility, on monetary policy. See P. Keefer and D. Stasavage, "When Does Delegation Improve Credibility? Central Bank Independence," Unpublished Paper Presented at the American Political Science Association Annual Meeting , Boston, MA., September 1998, 2-4.

195. Edwards, *op. cit.*, 86. For further discussion of tax reforms in Argentina and Mexico, see Sergio Berensztein, "Rebuilding State Capacity in Contemporary Latin America: The Politics of Taxation in Argentina and Mexico," in *Latin America in the World Economy*, eds., Roberto P. Korzeniewicz and William C. Smith (Westport: Connecticut, 1996), 229-248. In this essay, Berensztein argues that neoliberal tax reform coalitions in Argentina and Mexico reduced opposition by compensating losers of the new scheme through compensatory social policies. These efforts to eliminate opposition were complemented by the "complexity, scope and lack of information" about the actual or probable consequences of tax reforms.

196. The Von Hagen and Harden and Alesina and Perotti typology of budget institutions was introduced in Chapter Three.

197. See Alesina and Perotti, 6.

198. Von Hagen and Harden, 336-338.

199. See Alesina *et al.*, 13-14 and Von Hagen and Harden, 323. These authors argue that a budget lacking transparency can lead to "creative accounting." Politicians have incentives to hide current and future taxes, over emphasize the benefits of spending and hide government liabilities.

200. Edwards, 327.

201. See Mark P. Jones, "Evaluating Argentina's Democracy," in *Presidentialism and Democracy in Latin America*, eds., Scott Mainwaring and Matthew Soberg Shugart (Cambridge University Press, 1997), 282.

202. Lopez Murphy 1995, 84.

203. *Ibid.*, 105.

[204] Alesina *et al.*, 37.

[205] *Ibid.*, 39

[206] Arend Lijphart and Carlos Waisman, eds., *Institutional Design in New Democracies* (Boulder, CO: Westview Press, 1996), 46-49.

[207] Alesina, *et al.*, 35.

[208] Ibid., 36 and 39.

[209] Von Hagen and Harden, 379. This argument poses challenging questions about the accountability of hierarchical budget rules. If the authors' hypothesis is accepted, the less collegial (democratic) the budget rules, the more accountable governments are regarding their fiscal decisions. The trade off in this case is one between budget efficiency and democratic accountability. Thus, acceptance of the structural hypothesis in the context of democratic regimes assumes that efficiency and democratic accountability are compatible. Empirical comparative studies of European countries show that democratic regimes with hierarchical budget procedures, have achieved and sustained greater fiscal balance than those with collegial budget rules. Alesina and Perotti review this literature and conclude that collegial institutions do not necessarily cause budget deficits but delay adjustments in fiscal imbalances. See Alesina and Perotti, 18-23. For further details see Bayoumi T. and B. Eichengreen, "Restraining Yourself: The Implications of Fiscal Rules for Economic Stabilization,"(Washington DC: IMF Staff Papers, March 1995).

[210] Alesina and Perotti, 20-21.

[211] Lopez Murphy 162.

[212] Jose Pablo Arellano, "Commentary: Public Sector Deficits and Macroeconomic Stability in Developing Countries," in *Budget Deficits and Debt: Issues and Options* (Kansas City: Federal Reserve Bank Symposium, 1995), 376.

[213] *Ibid.*, 378.

[214] Oscar Munoz Goma and Carmen Caledon, "Chile in Transition: Economic and Political Strategies," in *Economic Policy and the Transition to Democracy,* eds., Juan Antonio Morales and Gary McMahon (New York, St.Martin's Press, 1996), 209-211.

[215] Edwards, 319. Note that economic services represents a category of expenditures related to state-owned firms. Once these firms were privatized, capital expenditures were no longer financed through either taxes or public debt. In greater detail, Edwards

acknowledges that fiscal adjustment in Latin America, translated into a reduction in social spending but that surprisingly, many social indicators such as infant mortality, school enrollment and life expectancy improved despite spending cuts, 254-55. Edward's findings are confirmed in the next section of this study.

216. Perry and Herrera, 38.

217. Cothran 1994, *Political Stability and Democracy in Mexico,* 180.

218. See Guillermo O'Donnell, "Illusions about Consolidation," in *Consolidating the Third Wave Democracies,* 40-57.

219. Glen C. Dealy, "Pipe Dreams: The Pluralistic Latins," *Foreign Policy* 57 (1984-85): 108-127 cited in *Politics and Social Change in Latin America,* ed., Howard Wiarda (Boulder, CO: Westview Press, 1992), 284-286.

220. S.M. Milesi-Ferretti and A. Razin, "The Sustainability of Current Account Deficits," ABER Working Paper, WP 5967 (Washington DC: ABER, 1996), 1.

221. Argentina, Chile and Mexico rely primarily on regressive taxes – taxes with an effective rate that is lower for high income than low income individuals (e.g. taxes on goods and services). For greater detail about regressive taxation, see John Mikesell, *Fiscal Administration, Analysis and Application for the Public Sector* (Belmont, CA: Wadsworth Publishing Company, 1995) , 282-4.

222. It should be noted that these findings are tentative in that they emerge from the analysis of budget data. The data allows for an analysis of public finance trends in each country but has important limitations. This sort of annual data limits the extent to which one can interpret the political strategies of policy makers engaged in the process of making budgetary decisions. Furthermore, national budget data limits the analysis of exogenous, economic variables. This limitation constrains the analysis of alternative explanations. For example, a decline in world oil or copper prices that may have contributed to reduced export revenues and thus triggered a need for debt financing in Mexico or Chile during the period under study.

223. Dennis Quinn, "The Correlates of Change in International Financial Regulation," *American Political Science Review* 91 (1997): 540-541.

224. Aspe 107.

225. The "crowding out effect" refers to the reduction in private spending and investing as a result of high interest rates produced by budget deficits that are financed by government

borrowing in the private loan markets. For further detail on the effects of fiscal policy, see James Gwartney and Richard Stroup, *Economics: Private and Public Choice,* 4th Edition (New York: Academic Press, 1987) Chapter 5, 99-121.

226. Alesina *et al.,* 40.

227. Two separate studies argue that hierarchical budget institutions lead to fiscal restraint. For example see Alesina and Perotti (1994), *op.cit.,* 18-21; and Von Hagen and Harden (1994). *op.cit.,* 345.

228. In both Argentina and Mexico weak constitutional commitments to rule transparency will have to be overcome before credible fiscal commitments can be sustained over the long term. A weak constitutional commitment to rule transparency means that rule learning for these countries will involve deep institutional reforms beyond budgeting. Reforming weak judicial systems may be a point of departure for the adoption of transparent budget rules. Without transparent rules governments cannot be accountable to markets or to voters.

229. Howard Wiarda, ed., *Politics and Social Change in Latin America* (Boulder, CO: Westview Press, 1992), 335. In the same volume see Glen C. Dealy, "Pipe Dreams: The Pluralistic Latins." Dealy discusses the authoritarian legacy in Latin America and its effect on integrating competing centers of power to create social unity.

230. See Edwards for a historical review of how Latin America reached this dubious distinction as a result of economic policies implemented since the mid 1940s, 1-13.

231. The proportion of urban populations in all three countries may help to explain why Argentina and Chile were able to ignore safe water services to rural areas. In Argentina, the urban population accounted for 85 percent of the total population from 1980 to 1985 and 96 percent from 1990 to 1995. The urban population of Chile was 83 percent of the total population from 1980 to 1985 and 84 percent from 1990 to 1995. Mexico's emphasis on service improvements in rural areas can be explained by the fact that 70 percent of the population was urban from 1980 to 1985 and 74 percent was urban from 1990 to 1995. In addition to a higher percentage of rural population, Mexico had the highest urban level of access to water safety of all three countries from 1980 to 1985 and from 1990 to 1995 improvements in safe water access shifted to the rural areas. See World Development Indicators, Social Indicators Data Sheet, CD-ROM, World Bank, Washington DC, 1998.

232. Educational expenditures do not just apply to primary education. Changes in educational expenditures also had a probable effect on secondary and post secondary education. Data on secondary and post secondary education is not available on an annual basis for each country. For details on educational expenditures in Argentina, Chile and Mexico see World Development Indicators, 1998, CD ROM, World Bank, *op. cit.*

233. Edgardo Boeninger, "Latin America's Multiple Challenges," in *Consolidating the Third Wave Democracies, op.cit.,* 41-43. Boeninger's definition of "social peace" is not equivalent to the definition of 'democratization.' While definitions of democratization focus on the political context of political change (decay of authoritarian rule, transition, consolidation and maturing of the democratic order), "social peace" refers to its social context.

234. Although international factors impact a government's ability to generate foreign exchange earnings, fiscal, monetary, trade and regulatory policy choices ultimately determine whether domestic borders remain open or closed to trade and capital flows. Trade and financial deregulation variables left out by the conceptual model emerge as significant throughout the qualitative analysis.

235. "Predictor" is not used here in the sense that we can predict market access, but rather in the sense that we can identify the most significant explanatory variables for market access.

236. For a detailed discussion of data mining see Kenneth Collier *et al., op.cit.*, 19-25. These authors argue that data mining relies on multivariate regression analysis, the chi-square test of statistical significance, rule association (clustering analysis), neural networks (classification and pattern mapping) and other statistical techniques. For additional detailed descriptions of data mining methods and applications see Usama M. Fayyad, Gregory Piatetsky-Shapiro, Padhraic Smyth and Ramasamy Uthurusamy, eds., *Advances in Knowledge, Discovery and Data Mining* (Cambridge: MIT Press, 1996); Ruby Kennedy, Benjamin van Roy and Christopher D. Reed, *Solving Data Mining Problems through Pattern Recognition* (New York: McGraw Hill, 1997); Joseph P. Bigus, *Data Mining with Neural Network* (New York: Mc Graw Hill, 1996).

237. David Marsh and Gerry Stoker, 9.

238. See Kurt Thealing, "Understanding Data Mining: It's All in the Interaction," White Paper, Data Mining Analytics Exchange Applications, December 1997, *http://www3 shore net/~kht/index htm.* For recent advances in data mining applications see "Data Mining and Knowledge Discovery, An International Journal," Microsoft Research, Redmond, WA , 1997, *http://research.microsoft.com/research/datamine.* In addition, for case studies on the application of data mining, see "Discovering Data Mining," IBM Redbook, 1997, *http://www.redbooks.ibm.com.*

239. The availability of institutional data from only 1980 to 1993 for Chile required that all institutional and policy variables for all countries for 1994 and 1995 be eliminated from the quantitative analysis. Keeping the data for 1994 and 1995 for two of the cases would have left too many missing values for purposes of data mining. Data mining tools do not perform well with an incomplete data set. Although data for all policy variables were available for

all three countries from 1980-1995, values for 1994 and 1995 were eliminated to reduce the probability of errors in data mining analysis.

240. For a detailed description of each variable, variable value and discussion of how Alesina *et al.* constructed the index of budgetary institutions, see Alesina *et al.*, "Budget Institutions and Fiscal Performance in Latin America," 9-15.

241. To complement measures of public finance capacity, revenue variables are added to the analysis because these measures are important tax financing sources that complement debt financing sources considered as part of a government's capacity to finance public expenditures. Central government revenues are defined as taxes on income, profits and capital gains, social security taxes, taxes on goods and services, taxes on international trade, other taxes and non-tax revenue. These categories are consistent with the government finance statistics included in the Global Development Finance database of the World Bank, CD-ROM 1998.

242. For a detailed discussion of sovereign credit analysis measures see Aida Der Hovanessian, 163-169.

243. Data sources included the Global Development Finance, World Bank database on CD-ROM, 1998; the World Development Indicators database on CD-ROM, 1998; Inter-American Development Bank, data set for budget institutions in Latin America from 1980-1995(Excel 97 version) provided by Ernesto Stein of the Office of the Chief Economist of the IDB, Washington DC; Government Finance Statistics data set (Excel 97 version) provided by Alison Roth of the Government Statistics Division of the International Monetary Fund, Washington DC and the data set of international bonds and notes issued by Argentina, Chile and Mexico from 1980-1995 prepared by the Bank for International Settlements (Excel 97) and provided by Denis Petre of the International Financial Statistics Department of the Bank for International Settlements, Geneva, Switzerland. All data have limitations. These limitation are well documented in all the annual reports for each one of these international financial institutions which produce the most standardized set of statistical data available for cross-national economic analysis.

244. Many of the data mining tools available at the Center for Data Insight are highly specialized for various business applications such as marketing. The selection of mining tools capable of analyzing the institutional and policy variables of this study focused on finding non-specialized tools capable of addressing the research hypotheses.

245. For a detailed discussion of the types of algorithms used in data mining and a description of each tool used in this analysis, see Kenneth Collier *et al.*), 27-32.

[246] Sensitivity is a relative measure of the importance of each input (e.g., independent variable) to the output (e.g. dependent variable) of the network. See Micheal J. A. Berry and Gordon S. Linoff, *Data Mining Techniques* (New York, NY: John Wiley and Sons, 1997), 324-325.

[247] See Fayyad *et al.*, 198.

[248] For a detailed description of the steps used in data mining, the KDD cycle (Knowledge Discovery in Databases) see Kenneth Collier *et al.*, *op. cit.*, 2-4.

[249] Alesina *et al,* 1.

[250] For a technical explanation of the structure of rule induction, decision trees and neural network algorithms, see Joseph Bigus, 98-101.

[251] See Miller and Russek, 612.

[252] Openness of the economy is measured as follows: aggregate net resource flows+ exports and imports of goods and services/ GNP. A more conventional measure of openness only considers trade flows. In the context of the global economy, it is relevant to incorporate both capital and trade flows to more accurately reflect both dimensions of contemporary open, domestic economies.

[253] Note that the process of filtering out variables automatically eliminates highly correlated independent variables, in effect setting up the equivalent of a correlation matrix to check for multicollinearity. Multicollinearity arises when the independent variables are themselves correlated.

[254] Increased equity portfolio flows resulting from privatization initiatives in Argentina, Chile and Mexico can be attributed to the main mode (initial public offerings of stock shares on either domestic or international stock exchanges) for selling state-owned firms in Argentina, Chile and Mexico. For a detailed discussion of the impact of privatization on public finance and on equity markets see Sebastian Edwards, *Crisis and Reform in Latin America*, 174-180.

[255] The World Bank data set for the three expenditure categories used to build the dependent variable had several missing values ranging from 1980 to 1981 for Argentina and from 1988 to 1993 for Chile. In addition, variable V4 (Access to the Sovereign Debt Market) had some zero or near zero values followed by some very large values for all three countries, as illustrated in Figure 4.1.

[256] In addition to market access (V4), eleven other variables were used as independent variables: tax revenues as a percentage of GDP (V77), exports of goods and services as a percentage of GDP (V28); domestic financing as a percentage of GDP (V23); average maturity of private sector debt (V94); net foreign direct investment (32); average maturity of official debt (93); interest rate spread -lending rate minus deposit rate (48); domestic credit provided by banking sector as percentage of GDP (V22), financing from abroad as percent of GDP(31); gross national savings as percent of GDP(39) and use of IMF credit (V86).

[257] Stepwise selection (SPSS enter method) is a useful method of variable selection, when the independent variables are highly intercorrelated. This is known as the problem of multicollinearity. For example, when a variable is entered and it reduces the importance of an already entered variable, the already entered variable is automatically removed from the model. Note that in Models 1 and 2 no variables were removed. The problem of autocorrelation appears when successive observations of the dependent variable are correlated because the data are collected over a period of time. Heteroscedasticity occurs when the variations in the difference between the actual and the predicted values are not the same for all the fitted values of the dependent variable. See Robert Mason and Douglas A. Lind, *Statistical Techniques in Business and Economics,* Seventh Edition (Homewood, Illinois: Irwin, Inc., 1990) , 569-570.

[258] SPSS Applications Guide, *op.cit.,* 209. This manual points out that *Beta* coefficients make regression coefficients simply more comparable.

[259] *Ibid.,* 209.

[260] See William H. Crown, *Statistical Models for the Social and Behavioral Sciences: Multiple Regression and Limited-Dependent Variable Models* (Westport, Connecticut: Praeger, 1998), 42.

[261] Other variables, including domestic financing as a percent of GDP (23), domestic credit provided by the banking sector (V22), net foreign direct investment (V32), the interest rate spread (V48) and the average maturity of private sector debt (V94) have low and negative t values falling in the +2 and -2 t value guideline range.

[262] *Ibid.,* 208. The SPSS output tables showing probabilities under column label *Sig.* have a value of less than 0.0005 when listed as values of .000.

[263] These three expenditure categories combine growth-oriented public investment elements of the new economic growth model with emphasis on human capital expenditures (education and health care) and the postwar traditional development model emphasizing

infrastructure investments in transportation and communications. For an extended analysis of the effects of education and health care expenditures on economic growth in Latin America, see Nancy Birdsall and Juan Luis Lodono, "No Tradeoff: Efficient Growth Via More Equal Human Capital Accumulation," in Nancy Birdsall, Carol Graham and Richard H. Sabot, eds., *Beyond Tradeoffs: Market Reform and Equitable Growth in Latin America, op.cit.,* 111-121.

264. The standard deviation is used to compare dispersions. It is a measure that compares the spread in two or more sets of observations. See Mason and Lind, 134.

265. Non-linear regression does not solve all problems, however. For example, when several explanatory variables involving higher order terms are used in a polynomial regression, and the small sample size is not large enough relative to the number of variables added to the equation, the degrees of freedom lost could reduce the statistical significance of the model. See William H. Crown, 55.

266. It should be noted that due to the problems with missing values in the data used, as well as the problems regarding the linear regression technique acknowledged in this chapter, the conclusions reached may not be useful for specific policy applications.

267. See Milesi, Ferretti and Razin, 1996; Alesina et al., 1995 and "Private Market Financing, IMF, 1995. My argument in chapter 3 about transparency being perhaps more significant than hierarchy also seems to be matched by these partial quantitative findings. My argument was premised on the importance of transparency as a function of the instant information flow that characterized financial transactions in the world economy.

268. As stated in chapter 1, these pillars are transparency, credibility and accountability representing the rules of the international financing game. Governments that play by these rules tend to increase their ability to access the international sovereign debt markets.

269. The phenomenon of learning across national borders has been studied primarily in the context of military international relations, specifically as it relates to "shared policy learning" aimed at reducing conflict, promoting cooperation and raising awareness of global interdependence. For a comprehensive review of the realist-idealist debates on international policy learning see Jeffrey W. Knopf, "The Importance of International Learning," Center for Nonproliferation Studies, Monterey Institute of International Studies, unpublished paper presented at the Annual Meeting of the American Political Science Association, Boston, September 1998. For a detailed account of US foreign policy lessons drawn from similar political situations see Lloyd S. Etheredge, *Can Governments Learn? American Foreign Policy and Central American Revolutions* (New York: Pergamon Press, 1985).

[270] For a recent example of how policy makers in Venezuela failed to engage in precision politics with financial market participants, see Thomas, T. Vogel Jr., "Critics Assail Venezuela's Chavez for Imprecision in Economic Plan," *The Wall Street Journal,* 10 February 1999, final edition, A19. This article highlights the growing Venezuelan fiscal deficit and the negative effects of vague commitments to fiscal restraint. While favoring social spending, President Chavez is unwilling to provide a precise explanation on how he plans to reduce Venezuela's fiscal deficit.

[271] Financial markets are considered 'rudimentary' and 'shallow' when they lack liquidity and offer a limited selection of tradable instruments. For example, Latin American sovereign debt issues are highly illiquid in domestic markets -it is not possible to trade these debt instruments readily. Additionally, only short and intermediate-term Latin American debt issues can be traded in international sovereign debt markets.

[272] IMF, *op cit., Private Market Financing* (1995), 19.

[273] Buscaglia and Long argue that legal and economic integration results from compatible political systems, the public sector's expectations of gains from trade liberalization and the private sector's expectations of gains from regionalizing production, transferring capital and technology. See Edgardo Buscaglia and Clarisa Long, "An Economic Analysis of Legal Integration in Latin America," *Policy Studies Review* 15 (1998): 56-59.

[274] See B. Eichengreen and Richard Portes in *Crisis? What Crisis? Orderly Workouts for Sovereign Debtors,* (London: Centre For Economic Policy Research, 1995), 56. The authors contend that financial markets are social institutions that can only function within a well defined legal and institutional framework.

[275] See George Macesich, 36.

[276] Tax revenues do not appear to be strongly associated with market access because tax financing strategies remained limited in Argentina, Chile, and Mexico from 1980-1995. Although tax revenues directly reflect domestic fiscal policy choices, export revenues do not. Export revenues not only depend on trade policy choices but also depend on domestic and international economic and political conditions. Policy makers have more discretion and control over tax revenues than over export revenues.

[277] Relative to education, these findings corroborate the empirical findings of Sheahan and Iglesias who conclude that inequality of educational opportunities in Latin America, including Argentina, Chile and Mexico, has aggravated the inequality of incomes and possibly health. Consistent with the social indicator trends outlined in Chapter four of this study, Sheahan and Iglesias argue that rural residents and much of the urban poor lacked access to primary education up to the mid 1950s. In their view, the historical neglect of

mass education overshadowed the literacy improvements since the 1960s. These improvements in educational access still have not closed the unusually large educational gap between the poor and upper-income families. For greater detail see Sheahan and Iglesias in *Beyond Trade-Offs: Market Reform and Equitable Growth in Latin America, op cit.*, 30-39.

278. For a comprehensive analysis of questions related to the social context of government formation, administrative reform and policy credibility see Michael Laver and Kenneth A. Shepsle, *Making and Breaking Governments: Cabinets and Legislatures in Parliamentary Democracies* (Cambridge: Cambridge University Press, 1996) , 18-42.

279. One example of budget rules that introduce incentives for greater budget efficiency is the concept of "entrepreneurial budgeting." According to Dan A. Cothran, this concept entails "*central* control of total spending, *decentralization* of authority to departments in the use of funds and enhanced *accountability* for results" (447) [*emphasis in original*]. Entrepreneurial budgeting has been used in the United States, Australia, Canada, Denmark, Sweden and Britain and could perhaps be used in Latin America to give budget participants within spending ministries greater decision making discretion with built-in incentives to achieve greater efficiency and accountability. For a detailed analysis of the benefits and limitations of this budgeting approach see Dan A. Cothran, "Entrepreneurial Budgeting," *Public Administration Review* 53 (1993): 445-454.

280. In their recent essay, C. Graham and Moises Naim argue that institutional reforms in the rulemaking arena take time. These authors distinguish between operational rules (e.g. tax collection) and meta institutions reflecting social traits. Based on this distinction, hierarchical budget institutions in Argentina, Chile and Mexico can be considered meta institutions because they reflect Latin America's Catholic and Spanish heritage of hierarchical society. Recognizing the slow and cautious nature of institutional change, Graham and Naim suggest that coalition building strategies can be effective in implementing reforms that introduce budget choices. From their perspective, coalition building amounts to engaging influential actors and giving them a stake in the reforms. See "The Political Economy of Institutional Reform in Latin America," in *Beyond Tradeoffs: Market Reform and Equitable Growth in Latin America,* 336-338. Adopting Graham and Naim's, institutional typology, I would argue that engaging financial market participants in coalitions with fiscal policy makers could promote learning of transparent budget rules and contribute to democratic consolidation and stability in the region.

281. For example, the model of interactive choice can be applied to study the effects of domestic educational policy choices on global competitiveness. The spheres of interactive choice include educational institutions, the policy process and the global political economy. The actors are educators, education policy makers and employers. The interactive choice centers on educational reform and global competitiveness. The effects of interactive choice

are economic growth and higher living standards. The conditions of interaction involve rule learning, path dependence, uncertainty, conflict and information (see Figure 3.2).

282. At the present time, not all available data mining tools are efficient in handling small, complex data bases. Additionally each software manufacturer has different requirements for the preprocessing of data in order to protect proprietary information. This makes comparisons of data across different data mining tools cumbersome because data that is preprocessed for one application may not be adequate for another. Each time one uses a different tool, one has to preprocess data to match the tool.

283. For a detailed analysis of the Lazard Freres proposal and the volatility in Latin American bond placements in the last three years, see *The Wall Street Journal*, "Lazard Partner Has Idea for Halting Crisis in Financial Markets," 15 October , 1998, final edition, A18 and "Latin America Faces a Brutal 1999 After Years of Growth, Economists Say," 16 December, 1998, final edition, A15. For a detailed Latin American analysis of financial contagion and its related conceptual issues (the quest for liquidity, lack of information, investors' risk aversion and uncertainty) resulting from the global financial crisis in Asia, see Grupo Financiero Banamex -Accival, *Review of the Economic Situation of Mexico* 74 (September 1998): 330-332.

284. See Milesi-Ferretti, S. M. and A. Razin, "The Sustainability of Current Account Deficits," ABER Working Paper 5667 (Washington DC: ABER, 1996). These authors examine the difference in deficit thresholds between industrialized and developing countries. They adopt a macroeconomic perspective ignoring institutional analysis.

285. Note that preliminary discussions between the Presidents of Argentina and Brazil and the US Treasury are now underway to establish a common currency in Latin America. A regional monetary union is still far off and faces many political hurdles – not unlike those confronted by the European Community prior to the establishment of the "euro' earlier this year. Nevertheless, such discussions represent a clear signal that regional financial cooperation is likely to follow. See David Wessel, Craig Torres and Jose de Cordoba, "Argentina Considers a Radical Peso Defense: Use Dollars Instead," *The Wall Street Journal,* 18 January 1999, final edition, A2 and A8.

Bibliography

Ahgion, P. and P. Bolton. 1990. "Government Debt and the Risk of Default: A Political Economic Model of the Strategic Role of Debt." In *Public Debt Management: Theory and Practice,* R. Dornbush and M. Draghi, eds. Cambridge: Cambridge University Press. 315-45.

Alesina, Alberto and Roberto Perotti. 1994. "The Political Economy of Budget Deficits."*NBER Working Paper* 4631, Cambridge: NBER.

_____. 1996. "Budget Deficits and Budget Institutions." IMF *Working Paper.* Washington DC: International Monetary Fund.

Alesina, A. and G. Tabellini. 1990. "A Positive Theory of Budget Deficits and Government Debt." *Review of Economic Studies*, 57: 403-14.

Alesina, Alberto, Ricardo Hausmann, Rudolf Hommes and Ernesto Stein. 1995. "Budget Institutions and Fiscal Performance in Latin America. "Inter-American Development Bank. Washington DC: Inter-American Development Bank.

Alesina, Alberto and H.Rosenthal. 1995. *Partisan Politics, Divided Government and the Economy.* Cambridge, MA: Cambridge University Press.

Alt, James E. and A. Chrystal. 1983. *Political Economics.* Berkeley: University of California Press.

Alston, Lee J., Thrainn Eggertsson and Douglass C. North, eds. 1996. *Empirical Studies in Institutional Change.* Cambridge: Cambridge University Press.

Ames, Barry.1987.*Political Survival: Politicians and Public Policy in Latin America.* Berkeley, CA: University of California Press.

Arellano, Jose Pablo. 1995. "Commentary: Public Sector Deficits and Macroconomic Stability in Developing Countries." in *Budget Deficits and Debt: Issues and Options*. Kansas City: Federal Reserve Bank Symposium, 375-384.

Arrow, Kenneth. 1963. *Social Choice and Individual Values,* 2nd Edition New Haven: Yale University Press.

Aspe, Pedro. 1993. *Economic Transformation the Mexican Way.* Cambridge: The MIT Press.

Balze, Felipe De La. 1995. *Remaking The Argentine Economy.* New York: Council on Foreign Relations Press.

Bank for International Settlements. 1998. Data Set for International Bond and Notes Issues for Argentina, Chile and Mexico from 1980-1995 (Excel 97 version). Geneva, Switzerland: Bank for International Settlements.

Barfield, Claude E. 1996. *International Financial Markets: Harmonization versus Competition.* Washington DC: The AIE Press.

Barro, Robert. 1979. "On the Determination of Public Debt." *Journal of Political Economy*, 87: 940-947.

Bates, Robert H., Avner Greif, Margert Levi, Jean-Laurent Rosenthal and Barry Weingast. 1998. *Analytic Narratives.* Princeton, NJ: Princeton University Press.

Bayoumi T. and B. Eichengreen. 1995. "Restraining Yourself: The Implications of Fiscal Rules for Economic Stabilization." Washington DC: IMF Staff Papers.

Bernhard, William T. 1998. "A Political Explanation of Variations in Central Bank Independence." *American Political Science Review* 95: 311-327.

Berry Micheal J.A. and Gordon S. Linoff. 1997. *Data Mining Techniques.* New York: John Wiley and Sons, Inc.

Bigus, Joseph P. 1996. *Data Mining with Neural Networks.* New York: McGraw Hill.

Birdsall Nancy, Carol Graham and Richard H. Sabot, eds. 1998. *Beyond Tradeoffs: Market Reform and Equitable Growth in Latin America.* Washington DC: Brookings Institution Press.

Boothe, P.M. and B.G. Reid. 1989. "Asset Returns and Government Budgets in a Small Open Economy." *Journal of Monetary Economics* 23: 65-77

Bowles, Samuel. 1998. "Endogenous Preferences: The Cultural Consequences of Markets and Other Economic Institutions," *Journal of Economic Literature* 36 (March): 75-111.

Breton, Albert. 1996. *Competitive Governments: An Economic Theory of Politics and Public Finance.* Cambridge: Cambridge University Press.

Buchanan, James and Gordon Tullock. 1965. *The Calculus of Consent* (Ann Arbor: University of Michigan Press)

Buitelar, Ruud and Pitou van Dijck, eds. 1996. *Latin America's New Insertion in the World Economy*: New York: St. Martin's Press.

Burkhart, Ross E. and Michael S. Lewis-Beck. 1994. Comparative Democracy: The Economic Development Thesis. *American Political Science Review* 88: 903-909.

Buscaglia, Edgardo and Clarisa Long. 1998. "An Economic Analysis of Legal Integration in Latin America. *Policy Studies Review* 15: 52-79.

Caiden, Naomi. 1996. "Budgetary Processes." In *Encyclopedia of Government and Politics,* eds., Mary Hawkesworth and Maurice Kogane. London: Routledge Press.

Camp, Roderic Ai, ed. 1996. *Democracy in Latin America: Patterns and Cycles.* Wilmington, Delaware: S&R Inc.

Campos, Ed and Sanjay Pradhan. 1996. "Budgetary Institutions and Expenditure Outcomes - Binding Governments to Fiscal Performance." *Policy Research Working Paper,* 1646. Washington DC: The World Bank.

Cantor, Richard and Frank Packer. 1996. "Determinants and Impact of Sovereign Credit Ratings." Research Paper 9608, *Economic Policy Review* (October):37-53.

Carrasquilla, Alberto. 1998. "Financial Integration: Opportunities and Risks." *Latin American Economic Policies* 4. Washington DC: Inter-American Development Bank.

Carporaso, James and David Levine. 1997. *Theories of Political Economy.* Cambridge: Cambridge University Press.

Ciria, Alberto. 1997. "Class and Conservative Parties in Comparative Perspective-Book Review." *American Political Science Review* 91: 762-63.

Cerny, Philip G. 1994. "The Dynamics of Financial Globalization: Technology, Market Structure and Policy Response. *Policy Sciences* 27: 319-42.

Clarke, Thomas, ed. 1994. *International Privatization: Strategies and Practices.* New York: Walter de Gruyter Press.

Clegg, Stewart R. and Gill Palmer, eds. 1996. *The Politics of Management Knowledge.* London: Sage Publications.

Coleman, William D. and Tony Porter. 1994. "Regulating Banking and Securities: Emerging Cooperation among national authorities." In *Political Economy and the Changing Global Order.* New York: St. Martin's Press.

Collier, David. 1993. "The Comparative Method" in *Political Science: The State of the Discipline*, Ada W. Finifter, ed. Washington DC: American Political Science Association.

Collier, Kenneth, Bernard Carey, Ellen Grusy, Curt Marjaniemi and Donald Sautter. 1998. "A Perspective on Data Mining," Unpublished White Paper, Center for Data Mining, Flagstaff: Northern Arizona University.

Corrigan, Gerald E. 1990. "Central Banks and the Financial System." In *Central Banking Issues in Emerging Market Economies."* Kansas City: The Federal Reserve Bank.

Cothran, Dan A. 1994. "Mexican Economic and Fiscal Policies to Sustain Political Stability." *Public Budgeting and Finance*, Winter 1994: 98-119.

___.1994. *Political Stability and Democracy in Mexico The "Perfect Dictatorship"?* Westport, Connecticut: Praeger.

___. 1993. "Entrepreneurial Budgeting: An Emerging Reform?" *Public Administration Review* 53: 445-454.

Cozzetto, D., et al. *Public Budgeting.* 1995. Longman: University of North Dakota Press.

Crane, Dwight B. 1995. *The Global Financial System, A Functional Perspective.* Boston, MA.: Harvard Business School Press.

Crisp, Brian F. and Michael J. Kelly. 1997. "The Socioeconomic Impacts of Structural Adjustment in Latin America." Paper presented at the Western Political Science Association, Tucson, Arizona.

Crown, William H. 1998. *Statistical Models for the Social and Behavioral Sciences: Multiple Regression and Limited Dependent Variables.* Wesport, Connecticut: Praeger.

Cox, Gary W. 1997. *Making Votes Count: Strategic Coordination in the World's Electoral Systems.* New York: Cambridge University Press.

Cukierman, Alex. 1992. *Central Bank Strategy, Credibility and Independence.* Cambridge: MIT Press.

Cuddington, John T. 1986. *Capital Flight: Estimates, Issues and Explanations.* Princeton Studies in International Finance No. 58. Princeton: Princeton University Press.

Czada, Roland, Adrienne Heritier and Hans Keman, eds. 1996. *Institutions and Political Choice, On the Limits of Rationality.* Amsterdam: VU University Press.

Dahl, Robert A. 1956. *A Preface to Democratic Theory.* Chicago: The University of Chicago Press.

De La Balze, Felipe. 1995. *Remaking the Argentine Economy.* NewYork: Council on Foreign Relations Press.

Detriagache, Erica. 1996. "Rational Liquidity Crisis in the Sovereign Debt Market: In Search for a Theory." IMF Working Paper 38. Washington DC: IMF.

Der Hovanessian, Aida. 1992. "Guide to Evaluating Sovereign Credits." Morgan Stanley, Fixed Income Credit Research Department. New York: Morgan Stanley.

Diamond, Larry, Marc F. Plattner, Yun-han Chu and Hung-mao Tien. 1997. *Consolidating the Third Wave Democracies.* Baltimore: The Johns Hopkins University Press.

Dombrowski, Peter. 1998. "Haute Finance and High Theory: Recent Scholarship on Global Financial Relations." *Mershon International Studies Review* 42: 1-28.

Dornbush, Rudiger, ed. 1993.*Policymaking in the Open Economy: Concepts and Cases in Economic Performance.* New York: Oxford University Press.

Douglas Mary and Aaron Wildavsky. 1982. *Risk and Culture. An Essay on the Selection of Technical and Environmental Dangers.* Berkeley: University of California Press.

Drake, Paul W., ed. 1994. *Money Doctors, Foreign Debts and Economic Reforms in Latin America from the 1890s to the Present.* Wilmington: SR Books.

Dye, Thomas R. 1995. *Understanding Public Policy,* Eight Edition. Englewoods Cliffs, New Jersey: Prentice Hall.

Easton, David. 1969. The New Revolution in Political Science. *The American Political Science Review* 63: 1051-1061.

Edwards, Sebastian. 1995. *Crisis and Reform in Latin America.* New York: Oxford University Press.

___. 1995. "Public Sector Deficits and Macroeconomic Stability in Developing Economies," in *Budget Deficits and Debt: Issues and Options.* Federal Reserve Bank of Kansas City. Kansas City: FRB. 307-369.

Eichengreen, Barry. 1994. *International Monetary Arrangements for the 21st Century.* Washington DC: The Brookings Institution.

Eichengreen, Barry and Richard Portes. 1995. *Crisis? What Crisis?Orderly Workout for Sovereign Debtors.* London: Centre for Economic Policy Research.

Erb, Claude B., Cambell R. Harvey and Tadas E. Viskanta. 1996. Political Risk, Economic Risk and Financial Risk. *CIBER Working Paper*. Durham: Duke University.

Epstein, Gerald A. And Herbert Gintis, "International Capital Markets and the Limits of National Economic Policy" in *International Capital Markets*.

Erro, David G. 1993. *Resolving the Argentine Paradox: Politics and Development.* Boulder, Lynne Rienner Publishers.

Etheredge, Lloyd S. 1985. *Can Governments Learn? American Foreign Policy and Central American Revolutions*. New York, NY: Pergamon Press.

Fabozzi, Frank J. 1993. *Bond Markets, Analysis and Strategies,* Second Edition. Englewood Cliffs, NJ: Prentice Hall.

Fabozzi, Frank J. and Irving M. Pollock, eds. 1987. *The Handbook of Fixed Income Securities.* Second Edition. Homewood, Illinois: Dow Jones- Irwing Press.

Fanelli, Jose Maria and Jose Luis Machinea. 1995. Capital Movements in Argentina. In *Coping with Capital Surges,* ed. Ricardo Ffrench-Davis and Stephany Griffith-Jones. Boulder: Lynne Rienner Publishers.

Farr, James and Raymond Seidelman, ed. 1993. *Discipline and History, Political Science in the United States.* Ann Arbor: The University of Michigan Press.

Fayyad, Usama M., Gregory Piatetsky-Shapiro, Pahdraic Smyth and Ramasamy Uthurusamy, eds. 1996. *Advances in Knowledge Discovery and Data Mining.* Cambridge: MIT Press.

Federal Reserve Bank. 1995. *Budget Deficits and Debt: Issue and Options.* New York, NY: Federal Reserve Bank.

Federal Reserve Bank of Kansas City. 1990. *Central Banking Issues in Emerging Market-Oriented Economies.* Kansas City, Kansas: The Federal Reserve Bank.

____. 1997. *Maintaining Financial Stability in a Global Economy.* Kansas City, Kansas: The Federal Reserve Bank.

Ferretti, Milese and A. Razin. 1996. "The Sustainability of Persistent Current Account Deficits" National Bureau of Economic Research. Working Paper. 1-23. Washington DC: National Bureau of Economic Research.

Fisher, Stanley, ed. 1980. *Rational Expectations and Economic Policy.* Chicago: The University of Chicago Press.

Frankel Jeffrey A. 1994. "The Internationalization of Equity Markets" National Bureau of Economic Research Reprint 1929. 1-19.

Frenkel Jacob and Assaf Razin. 1996. *Fiscal Policies and Growth in the World* Economy. Cambridge: MIT Press.

Ffrench-Davis, Ricardo and Stephany Griffith-Jones, eds. 1995. *Coping with Capital Surges.* Boulder: Lynne Rienner Publishers.

Ffrench- Davis, Ricardo, Manuel Agosin and Andras Uthoff. 1995. "Capital Movements, Export Strategy and Macroeconomic Stability in Chile." in *Coping With Capital Surges.* Boulder: Lynne Rienner Publishers.

Frenkel, Jacob A. and Assaf Razin. 1996. *Fiscal Policies and Growth in the World Economy.* Cambridge: MIT Press.

Frieden, Jeffry A. 1991. "Invested Interests: The Politics of National Economic Policies in a World of Global Finance. *International Organization* 45 (Autumn):425-451.

Frieden, Jeffry A. and Ronald Rogowski. 1996. The Impact of the International Economy on National Policies: An Analytical Overview. In *Internationalization and Domestic Policies,* eds. Robert O. Keohane and Helen V. Milner. Cambridge: Cambridge University Press.

Furubotn, Eirik G. and Rudolf Richter. 1997. *Institutions and Economic Theory: The Contributions of the New Institutional Economics.* Ann Arbor, MI: The University of Michigan Press.

Garreton, Manuel Antonio. 1995. Redemocratization in Chile. *Journal of Democracy* 6:146-158.

Geoffrey Garrett. 1998. *Partisan Politics in the Global Economy.* Cambridge, MA: Cambridge University Press.

___. 1995. "Capital Mobility, Trade and the Domestic Politics of Economic Policy." *International Organization* 49: 657-687.

Garrett, Geoffrey and Peter Lange. 1996. "Internationalization, Institutions and Political Change"in *Internationalization and Domestic Policies,* eds. Robert O. Keohane and Helen V. Milner. Cambridge: Cambridge University Press.

Geddes, Barbara. 1994. "Challenging the Conventional Wisdom." *The Journal of Democracy* 5: 161-175.

_____. 1994. *Politician's Dilemma: Building State Capacity in Latin America.* Berkeley: University of California Press.

Gill, Stephen. 1998. "European Governance and new Constitutionalism: Economic and Monetary Union and Alternatives to Disciplinary Neoliberalism In Europe." *New Political Economy* 3: 5-25.

Glasser, Bradley. 1995. "External Capital and Political Liberalizations." *Journal of International Affairs* 49 (Summer):45-73.

Goldstein, Morris, Donald J. Mathieson and Timothy Lane. 1991. "Determinants and Systemic Consequences of International Capital Flows." International Monetary Fund, Occasional paper 77. Washington DC : International Monetary Fund.

Goodman J., and L. Pauly. 1993. "The Obsolescence of Capital Controls? Economic Management in an Age of Global Markets. *World Politics.* 46: 50-82.

Grabel, Ilene. 1996. "Marketing the Third World: The Contradictions of Portfolio Investment in the Global Economy." *World Development,* 24: 1761-1776.

Grosse, Robert, ed. 1995. *Government Responses to the Latin American Problem.* Miami, Florida: North- South Center Press, University of Miami.

Grupo Financiero Banamex. 1998. *Review of the Economic Situation in Mexico* 74: 319-355.

Gummet, Philip, ed. 1996. *Globalization and Public Policy.* Cheltenham, Glos.UK: Edward Elgar Publishing.

Gwartney, James D. and Richard L. Stroup. 1987. *Economics, Private and Public Choice,* 4th Edition. Washington DC: Hartourt Brace Janovich.

Haas, E.B. 1990. *When Knowledge is Power: Three Models of Change in International Organizations.*Berkeley, CA: University of California Press.

Haber, Stephen. 1996. *How Latin America Fell Behind, Essays on the Economic Histories of Brazil and Mexico, 1800-1914.* Stanford: Stanford University Press.

Haggard, Stephen and Sylvia Maxfield. 1996. "The Political Economy of Financial Internationalization in the Developing World." *International Organization* 50: 35-68.

Haggard, Stephan, Chung H. Lee and Sylvia Maxfield, eds. 1993. *The Politics of Finance in Developing Countries.* Ithaca. NY: Cornell University Press.

Haggard, Stephen and Robert R. Kaufman. 1994. "The Challenges of Consolidation," *Journal of Democracy* 5: 5-16.

___. 1997. "The Political Economy of Democratic Transitions." *Comparative Politics.* (April): 263-281.

Hague, Rod, Martin Harrop and Shaun Breslin. 1992. *Comparative Government and Politics.* London: MacMillan.

Hall, Peter A. and Rosemary C.R.Taylor. 1996. "Political Science and the Three New Institutionalisms." *Political Studies* 64: 936- 957.

Hahm, S.D., M.S. Kamlet and DC Mowery. 1996. "The Political Economy of Deficit Spending in Nine Industrialized Parliamentary Democracies: The Role of Fiscal Institutions." *Comparative Political Studies* 29: 52-77.

Harberger, Arnold. 1985. "Observations on the Chilean Economy." *Economic Development and Cultural Change* 33: 451-68.

Hargreaves Heap, Shaun, et al. 1997. *The Theory of Choice, A critical Guide.* Oxford: Blackwell.

Hausmann, Ricardo and Roberto Rigobon. 1993. *Government Spending and Distribution in Latin America.* Washington DC: Inter-American Development Bank.

Hausmann, Ricardo and Liliana Rojas Suarez, eds. 1996. *Volatile Capital Flows: Taming Their Impact on Latin America.* Inter- American Development Bank. Washington DC.

Hay, Colin. 1995. "Structure and Agency." In *Theory and Methods in Political Science*, eds., David Marsh and Gerry Stoker. New York: St. Martin's Press.

Helleiner, Eric. 1994. From Bretton Woods to Global Finance. In *Political Economy and the Changing Global Order,* eds., Richard Stubbs and Geoffrey Underhill. New York: St. Martin's Press.

____. 1994. *States and the Reemergence of Global Finance.* Ithaca, NY: Cornell University Press.

Herring, Richard J. and Robert E. Litan. 1995. *Financial Regulation in the World Economy.* Washington DC: The Brookings Institution.

Hirschman, Albert O. 1993. *Journeys Toward Progress: Studies of Economic Policymaking in Latin America.* Boulder: Westview Press.

Hirst, Paul and Grahame Thompson. 1995. "Globalization and the Future of the Nation State." *Economy and Society,* 24: 408-442.

Huber, J. 1992. "Restrictive Legislative procedures in France and in the United States." *American Political Science Review* 34: 67-88.

Huntington, Samuel P. 1991. *The Third Wave: Democratization in the Late Twentieth Century.* Norman, OK: University of Oklahoma Press.

Inter-American Development Bank. 1995. Data set on Latin American Budget Institutions 1980- 1995 (Excel 97 version).

International Finance Corporation (IFC). 1994. *Emerging Stock Markets Factbook.* Washington DC: IFC.

International Monetary Fund (IMF). 1996. *International Capital Markets: Developments, Prospects and Key Policy Issues.* Washington DC: International Monetary Fund.

___ 1995. *Private Market Financing for Developing Countries.* Washington DC: IMF.

___. 1996. *The Determinants and Systemic Consequences of International Capital Flows.* Washington DC: IMF.

___. 1996. *The Role of Credit Markets in a Transition Economy with Incomplete Public Information.* Washington DC: IMF.

___. 1986, 1991 and 1996. *Government Finance Statistics Yearbook.* Washington DC: IMF.

___. 1998. Government Finance Statistics Data Set (Excell 97 version). Washington DC: IMF.

Johnson, David B. 1991. *Public Choice, An Introduction to the New Political Economy.* London: Bristlecone Books.

Kapstein E. 1992. "Between Power and Purpose: Central Bankers and the Politics of Regulatory Convergence." *International Organization.* 46:1, 265-287.

Katz, Daniel and Robert L.Kahn. 1996. "Organizations and the System Concept." In *Classics of Organizational Theory,* Fourth Edition, Jay Shafritz and Steven Ott, eds. Fort Worth, Texas: Harcourt Brace College Publishers.

Keefer, Philip and Stephen Knack. 1997. "Why Don't Poor Countries Catch Up? A Cross-National Test of an Institutional Explanation." *Economic Inquiry* 35: 590-602.

Keefer, Philip and David Stasavage. 1998. "When Does Delegation Improve Credibility? Central Bank Independence. Unpublished Paper presented at the American Political Science Association Annual Meeting, Boston, MA.

Kennedy, Ruby, Benjamin van Roy and Christopher D. Reed, eds. 1997. *Solving Data Mining Problems through Pattern Recognition.* New York: McGraw Hill.

Keohane, Robert O. and Helen Milner, eds. 1996. *Internationalization and Domestic Politics.* New York: Cambridge University Press.

King, Loren A. 1998. "Economic Growth and Basic Human Needs." *International Studies Quarterly* 42: 385-400.

Knowledge Seeker Data Mining Software. 1993. Angoss Software Corporation

Knopf, Jeffrey W. 1998. "The Importance of International Learning." Unpublished paper presented at the American Political Science Association Annual Meeting. Boston, MA.

Kontopoulos, John T. 1997. "Fiscal Policy and Electoral Competition." Ph.D. dissertation, Columbia University. Ann Arbor, MI: UMI Dissertation Services.

Korzeniewicz, Roberto P. and William C. Smith, eds. 1996. *Latin America in the World Economy.* Westport, Connecticut: Praeger.

Krueger, Ann O. 1974. "The Political Economy of the Rent-Seeking Society." *American Economic Review* 64: 291-303.

Laban, Raul and Felipe B. Larrain. 1994. The Chilean Experience with Capital Mobility. In *The Chilean Economy: Policy Lessons and Challenges,* eds., Barry P. Bosworth, Rudiger Dornbusch and Raul Laban. Washington DC: The Brookings Institution.

Laver, Michael and Kenneth A. Shepsle. 1996. *Making and Breaking Governments Cabinets and Legislatures in Parliamentary Democracies.* Cambridge, UK: Cambridge University Press.

Levi, Margaret.1988. *Of Rule and Revenue*. Berkeley, CA: University of California Press.

Levy Brian and Pablo T. Spiller, eds. 1996. *Regulations, Institutions and Commitment.* New York: Cambridge University Press.

Lijphart, Arend and Carlos Waisman, eds. 1996. *Institutional Design in New Democracies.* Boulder, CO.: Westview Press.

Lindblom Charles. 1959. "The Science of Muddling Through." *Public Administration Review* 19: 79-88. Cited in Stella Z. Theodolou and Matthew A. Cahn, eds., *Public Policy*. Englewoods Cliffs, New Jersey: Prentice Hall.

Linz, Juan J. and Alfred Stepan. 1996. *Problems of Democratic Transition and Consolidation: Southern Europe, South America and Post Communist Europe.* Baltimore, Maryland: The John Hopkins University Press.

Lopez Murphy, R. ed. 1995. *Fiscal Decentralization in Latin America.* Washington DC: InterAmerican Development Bank.

Macesich, George.1996. *Transformation and Emerging Markets.* Westport, Connecticut: Praeger.

Magill, Frank N., ed. 1996. *Survey of Social Science, Government and Politics Series.* Pasadena, Ca.: Salem Press.

Mahon, James E. Jr. 1996. *Mobile Capital and Latin American Development.* University Park, Pa.: The Pennsylvania State University Press.

Makin. A.J. 1994. *International Capital Mobility and External Account Determination.* London: St. Martin's Press.

Mainwaring, Scott and Matthew Soberg Shugart, eds. 1997. *Presidentialism and Democracy in Latin America.* New York: Cambridge University Press.

March, James G. and Johan P. Olsen. 1984 "The New Institutionalism: Organizational Factors in Political Life." *American Political Science Review* 78: 734-749.

___.1989. *Rediscovering Institutions, The Organizational Basis of Politics.* New York: The Free Press.

Marsh, David and Gerry Stoker. 1995. *Theory and Methods in Political Science.* New York: St. Martin Press.

Mason Robert D. and Douglas A.Lind. 1990. *Statistical Techniques in Business and Economics.* Boston, MA: Irwin Press.

Maxfield, Sylvia. 1994. "Financial Incentives and Central Bank Authority in Industrialized Nations." *World Politics* 46: 123-145.

McCool, Daniel C. 1995. *Public Policy Theories, Models and Concepts, An Anthology.* Englewoods Cliffs: Prentice Hall.

Milesi-Ferretti, S.M. and A.Razin. 1996. *The Sustainability of Current Account Deficits"* ABER Working Paper 5967. Washington DC: ABER.

Miller, Gary. 1997. "The Impact of Economics on Contemporary Political Science." *Journal of Economic Literature* 35: 1173-1204.

Miller, Stephen M. and Frank S. Russek. 1997. "Fiscal Structures and Economic Growth: International Evidence." *Economic Inquiry* 35 : 603-613.

Mitchell, William. 1983. "Fiscal Behavior of the Modern Democratic State: Public Choice Perspectives and Contributions" in *Political Economy: Recent Views,* ed. Larry Wade. Boston: Kluwer-Nijhoff.

Model 1 Data Mining Software. 1995. Unica Technologies, Inc., Boston , Massachusetts.

Moody's Investor Services. 1996. "Global Credit Research Report: Sovereign In Depth Analysis of Argentina." New York: Moody's Investor Services.

___. 1997. "Global Credit Research Report: Sovereign In Depth Analysis of Chile." New York: Moody's Investor Services.

___. 1997. " Global Credit Research Report- Sovereign In Depth Analysis of Mexico." New York: Moody's Investor Service.

Montiel, Peter J. 1993. "Capital Mobility in Developing Countries: Some Measurement Issues and Empirical Estimates. Working Paper 1103. Washington DC: World Bank.

Morales, Juan Antonio and Gary Mc Mahon, eds. 1996. *Economic Policy and the Transition to Democracy: The Latin American Experience.* New York: St. Martin Press.

Morrow, James D. 1994. *Game Theory for Political Scientists.* Princeton: Princeton University Press.

Mussa Michael and Morris Goldstein. 1993. "The Integration of World Capital Markets." In *Changing Capital Markets: Implications for Monetary Policy."* Proceedings of symposium sponsored by the Federal Reserve Bank of Kansas City. Jackson Hole, Wyoming: Federal Reserve Bank.

Murphy, Ricardo Lopez, ed. 1995. *Fiscal Decentralization in Latin America.* Washington DC: Inter-American Development Bank.

Nazmi, Nader. 1996. *Economic Policy and Stabilization in Latin America.* London: M.E. Sharpe.

Neubauer, Deane E. 1967. Some Conditions of Democracy. *American Political Science Review* 61: 1002-1009.

Needler, Martin C. 1995. *Mexican Politics: The Containment of Conflict.* Westport, Connecticut: Praeger.

Niskanen, William A. 1997. "Autocratic, Democratic and Optimal Government." *Economic Inquiry* 35 (July): 464-479.

Norlinger, Eric, A. 1988. "The Return to the State: Critiques." *American Political Science Review* 82: 875-885.

North, Douglass C. 1990. *Institutions, Institutional Change and Economic Performance.* Cambridge: Cambridge University Press.

___. 1984. "Transaction Costs, Institutions and Economic History." *Journal of Institutional and Theoretical Economics* 140: 7-17.

Norton, Joseph J. and Raymond M. Auerback, eds. 1993. *International Finance in the 1990s: Challenges and Opportunities.* London: Blackwell.

O'Donnell, Guillermo. 1995. Do Economists Know Best? *Journal of Democracy* 6:23-28

___. 1988. *Bureaucratic Authoritarianism: Argentina 1966-1973, in Comparative Perspective.* Berkeley: University of California Press.

Olson, Mancur. 1965. *The Logic of Collective Action: Public Goods and the Theory of Groups.* Cambridge, Mass.: Harvard University Press.

Ostrom, Elinor. 1998. "A Behavioral Approach to The Rational Choice Theory of Collective Action." *American Political Science Review,* Vol. 92, March: 1-22.

Patashnik, Eric M. 1996. "The Contractual Nature of Budgeting: A Transaction Cost Perspective on the Design of Budgeting Institutions." *Policy Sciences* 29: 189-212.

Pauly, Louis W. 1995. "Capital Mobility, State Autonomy and Political Legitimacy." *Journal of International Affairs* 48 (Winter): 368-388.

Peralta Ramos, Monica. 1991. *The Political Economy of Argentina: Power and Class Since 1930.* Boulder: Westview Press.

Perry, Guillermo and Ana Maria Herrera. 1994. *Public Finances, Stabilization and Structural Reform in Latin America.* Washington DC: Inter-American Development Bank.

Perry, Robert and John Robertson. 1998. "Political Markets, Bond Markets and Effects of Uncertainty: A Cross National Analysis." *International Studies Quarterly* 42: 131-160.

Philip, George. 1993. "The New Economic Liberalism and Democracy in Latin America: Friends or Enemies? *Third World Quarterly* 14: 555-571.

Posada Carbo, Eduardo. 1996. *Elections before Democracy: The History of Elections in Europe and Latin America.* London: Institute of Latin American Studies, University of London.

Pollins, Brian M. 1993. "Global Capital: Two Financial Booms Compared." Unpublished Paper.

Posen, Adam S. 1997. "Monetary Realism: Central Banks and The Political Economy of Disinflation." Ph.D. dissertation, Harvard University.

Przeworski, Adam and Henry Teune. 1970. *The Logic of Comparative Social Inquiry.* New York: Wiley-Interscience.

Putterman, Louis, John E. Roemer and Joaquim Silvestre. 1998. "Does Egalitarianism Have a Future?" *Journal Of Economic Literature* 36: 861-902.

Quinn, Dennis. 1997. "The Correlates of Change in International Financial Regulation." *American Political Science Review* 91: 531-551.

Ragin, Charles C. 1987. *The Comparative Method, Moving Beyond Qualitative and Quantitative Strategies.* Berkeley: University of California Press

Reisen, Helmut. 1990. *Public Debt, External Competitiveness and Fiscal Discipline in Developing Countries.* Princeton Studies in International Finance. Princeton University.

Reeves, Clyde H. 1986. *Measuring Fiscal Capacity.* Boston, MA: Oegleschlager, Gunn and Hain.

Remmer, Karen L.1996. "Democracy and Economic Crisis: The Latin American Experience." In *Democracy in Latin America: Patterns and Cycles,* ed. Roderic Ai Camp, 269-291. Wilmington:SR Books.

Riker, William. 1990. "Political Science and Rational Choice." In *Perspectives on Positive Political Economy,* eds. James E. Alt and Kenneth A. Shepsle. New York: Cambridge University Press.

___. 1980. "Implications for the Disequilibrium of Majority Rule for the Study of Institutions." *American Political Science Review* 74: 432-47.

Roett, Riordan. 1995. *The Challenge of Institutional Reform in Mexico.* Boulder,CO.: Lynne Rienner Publishers.

Rojas-Suarez, Liliana. "Risk and Capital Flight in Developing Countries." Occasional Paper 77. Washington DC: International Monetary Fund.

Rose, Richard. 1995. *Lesson Drawing in Public Policy, A Guide to Learning Across Time and Space.* Chatham: Chatham House Publishers.

Rosenau, James N. and Mary Durfee. 1995. *Thinking Theory Thoroughly, Coherent Approaches to an Incoherent World.* Boulder: Westview Press.

Rothstein, Bo. 1996. "Political Institutions: An Overview." In Robert Goodin and Hans Dieter Klingemann, eds., *A New Handbook of Political Science* (Oxford: Oxford University Press. 133-166.

Roubini, N. and J. Sachs. 1989. "Government Spending and Budget Deficits in the Industrialized Countries." *Economic Policy* 8: 99-132.

Sabatier, Paul. 1988. "An Advocacy Coalition Framework of Policy Change and the Role of Policy-oriented Learning Therein." *Policy Sciences* 21: 129-168.

Sanchez, Manuel.1992. *Mexico y el Tratado Trilateral de Libre Comercio.* Mexico City: ITAM and McGrawHill.

Sartori, Giovanni. 1991. "Comparing and Miscomparing." *Journal of Theoretical Politics* 3: 243-257.

Scenario Data Mining Software. 1997. Cognos Corporation. Ottawa, Canada

Schmitter, Philippe C. 1989. "Corporatism is Dead! Long Live Corporatism." *Government and Opposition* 24: 54-73.

Schroeder, Larry. 1994. "Comparative Perspectives on Public Finance" in Randall Baker, ed., *Comparative Public Management: Putting US Policy in Context.* Westport, Ct.: Praeger Publishers.

Scokpol, Theda and Margaret Somers. 1994. "The Uses of Comparative History in Macrosocial Inquiry." In *Social Revolutions in the Modern World,* Theda Skocpol. Cambridge, Cambridge University Press.

Shepsle Kenneth A. and Barry Weingast. 1984. "Uncovered Sets and Sophisticated Voting Outcomes with Implications for Agenda Institutions," *American Journal of Political Science* 28: 50-73.

Simon, Herbert. 1982. *Models of Bounded Rationality,* Vol.2. Cambridge, Mass.: MIT Press.

Simmons, Beth A. 1994. *Who Adjusts? Domestic Sources of Economic Policy.* Princeton: Princeton University Press

Sinclair, Timothy. 1995. Economic and Financial Analysis Considered as Knowledge Dynamics of Global Governance. Political Science Department, York University. *Paper presented at the annual meeting of the International Studies Association*, Chicago.

Singer, Peter.1981. "The Right to be Rich or Poor." In *Reading Nozick*, ed., Jeffrey Paul. Totowa, NJ: Rowman and Littlefield.

Smith, William C., Carlos Acuna and Eduardo Gamarra, eds. 1994. *Democracy, Markets and Structural Reform in Latin America.* Miami: University of Miami Press.

Stallings, Barbara, ed. 1995. *Global Change, Regional Response: The New International Context of Development.* New York: Cambridge University Press.

Statistical Package for the Social Sciences. 1998. Software Version 8.0. SPSS, Chicago.

___. 1998. Applications Base 8.0 Guide. Chicago, IL: SPSS, Inc.

Stein, Robert . 1995. *Perpetuating the Pork Barrel.* New York: Cambridge University Press.

Steinmo, Sven, Kathleen Thelen and Frank Longstreth, eds. 1992. *Structuring Politics: Historical Institutionalism in Comparative Analysis*. New York: Cambridge University Press.

___. 1990. "Finance, Information and Power" *Review of International Studies.* 16: 259-74.

Stubbs, Richard and Geoffrey R.D. Underhill, eds. 1994. *Political Economy and the Changing Global Order.* New York: St. Martin's Press.

Tarrow, Sidney. 1995. "Bridging the Quantitative - Qualitative Divide in Political Science." *American Political Science Review* 89 (June): 471-476.

The Wall Street Journal. 15 October and 16 December 1988 and 18 January, 1999. Final Editions.

Thealing, Kurt. 1997. "Understanding data Mining: It's all in the Interaction." White Paper, Dta Mining Analytics Exchange Applications. http://www3shore net/~kht/index htm.

Theodolou, Stella Z. and Matthew A. Cahn. 1995. *Public Policy, The Essential Readings.* Englewood Cliffs: Prentice Hall.

Thurber, Clarence E. and Lawrence S. Graham, eds. 1973. *Development Administration in Latin America.* Durham: Duke University Press.

Tsebelis, George. 1990. *Nested Games.* Berkeley: University of California Press.

___. 1995. "Decision Making in Political Systems." *British Journal of Political Science* 25: 289-325.

Varman-Schneider, Benu. 1991. *Capital Flight from Developing Countries.* Boulder: Westview Press.

Verdier, Daniel. 1998. "Domestic Responses to Capital Market Internationalization Under the Gold Standard, 1870-1914." *International Organization* 52 (Winter): 1-34.

Von Hagen, Jurgen and I.J. Harden. 1994. "National Budget Process and Fiscal Performance." Unpublished Manuscript.

Walsh, Carl. 1995. "Optimal Contracts for Central Bankers." *American Economic Review* 85: 193-218.

Weber, Max. 1949. "The Meaning of Ethical Neutrality." In *The Methodology of the Social Sciences*, trans., Edward Shils and Henry Finch. Glencoe, Illinois: The Free Press.

Webb M. 1991. "International Economic Structures, Government Interests and International Coordination of Macroeconomics Adjustment Policies, " *International Organization* 45 (Spring): 309-42.

Weingast, Barry and Kenneth A. Shepsle and C. Johnson. 1981. "The Political Economy of Benefits and Costs: A Neoclassical Approach to Distributive Politics." *Journal of Political Economy* 89: 642-64.

Wiarda, Howard J., ed. 1992. *Politics and Social Change in Latin America, Still a Distinct Tradition?* Boulder: Westview Press.

Wildavsky, Aaron. 1992. *The New Politics of the Budgetary Process, Second Edition.* New York: Harper Collins Press.

Wilke, James W. et al., eds. 1995. *Statistical Abstract of Latin America.* 31, Part 2. Los Angeles: UCLA Latin American Center Publications.

Williamson, John. 1990. *The Progress of Policy Reform in Latin America.* Washington D. C.: Institute for International Economics.

___.1990. *Latin American Adjustment: How Much has Happened?* Washington DC: Institute for International Economics.

Williamson, Oliver E. 1983. "Credible Commitments," *American Economic Review* 73: 519-540.

World Bank. 1998. "Delegation, Credibility and Efficiency - The Role of Agency Independence and Fixed Policy Rules in Policy Making." Unpublished Draft Research Proposal, prepared by Philip Keefer and Davis Stasavage. Washington DC: World Bank.

___. 1998. Global Development Finance Database on CD-ROM.

___. 1998. World Development Indicators Datbase on CD-ROM.

___. 1996. "Financial Restructuring in Chile, *OED Precis 101.*" Washington DC: World Bank.

___. 1996. "Budgetary Institutions and Expenditure Outcomes." Policy Research Working Paper 1646, prepared by Ed Campos and Sanjay Pradhan. Washington DC: World Bank

___. 1995. "Privatization and Deregulation in Mexico" *OED Precis 97.* Washington DC: World Bank.

___. 1995. "Privatizing Argentina's Public Enterprises" *OED Precis 100.* Washington DC: World Bank.

Index

J

K

*

STUDIES IN POLITICAL SCIENCE

1. David R. Jones, **Political Parties and Policy Gridlock in American Government**
2. Jong-Sup Lee and Uk Heo, **The U.S.-South Korean Alliance, 1961-1988: Free-Riding or Bargaining?**
3. Rachel K. Gibson, **The Growth of Anti-Immigrant Parties in Western Europe**
4. Derek S. Reveron, **Promoting Democracy in the Post-Soviet Region**
5. James R. Hedtke, **Lame Duck Presidents–Myth or Reality**
6. Gerson Moreno-Riaño, **Political Tolerance, Culture, and the Individual**
7. Rosa Gomez Dierks, **Credible Fiscal Policy Commitments and Market Access—Case Studies of Argentina, Chile, and Mexico, 1980-1995**